SITTANG
THE LAST BATTLE

SITTANG
THE LAST BATTLE

THE END OF THE JAPANESE IN BURMA,
JULY–AUGUST 1945

LOUIS ALLEN

MACDONALD · LONDON

Natsu-gusa ya
tsuwamono-domo no
yume no ato

('Summer grasses...
all that is left of
the dreams of warriors')

Bashō

FIRST PUBLISHED IN GREAT BRITAIN IN 1973
BY MACDONALD AND CO. (PUBLISHERS) LTD,
ST GILES HOUSE, 49-50 POLAND STREET,
LONDON, W.1.

© LOUIS ALLEN, 1973

REPRINTED 1974

ISBN 0 356 04219 7

MADE AND PRINTED IN GREAT BRITAIN BY
REDWOOD BURN LIMITED, TROWBRIDGE AND ESHER

CONTENTS

LIST OF ILLUSTRATIONS

ACKNOWLEDGEMENTS

I owe a great debt of gratitude to Mr Tsuchiya Eiichi, who has provided me with many of the Japanese texts used in *Sittang*, has answered many questions on the break-out, and has regularly sent me a copy of 28 Army's bulletin, *Nansō*. He has also sent me a number of photographs. To Mr Hachisuka Mitsuo I am indebted not merely for answering questions on *Hayate Tai* but also for arranging for me to meet Mr Tsuchiya and Mr Wakō in Tokyo. To Mr Tsutsumi Shinzo I am indebted for hospitality in London on a number of occasions, and for permission to use *Tenshin*, his narrative of 13 Naval Guard Force during the break-out. I thank the Imperial War Museum for permission to use its library of photographs; and my wife and family for their forbearance while the book was being written.

INTRODUCTION

X-Day is what the Japanese in Burma called it. In the calendar it was 20 July 1945, just over three weeks before the war in the Far East came to an end. On that day, thousands of Japanese troops belonging to 28 Army came out of the rain-sodden fastness of the hills of the Pegu Yomas and attempted to break through the cordon of British and Indian divisions which held the line of the long road that led from Mandalay to Rangoon. It was the very last battle which the British Army fought in the Second World War, the last battle of the Japanese forces in South-East Asia, the last battle of a united Indian Army before partition into India and Pakistan split up for ever one of the finest armies in the history of warfare. The battle involved some extraordinary coincidences, and some fantastic disproportions in casualties. Yet as far as the British official history is concerned, the drama of the break-out over the Sittang seems to have been missed. 'No attempt will be made to describe in detail the fighting during the break-out,' writes the official historian.[1] 'It is a story of interceptions on the main Pegu-Toungoo road with brief, hard-fought actions in darkness and pouring rain.' It was, that is to say, like Inkerman, a soldiers' battle rather than a generals' battle, with this difference: Inkerman was a matter of slogging hand-to-hand struggles in the gun-lit darkness, while the Battle of the Break-out was a battle of man against the elements, in which the protagonists were not so much men wielding rifle, bayonet and machine-gun, as men with malaria, dysentery and tortured feet swollen with beri-beri, men plunging in the terror of a midsummer night into a land of endless swamp, men screaming as the remorseless current of the Sittang bore them downstream, seawards, until their bodies floated far out into the Gulf of Martaban.

Interpretations of the success or failure of the battle vary enormously. In terms of sheer number, the British claim to victory is incontrovertible. Of an initial force of at least 20,000 men, the Japanese finally managed to collect into camps in Tenasserim, at the time of the surrender, about 7,000 survivors. In other words, in a matter of three weeks, an entire Japanese army had lost over half its strength. During the same period, the combined British and Indian forces, including a Burmese guerrilla force, had lost precisely ninety-five men — a ratio of about a hundred to one. There was another difference, too, from most of the other battles the Japanese had fought in Burma. Their losses in prisoners were relatively high. Only relatively — because their stern code excluded a soldier who became a prisoner-of-war from Japanese society should he ever attempt to return home. This ensured that men were captured, as a rule, only when unconscious, dying from fever or wounds, or unable somehow to reach the pin of the hand-grenade that would allow them to commit suicide and so redeem their shame. Nonetheless, many Japanese had reached breaking point by July 1945. Seven hundred and forty prisoners were brought into the cages of 17 and 19 Indian Divisions in a couple of weeks, and these included the highest ranking officers ever taken in the Burma campaign — captains and lieutenants. The ratio of prisoners to killed was higher than ever before, ten times as high, in fact. As Field-Marshal Slim writes, 'this final disaster had not only destroyed the Twenty-eighth Army, but had struck a mortal blow at the fighting spirit of the whole Japanese Army in Burma.'[2]

How is it, then, that the Japanese generals who planned and fought this battle can still believe that the victory was theirs, even though it was a costly one? Interviewed by *The Sunday Times* twenty years later, for a feature about modern Japan, the commander of 28 Army, Lieutenant-General Sakurai Shōzō, and his Chief of Staff, Major-General Iwakuro Hideo, both declared they had achieved the impossible by bringing 50 per cent of their force out of a British trap which might have destroyed them all. It was his best campaign, Sakurai told the interviewer, 'we would have been decimated if the war had gone on, because individually we could not surrender.' The general who commanded one of his brigade groups, Nagazawa Kanichi, declared in the Japanese magazine *Nansō*, '28 Army's bold determination to seek life in the midst of death and break defiantly through the enemy was a success. What changed our joy into sadness was that it was followed so soon by the surrender of Japan.'[3] When that happened, Nagazawa writes, he was moved to commit suicide as a way of showing he shared in the responsibility for all that had happened, but was restrained from doing so by the Emperor's command that all Japanese should continue to work for the well-being of their country in peaceful ways.

The sacrifice of thousands upon thousands of men was a heavy price to pay, and it was a cruel fate which made them pay this price only a matter of weeks before the entire Imperial Army surrendered unconditionally − a possibility which had not occurred to any of the officers of 28 Army in the worst moments of their tragedy. Nonetheless, the exacting of this price made it possible to bring the survivors back into what might have become a readjusted Burma front to prepare the defence of Tenasserim against a British thrust down the coast towards Malaya or across into Siam, had the war continued. Seen in these terms, Sakurai did the only possible thing: once it was laid down − or rather taken for granted − that individual or unit surrender was out of the question, it was unthinkable to let his men slowly rot in the monsoon rains or die of starvation in the Pegu Yomas. Break-out or die, that was the alternative. Put in this way, the answer was plain.

Most armies talk about fighting to the last man and the last round, Field-Marshal Slim once pointed out − the Japanese actually did it. The respect for Sakurai and his refusal to surrender, even in intolerable conditions, which is evident in the final pages of Slim's *Defeat into Victory*, is echoed by the

Indian historian of the reconquest of Burma:[4]

Starving, stricken by disease, harassed by the Royal Air Force and active patrolling by land forces, with no cover from the unending rains, any other adversary would have surrendered his whole force. But Lieut. General Sakurai, true to the traditions of his brave race — not unlike the Rajputs of the Middle Ages in India — did not consider surrender and paid the price.

Yet, from the British side, one can see why the battle takes up little space in the official history. In no sense did it have the strategic significance of the struggle for Imphal, which decided the success or failure of Japan's plans for the conquest of India, nor that of the battle of Meiktila, which settled the final outcome of the Burma campaign and is one of the most underestimated strategic master-strokes in the history of the Second World War. Except in terms of scale, it was basically a mopping-up operation, and its outcome would not radically have altered the shape of future campaigns in South-East Asia, though the presence of 28 Army in the Pegu Yomas might have constituted an irritation, if not a dire threat, to lines of communication. This is why the British IV Corps dealt with the problem posed by Sakurai in an almost comfortable manner. The terrain of the Rangoon-Mandalay Road between Toungoo and Pegu where the battle was fought, and the Sittang Valley in which it continued, was utterly unsuitable in mid-July for any kind of large-scale infantry conflict. Battles between opposing groups of infantry were very few. Instead, the Japanese were harried from the air, and although they marched by night and hid up in villages by day, their paths of advance were fully known beforehand, and British artillery ranged on them pitilessly and unceasingly as they plunged deeper and deeper into the morass that led to the Sittang. Here, though, there was no respite.

The Burma National Army, which had been a puppet creation of the Japanese invaders in 1942, had become aware that by early 1945 Japan had more or less lost the war. So they changed sides. British officers had taken command of groups of Burmese guerrillas in the no man's land that was the Sittang Valley, and constantly pursued broken groups of Japanese, cut them up piecemeal, and completed what air strikes and British-Indian guns had begun. The river did the rest. In many places as much as 440 yards wide, and turned by the monsoon into a fast-flowing merciless torrent, the river played havoc even with those troops who had been drilled to meet its dangers and had trained with bamboo poles as crossing-supports. To no avail: the river took them, ate them greedily, and sent them downstream as swollen corpses in their hundreds.

This is where the tragic paradox of the story of the Sittang Battle lies. That river, which had witnessed the greatest defeat of the British Army in Burma in the disastrous campaign of early 1942, now not merely watched but actively assisted in the final disintegration of an entire Japanese army. There were other coincidences too. The British-Indian Division which was split in two by the blowing of the Sittang Bridge in February 1942 was 17 Division, under Major-General 'Jackie' Smyth, VC, MC, who had to take one of the most agonizing decisions facing any British commander during the war. Should he delay blowing the Sittang Bridge until all his division — retreating from the victorious Japanese — was across? Or should he blow it at once to prevent the Japanese using it to speed their advance on the city of Rangoon? He chose the latter course, and left two-thirds of his division on the opposite bank as a result, either to make their way across the Sittang by swimming where the bridge had been blown, or to move northwards where the river narrowed and try their luck there. Now, three-and-a-half years later, that very same division was blocking the path to the Sittang of the Japanese 28 Army, holding an area stretching from Pyu to Pegu.

Another coincidence: constituting the central group of 28 Army was the force known as *Shimbu Heidan* (Shimbu Force), the infantry group of 55 Division. It was 55 Division which had invaded Burma in 1942 and accomplished the downfall of 17 Division. Yet again, its fellow division in the 1942 days, 33

Division, which had gone on to take part in the attempted
invasion of India, had been commanded in those first triumphant months in Burma by Sakurai Shōzō, the man who was
now facing the crossing of the Sittang from the west. This
time it was he who was in full retreat, and thinking not in
terms of a glorious victory but of rescuing whatever could be
rescued of the shattered Japanese Army in Central and Lower
Burma.

The impression should not be given, though, that the
Japanese break-out operation across the Mandalay Road and
the Sittang River was a last-minute act of despair, unplanned
and unprepared. This was not the case at all. It was considered
as a possibility months before it took place, the plans and orders for it were drafted with almost every kind of adverse cir-
cumstance in mind, and even in the reduced conditions of life
in the Pegu Yomas, strict training was carried out to fit the
thousands of Japanese troops for the break-out and the river
crossing. But the timing was against them. The monsoon made
movement intolerably difficult. Disease had weakened the
men's physique. Allied intelligence had discovered when and
where the break-out was to be made, weeks before it took
place, what units would take part, along which tracks they
would come, how many men were in each, what kind of
weapons they carried, how much ammunition they had left,
even what were their rations and their state of mind. 28 Army
had completely lost the element of surprise. They were to
attempt a break-out through a triumphant and determined
enemy, fully acquainted with their plans, possessed of incom-
parably greater firepower, and sitting firmly athwart every
one of their escape routes from the hills.

Against odds of this kind, even skill and fanatical bravery
were of little account. There could be no real doubt of the
final outcome. So was accomplished the tragedy of the last
intact Japanese battle formation in Burma, which was cut to
pieces in the Sittang Valley in the last few weeks of the
Second World War.

Perhaps I should say what my own qualifications are for writing about the break-out. In the first place, I saw the battle from start to finish, from a number of Burmese villages strung out along the Rangoon-Mandalay Road and along the track which leads into the foothills of the Pegu Yomas from Penwegon to Yee. Before the battle began, I translated the Shimbu Force Operation order later referred to in Appendix A and, together with a Nisei sergeant from Hawaii and another Japanese-speaking British officer, interrogated every prisoner who fell into the British net along the front of 17 Indian Division, from Pyu in the North to Nyaunglebin and Daiku in the south. I was the young lieutenant referred to in the account of Tsutsumi's wanderings that forms the last chapter of this book.

At the war's end I met most of the Japanese survivors — from generals to privates — in the surrender camps set up in Burma, Siam, and French Indo-China (as it was then) and talked about the Sittang operation while it was still a vivid memory for them. I have kept in touch with several of them since those days, and visited them in Japan during the year of the Tokyo Olympics, 1964, when I was in the country as a guest of the Japanese Foreign Office. One of them, Lieutenant-Colonel Tsuchiya Eiichi, who is now the head of a Japanese light-vehicles industry, runs a bulletin called Window on the South (Nansō) which is the record of the Sittang-Kai, the 'old comrades' association'of the officers and men of 28 Army and its subordinate units. The pages of that bulletin, with their memories of Burma, its people, its climate, its language, and the events which took place there between 1942 and 1945, show how strongly the images of the past are embedded in the minds of the men who made that historic crossing of the Sittang in the summer of 1945, even now, after the lapse of more than a quarter of a century. Some of them, like Tsuchiya himself, and Lieutenant-Commander Tsutsumi, of the 13 Naval Guard Unit, have committed their reminiscences to paper. I have had verbal accounts from others, like Major

Hachisuka, who is an old friend from the day he came into the village of Shwegyin as a peace envoy, with whom I wandered later in Tokyo to the Yasukuni Shrine and round the bookshops of Kanda, and who brought together a group of friends in a Ginza restaurant to talk about the battle.

In Burma itself I have been over much of the ground of the battle several times, either waterlogged as it was in the height of the monsoon season, or green and pleasant in later, drier months: the foothills of the Pegu Yomas, the tracks of the railway, the stretch of the Rangoon-Mandalay Road which runs between Toungoo and Pegu and which was once as familiar to me as the road between Durham and Newcastle is now; I have swum in the *chaungs* that feed the Sittang, and in the river itself, which can change in a brief space of time from a tranquil stream in which you can lazily swim and boat into a lethal maelstrom hurling itself in a frenzy towards the sea.

In a very real sense, therefore, those few weeks of July and August 1945 are as strongly imprinted on my mind as on the minds of the Japanese themselves. And because I was caught up in those events as irrevocably as they were, I have tried, at a distance of time which was not easily imaginable to me then, to look at what happened almost exclusively from their point of view. I have tried to tell the story of the battle as the Japanese saw it, and to convey their attitudes of mind. There have been many accounts of the campaigns in Burma, in English, but they have chiefly been written, naturally enough, from the viewpoint of the British or Indian soldier. There is a case, I hope, for seeing it as the enemy saw it, through his eyes, and bearing in mind his aspirations, his emotions, and his memories.

I have put as epigraph to *Sittang* a short poem by the seventeenth-century Japanese poet Basho. It has always seemed to me the perfect epitaph for those who fell in the Battle of the Break-out. The actual significance of the words is sorrow and regret; of the clash of arms, of the fierce cries and the bloodshed, of all the clamour and din of war, nothing is left but a flat green plain of summer grass, blown by a breeze. The nostalgia and the regret are both trite and universal. But Bashō, with the sounding trumpets of those vowels in the phrase for 'soldiers' which is the whole of the second line, *'tsuwamono - domo no,'* has infused the sadness with an echo of courage, glory, and idealism which, however out of place they may seem now, were truth and reality for many of these Japanese soldiers and sailors in the last weeks of the war.

Part 1 Prelude

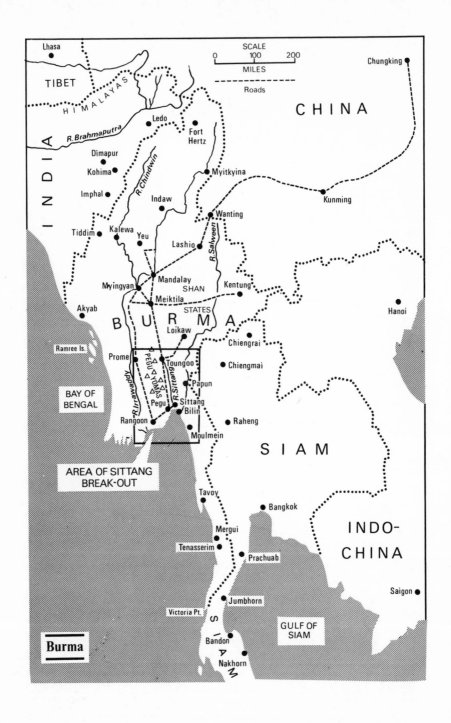

Burma

CHAPTER ONE

FORCES IN PRESENCE

The Japanese forces in Burma were divided into three Armies, 15, 28 and 33, under the overall command of Burma Area Army (Lt.-Gen. Kimura Hyōtarō) in Rangoon. In its turn, Burma Area Army came under the command of Field-Marshal Terauchi's Southern Area Army in Saigon, which was responsible to Imperial General Headquarters in Tokyo. In 1944 and 1945, 15 Army was destroyed when it attempted to invade India and 33 Army was defeated in the Irrawaddy battles which resulted in the loss of Central and Lower Burma by the Japanese. By the summer of 1945, Rangoon had fallen to the British and 15 and 33 Armies were retreating into Tenasserim, the south-east corner of Burma. To avoid being cut off in the Arakan, 28 Army was to cross the Irrawaddy, shelter in the Pegu Hills or 'Yomas', and then break out across the Sittang River to join the remnants of the other two Armies in Tenasserim. That is the situation at the beginning of this book.

28 Army

28 Army was founded for a specific limited purpose: to be the left flank of the Japanese invasion of India in 1944. The main thrust of the invasion would be made by 15 Army under Lieutenant-General Mutaguchi, who intended to pierce through the Chin Hills, debouch on to the Manipur Plain and seize Imphal, the capital of Manipur State and headquarters of British IV Corps. After this he was to make for the Brahmaputra while the news of his advance caused the discontented masses of Bengal to rise against the British oppressor and open the gates of India to the Japanese. At

any rate, that was the theory. To ensure the safety of 15 Army's left flank against possible sea-borne invasion of the Arakan, or a downward thrust from Chittagong, the coasts of Burma had to be watched. Three divisions were put at the disposal of 28 Army: 2 Division, which was later moved to Central Burma and then to French Indo-China, and plays no part in this narrative, and 54 and 55 Divisions, which are our main concern. In addition there were other units which were to play a dramatic role in the events of July 1945. In its seaward watch, the army had the collaboration of the Japanese Navy. 13 Base Unit, under Rear-Admiral Tanaka Raizō, who had made his reputation in the South-West Pacific, had headquarters in Rangoon and two of its guard units, or *keibitai* (12 and 13), were located in Rangoon and Taungup. Their chief task was to keep a watch on the coast for enemy ships, the blocking of rivers, and minesweeping. Each guard unit was about 600 men strong, with a mixed bag of small vessels, fifteen landing craft, four or five torpedo boats, and a number of minesweepers. Finally, in the summer of 1945, the various units of the Rangoon garrison, including hastily mobilized civilians, were grouped together into a formation called 105 Independent Mixed Brigade, and put under the command of 28 Army in the Pegu Yomas.

Of these formations, 55 Division had most experience of Burma. Raised in Shikoku from the four prefectures of Takamatsu, Tokushima, Kōchi and Matsuyama, it had invaded Burma from Siam in December 1941 and in a series of hard-fought battles had compelled the British 17 Division to retreat across the Sittang. Leaving its companion division (33) to take Rangoon, 55 Division had moved north to attack the Chinese, who had come south as far as Toungoo to act as belated reinforcements for the defeated British, but 55 Division rolled them back, took Mandalay in the process, and in one swoop after another, occupied the rest of North Burma. It was a triumphal progress.

When he took over his new army in January 1944,

Lieutenant-General Sakurai Shōzō was well acquainted with the history of 55 Division, and indeed with Burma as a whole, since it was he who had commanded 33 Division in the 1942 invasion. As a young officer Sakurai had seen service as a military attaché in France, had served on the General Staff at the War Ministry during the China Incident, and after his breathtaking capture of Rangoon in 1942 had become chief of the Mechanized Warfare Department at General Headquarters in Tokyo. His officers respected him for his integrity and decisiveness, and for his scrupulous private life, which set him apart from some of his colleagues among the Japanese generals in Burma. Of the two other army commanders who were his contemporaries, Mutaguchi of 15 Army had the reputation of being a womanizer, and Honda of 33 Army was regarded as an inexhaustible store of filthy stories, though his peccadilloes seem to have been verbal rather than behavioural. Tall for a Japanese, thin and bony in appearance, Sakurai has survived to a great age. It says a great deal for the case he makes for the rightness of his conduct of the suicidal Battle of the Break-out that his officers are still intensely loyal to him, and in fact his staff still congregate annually at his home to be photographed with him on his birthday. 'The Commander-in-chief', Lieutenant-Colonel Saito of 55 Division once said of him, 'had such a character as would remind you of the grace and grandeur of Mount Fuji', and he added, perhaps more to the point, 'he was well conversant with the power of the British-Indian forces and the geography of the battlefields of Burma.'

On 18 January, 1944, he was joined by his Chief of Staff, Major-General Iwakuro Hideo. Iwakuro was perhaps the most variously talented man in the Japanese Army in Burma, and had already been through many crucial experiences before he came to join Sakurai. The term is over-used, but Iwakuro had in his time been a real man of destiny for the Japanese Army. He had drawn up an influential document on the Japanese Army's policy in Manchuria in 1932 ('The Guiding

Principle of Manchukuo') and had been on the staff of General Muto, head of the Military Affairs Bureau. Later still, in 1941, when some American missionaries persuaded Roosevelt's Postmaster-General, James Walker, to put the views of a group of Japanese soldiers and businessmen direct to the President, bypassing the State Department in the hope of arranging a peace and acceptance by the U.S.A. of some of the conquests of the Army in China, it was Iwakuro who was chosen by the Japanese Army as its representative. He spent months in America involved in secret negotiations at the highest level in New York and Washington, before the inability of either side to compromise on essentials led to the breakdown of the talks. The Americans who dealt with him described him as an attractive and vigorous personality, and although some historians have doubted whether he was genuinely working for reconciliation and think he was simply carrying out an intelligence operation to gauge America's will to war, it is not unlikely that he represented a section of Army opinion which would have liked to preserve peace with the Americans if they could have been sure of a free hand in China.

A few months after the breakdown of the talks, Iwakuro was in French Indo-China, waiting for the signal to set his men against the British in Malaya. He was by this time in command of 5 Guards Regiment, and his swift and ruthless drive south to Singapore is described in his book *Seiki no sōkōgeki (The Campaign of the Century—the Assault on Singapore),* the draft of which, in the form of a war diary, he carried with him in the Pegu Yomas. But Iwakuro was a political soldier. Once the war was at an end in Malaya, he became involved in Indian politics, at the head of the organization which controlled Japan's relations with the *Azad Hind Fauj* ('Indian National Army'). The Iwakuro Organization, which later became the Hikari ('Light') Organization, was responsible for liaison between the Japanese Army and the Indians, and for arranging supplies. It was a constant source of friction and dissatisfaction, and

Iwakuro seems to have been less successful at smoothing matters over than his predecessor, Major Fujiwara. In fact at one time he was forced to place the Indian commander, Mohan Singh, under arrest. In time Iwakuro was replaced at the head of the Organization by the Japanese military attaché in Berlin, Colonel Yamamoto, and transferred to military government in Sumatra. From there he came to join Sakurai and 28 Army in South-West Burma.

54 Division

The largest unit under 28 Army's command in the summer of 1945 was 54 Division. The code-name for this formation was the Japanese ideogram for 'warrior'—*tsuwamono*—but like most other Japanese words this one has other readings, *hei* and *hyō*, which are derived from the way the Chinese used to pronounce the character at the time it was borrowed from their language over a thousand years ago. This multiplicity of readings allows Japanese to be a very allusive language, and in the case of 54 Division's code-name we see this allusiveness at work, as in the other code-names of 28 Army. The noun *tsuwamono* itself resounds like a claim to courage, and is the old Japanese way of reading the character. The reading *hyō* is the first part of the name of the prefecture Hyōgo which lies along the Inland Sea of Japan and of which the prefectural city is the beautiful castle town of Himeji. So the code-name serves both as encouragement to valour, as a reminder of Japan's military past (*tsuwamono* has a mediaeval flavour about it) and also as a means of recalling the local attachment of the division.

Under Lieutenant-General Katamura Shihachi, 54 Division arrived in Burma in September 1943 to take over the defence of the Arakan coast, including the islands of Ramree and Cheduba. The relentless pressure of XV Corps gradually forced the division out of the Arakan by the spring of 1945, by which time it had become clear that, like the other formations of 28 Army, 54 Division would be cut off and

surrounded by the British if it did not escape from the
Arakan across the Irrawaddy. So began a fighting retreat
towards the great river. The division had had a new
commander since September 1944, when Katamura was
succeeded by the gallant, puckish figure of Lieutenant-
General Miyazaki Shigesaburō, a tiny general with the heart
of a lion who had fought several desperate actions during the
retreat from Kohima in command of the rearguard of
31 Division.

He had originally intended to cross the Irrawaddy at
Thayetmyo, but the speed of the British advance made this
impossible, so Miyazaki began to probe frantically down the
west bank for a suitable crossing point. Finally he opted for
Kama. It was a far from perfect choice. He was open to
British attacks from the north, north-west, and west which
he had to fend off while preparing his forces to cross. Once
on the other side he had to break through a cordon set up by
7 Indian Division to trap him. In fact there were two cordons,
an inner one consisting of a 4-mile arc on the east bank of the
Irrawaddy south of Kama, three battalions strong, in high
ground and thick jungle, and an outer cordon or screen of two
battalions in the scrub country behind, blocking 54 Division's
path into the Pegu Yomas. Only after stiff fighting did the
Japanese manage to break through the cordon and reach the
village of Paukkaung, where they were to concentrate before
moving into the shelter of the mountains. Miyazaki had lost
heavily: in the fighting round Kama, both to preserve and
pass through his bridgehead on the Irrawaddy and the cordons
lying in wait for him, he lost most of his transport and
artillery and over 1,400 men. More than seventy prisoners
were taken, a very high figure for the time, which showed that
divisional morale was cracking. But in spite of these losses
Miyazaki managed to assemble the greater part of his division
at a rendezvous called Point 536, a hill east of the Irrawaddy,
by the end of May 1945. From there he moved to Paukkaung,
to recuperate his battered strength and prepare for the move

into the Pegu Yomas.

55 Division

55 Division was already split up into a number of separate forces long before 28 Army moved into the Pegu Yomas. A unit called Kanjō Force consisting chiefly of 112 Infantry Regiment had been sent to stop the southward advance of British-Indian armoured units from the Mount Popa area in March 1945. And the 143 Infantry Regiment provided the nucleus of what was called Chū ('Loyal') Force, which was put first under the command of 33 Army and then under the direct command of Burma Area Army, to stem the flood of Allied troops between Meiktila and Rangoon. Chū Force was commanded by the divisional commander in person, Lieutenant-General Hanaya Tadashi, while what was left of the division, namely its infantry group, was reformed under the name of Shimbu Force under the infantry group commander, Colonel Nagazawa Kanichi, who was later promoted to Major-General. The fact that such large segments were cut off from the division naturally weakened it considerably, and Hanaya's absence in Central Burma lowered the morale of the troops, who admired him as a tough old man in the uncompromising tradition of the Japanese *samurai*. The opinion was not shared by many of his officers. I had several conversations with Hanaya in Siam in 1946, and he seemed to me then the bluff, hearty, fatherly figure he appears to be in photographs of the period. In fact he was a crafty bully, who treated his junior officers with the same contemptuous disregard for them as human beings with which he viewed the population of Manchuria, who had been pawns in the political game Hanaya and his friends had played in the years leading to the Marco Polo Bridge Incident. There are innumerable stories of his beating quite senior officers over the face with his fists, not merely when he was irritated with them, but *pour encourager les autres,* and pointing out in a bull-like bellow that they had no operational experience or

knowledge of battle conditions and were utterly useless and incompetent. In some cases the observations were no doubt accurate. But it hardly improved matters or fostered mutual confidence for the commanding general of the division to beat up a lieutenant-colonel before his own orderly, so frequently and to such effect—the colonel retired from these sessions with purple bruises or blood flowing from his face— that the victim seriously thought of taking his own life by the traditional *samurai* method of cutting his stomach open with his sword *(seppuku).*

Not that this would have had the slightest effect on Hanaya. Rather the contrary. He is known to have told a number of his officers to commit suicide by *seppuku,* when he was dissatisfied with their bearing or conduct of operations. When a young lieutenant asked for artillery support to cut British wire entanglements during a particularly fierce engagement in the Arakan, Hanaya accused him of cowardice. 'Get on with the attack without artillery!' he yelled. 'Put in a night attack! What's the matter with you, are you afraid of attacking by night? Go and cut your guts out! Go on, do it here and now; if your sword's rusty you can borrow mine!' The young lieutenant was battle-hardened enough to have seen worse things than an angry general, and faced the wild eyes unmoved. But there were even worse instances. Hanaya once came upon the commander of his divisional engineers, Murayama, stripped almost naked as he was helping his men on a difficult job. 'Hey, you!' Hanaya burst out. 'Is that the way you normally dress? What sort of an example do you think you're setting? And you're supposed to be a regimental commander!' Murayama was furious at being rebuked in this way in front of his men, and swore to his officers that if Hanaya repeated the performance he would cut him down with his sword on the spot.

On the lower ranks, Hanaya's impact was different. When he spoke to them, his message was of the tough and simple kind they understood: 'Whatever situation you're in, you fight to the last, d'you hear? Keep on firing until your last round's gone. Then fight on with your sword. When your sword's broken, turn yourself into a human bullet and charge into the enemy, even if the odds are ten to one! Keep shouting "Long live the Emperor" until the very end! Then you can die bravely!'

There was something else about Hanaya which had a great influence on the division and 28 Army as a whole. Like Iwakuro, the Army Chief of Staff, Hanaya had had great experience of espionage and of the value of subversion in warfare. During the 1930s he was one of a group of officers in the Japanese Army in Manchuria who had worked constantly to extend the war in North China and complete the Japanese hold over the entire Chinese mainland. Manchuria was only the first step in this. Night after night, in his mess in the Arakan, Hanaya told the officers of 55 Division how he, Hanaya, had created the state of Manchukuo almost single-handed: *'Manshū wo ore ga tsukutta no da!'* ('I made Manchukuo!') He never tired of telling the story of how, on 16 September 1931, when everything hung in the balance between Chinese and Japanese and after endless discussion about blowing up a piece of railway to serve as an act of provocation which would allow the Japanese to commence hostilities, Colonel Itagaki, another army conspirator, had decided to let everything hang on the fall of a chopstick. 'I'll stand it up,' he had said, 'and if it falls to the right we call the whole thing off. If it falls to the left, we go ahead.' The chopstick fell to the right. One young captain, Imada, bounded up from his seat and cried out, 'Life is too important for men like you—stop all this nonsense with chopsticks, I'll go ahead and do it myself!' He dashed from the room, and Hanaya, who was at the time head of a Special Duties Organization *(Tokumu Kikan)* in the city of Mukden, said briefly to the others, 'We can't have him stealing a march on us like this. I'll go too!' With Hanaya's intervention the line was duly blown, and the Japanese Army took advantage of the incident to make war on the Chinese who were framed into responsibility for it. From that time on, the road to the Pacific War was open. So Hanaya could well claim that he had played a significant part in Japan's destiny.[1]

Spies in the Hills

Although he was away in Central Burma in command of Chū Force when his division began to move out of the Arakan across the Irrawaddy, Hanaya had left his mark on it, particularly in the encouragement given to the use of secret agents as an instrument of war. Not that he had begun this: 28 Army as a whole was intelligence-minded and contained a number of generals and staff officers who had either shared Hanaya's Manchurian background or acquired experience of intelligence work elsewhere. Major-General Sakurai Tokutaro (not to be confused with the Army commander, who bore the same surname), the commander of the 55 Division Infantry Group before the creation of Shimbu Force, had served in China, and although he had the reputation of being a frank, open and rather solid-minded man, he had used rough and ready methods of gathering intelligence. Gangsters and political fortune-hunters had been brought in to extract information from the local people and pass it on to the Japanese command. *Shinagoro* was the term the Japanese used for these strong-arm agents whose effectiveness was as might be expected: the short-term results were reasonable, but the long-term effect of allowing these toughs to oppress the population was to alienate the Chinese. Hanaya's and Sakurai's addiction to strong-arm methods was one of the reasons why Burma Area Army thought that in these two generals they had a couple of real tough nuts, one of whom, inside the army and out, had the reputation of being quite *'mucha-kucha'*–'unbalanced', if not immediately certifiable. Small wonder that one Japanese journalist referred to them both as 'a prize pair of lunatics' *('kijin no kōittsui')*. Yet, repugnant as they are bound to seem, Hanaya's brutal methods were not pure sadism. They had a purpose, and sometimes achieved it. He believed intensely in *Yamato-damashii*, that 'spirit of Japan' which would drive soldiers on to impossible tasks, well beyond the endurance of the individual, and which could yet be exacted of them, like the supreme sacrifice, in the name of their country.

Some intelligence organizations were already functioning when Hanaya took over his command. The Indian National Army, or *Azad Hind Fauj*, which had been formed from Indian prisoners-of-war captured in Malaya and Singapore and then trained to fight against the British, had set up a number of intelligence agencies on the Indian border under Japanese auspices, to subvert Indian loyalty to the British and send agents into India. The Japanese liaison organization which worked with the Indian National Army, as mentioned above, was called the *Hikari Kikan*, or 'Light Organization'. The Akyab agency of this organization was headed by a Captain Hattori, who had been trained in the Japanese Army's intelligence training centre, the Nakano School in Tokyo, after graduating from Waseda University in political science. Hattori had helped to train the rebel Burmese Aung San and his fellow Thakins on Hainan Island in 1941 and his Akyab agency ran a network of agents throughout the Arakan, across the British lines and over the frontier into India. In addition to other officers and N.C.O.s from the Nakano School, the Akyab agency employed three Japanese civilians *(shokutaku)* who between them formed an unprecedented cross-section of Japanese religious life in the service of the army.

One of them, Maruyama Gyōryō, was a Buddhist priest who belonged to that most fanatically ultra-nationalist of sects, the Nichiren sect. Most unusually for a Japanese, he had a working knowledge of Urdu, and was involved in recruiting agents from the Kaladan Valley to send into Bengal. The fact that he was a Buddhist priest was not unconnected with his success. Maruyama had been in India before the war, proselytizing on behalf of his sect. Once the Japanese had conquered the Arakan, he set up a network of Arakanese to work into India from bases near the frontier, travelling through the war zones without let or hindrance. His Arakanese always tipped him off whenever there was any danger of the British trapping him, and his two-fold contacts with Buddhist priests *(pongyis)* on the one hand and local tribal dignitaries on the other were ideal sources of intelligence for the Japanese. Maruyama impressed the Arakanese by his imperturbable courage under shellfire or bombing. During an air-raid or an artillery barrage he would beat his priest's drum and intone aloud the invocation of his sect, *'Namu myōhō renge kyō'* ('We pray to the Lotus Sutra of the Wonderful Law'), which has a hypnotic effect when reiterated constantly like a rosary; or he would recite prayers for those fallen in battle. 'The impact of this holy man on the hearts of the natives', one Japanese writer puts it, 'greatly simplified the collecting of intelligence.'

Kayabuki was even stranger. A Muslim, and one of the very few Japanese ever to have performed the *Hajj,* or pilgrimage to Mecca, he organized a network of Arakanese agents who moved with great freedom from Japanese-held areas to British. Indeed one of them once strolled into a British headquarters, stored in his mind for future reference what he saw, and calmly walked out again, his presence unqueried by anyone. As a *hajji,* Kayabuki was much revered by the Arakanese Muslims, and this enabled him to recruit agents in the Alethangyaw area for despatch by sea into India. The news of the presence of a *hajji* swept like wildfire across the Arakan, and volunteers were not lacking for Kayabuki's build-up of spy networks along the Bay of Bengal from Akyab to the little port of Maungdaw, until he had an ear in every village.

Lieutenant-General Hanaya was not content with organizations which simply ran agents into India. There are a number of primitive hill tribes in the Arakan, and he decided there was much to be gained by working with them as well as with the more sophisticated communities of Indians and Burmese. From a number of army graduates of the Nakano School he set up the *Akira Kikan* ('Radiance Organization') under the command of Captain Tanaka Seirokurō and with a nucleus of three N.C.O.s. Tanaka already had experience of working with Burmese. At the time of the first invasion of Burma in 1942 he had marched with a unit of the Burma National Army—a group of 300 men under one of the Thakins—right through the pass in the hills which leads to Taungup and on to Akyab, arriving there well ahead of the main body of Japanese infantry. He was particularly well versed in the topography and peoples of the Kaladan Valley and set up a base in the Mayu Range using forty Arakanese and Kamui agents, who spread out in the hills around Modok and passed him news on the movements of the West African division as it moved south down the Kaladan Valley.

Some of the tribesmen with whom he came in contact were unusually fierce, and the Japanese supplied him with *saké* and vegetables to win them over. The expenditure was not great, and the prize considerable. The tribes knew nothing about political demarcations and cared less, and their areas spanned the frontier between India and Burma, so agents sent into Bandurban and Chiringa could easily infiltrate into Chittagong and head west into Bengal. Tanaka himself was guerrilla-minded as well as being involved in intelligence-gathering. He put up a plan to send a flying column of the Burma National Army to take Chittagong, in Bengal, from the rear, but nothing came of it. The Mru and Kamui tribes were his special concern, and he shared so fully in their simple life and customs that he was once offered the highest priced local bride. 200 *yen* was the asking rate, but since the Kamui pride themselves on distended stomachs and protruding navels and buttocks, she hardly corresponded to Tanaka's ideal of beauty, and he was compelled to decline what developed into a very pressing offer.

Of course this type of intelligence work, involving funds

and prestige, was dependent on the close proximity of a large armed force. When the Japanese began to withdraw from the Arakan at the beginning of 1945 Tanaka's men stayed behind in the hills around Modok. It was a hazardous proposition. They lived in thick creeper-covered jungle alive with poisonous snakes and were cut off from any sources of food-supplies. Tanaka's little group was very soon reduced to near-starvation, and malaria and beri-beri robbed them of what little energy remained. They moved east of the Arakan Yomas and finally concentrated in the village of Myohaung. One night the hut they were living in was surrounded by natives and attacked, and the unit was slaughtered almost to a man. It was a fate which, in its details if not its tragic completeness, was to overtake many of 28 Army's intelligence units before the war was over.

As often happens in the use of agents, personal tragedies became involved with military collapse. There were two Japanese agents in the Pegu Yomas in 1945 who were of a very different nature from the tough guerrilla-trained men who characterized most of 28 Army's intelligence units. These were the Japanese civilian Mizushima and his wife, who was a Karen woman from Bassein in the Delta. Mizushima lived very happily in Bassein with his Karen, but as the British advance crept further and further south it was obvious that he would not, as a Japanese, be able to conceal himself for long in what would soon be British-occupied territory. There was no need for his wife to leave their home, he thought. He was prepared to bow to the inevitable himself and escape while the routes were still open, knowing that he and his wife could meet again once the war was over—though that prospect seemed very remote. When he broke the news to her that he intended to follow Shimbu Force into the mountains, she clung to him and wept, pleading and protesting. Finally Mizushima gave way, and when he went into the Yomas his Karen wife was with him. They were a godsend to the intelligence gatherers of Shimbu Force: a Japanese familiar with Burmese life, and a Karen woman who could move about unquestioned—or relatively so—in Burmese surroundings. Soon they were travelling from place to place in the eastern foothills of the Pegu Yomas, watching the assembly points of units of the Burma National Army, which was now co-operating with the British.

In theory, the turbulent times themselves might have afforded protection for these two; many families had been uprooted by the campaigning armies, food supplies were chaotic, all kinds of reasons could have caused them to move from one village to another. But then the coincidence began to be too obvious, and the couple began to be talked about in the eastern Yomas villages. It was not long before the Burma National Army decided to pull them in for questioning.

They were not, as it happened, difficult to find. They always moved together as a couple, however dangerous the territory. One day they came into a village and at once sensed from the tension in the atmosphere that this was not going to be a visit like any other. The villagers were ill at ease, and Mizushima and his wife became aware of the presence of strangers like themselves, as if little groups of men were quietly slipping into the huts and the surrounding forest edge and blocking the way out. The Burma National Army had in fact ringed the village as soon as it was known the Mizushimas had arrived. Suddenly there was no more time even to plan a quick escape. Three or four strangers made a concerted move towards Mizushima, who pulled out his pistol, not for his own defence, but to ensure that neither he nor his wife fell into Burmese (and hence British) hands. He pointed the gun at her breast and fired. Before the Burmese reached him he turned the gun on himself, and as his wife's body slid to the wet earth he put the second bullet in his brain.

I have purposely left consideration of the most important operative group to the last, since its activities had most effect on the planning and running of the break-out operation in the summer of 1945. Unlike some of the other spy organizations,

which had links with a division or a particular area of the
Arakan, *Hayate Tai* ('Rushing Wind Unit') derived from
28 Army as a whole. It was set up at Taikkyi in October
1944, and its purpose was—at first—a long-range one rather
than the gathering of intelligence of immediate tactical value.
Sakurai, the commander of 28 Army, had foreseen even at
this stage the possibility that at some future date his army
might be involved in guerrilla warfare in Lower Burma, and he
wanted to be sure he had men equipped to face it, who knew
the ground they would be fighting over and could move easily
among the native peoples. This explains the selectiveness of
the first set-up. Recruits were to be chosen on two counts,
one of them being the ability to resemble the Burmese and
mix with them without being noticed, and the other being a
high standard of mental and physical fitness. Its purpose was
thus summed up in a short Japanese phrase of four characters:
'*Kōshin Menkei*', 'a Japanese heart in a Burmese skin'. Great
care was taken in the correct study and adoption of Burmese
customs. The trainees had to learn to like Burmese food
which, like Indian curries, is usually too hot and bitter
for Japanese palates accustomed to subtler flavourings of
vegetables and fish. They were even instructed in the
different postures for micturition and defecation peculiar to
the Burmese.

Curiously enough, apart from one member of the training
staff, Captain Suganaga, who had belonged to the *Hikari
Kikan* and had some experience of working with agents and
troops other than Japanese, none of the *Hayate Tai* training
staff had much, if any, acquaintance with intelligence work.
The commanding officer was Major Hachisuka Mitsuo, of
28 Army staff. He was a good choice, resilient and humorous,
fair-minded, small and tanned enough to be taken for a
Burmese but broad-shouldered and muscular, and with
reserves of toughness that were moral as well as physical. He
and the rest of the staff were trained along with the trainees
in those things they were learning about for the first time,

particularly the details about the Burmese way of life which were taught by a civilian born of a Japanese father and a Burmese mother.   Lectures on the broader aspects of the situation in Burma were given by old hands like Major-General Iwakuro and Lieutenant-Colonel Tsuchiya.   A total of 161 trainees passed through the hands of *Hayate Tai* in the few short months of its existence. Twenty-one of these were kept back to act as nucleus for a second course which never materialized, since 28 Army had already begun its retreat into the Pegu Yomas.   The rest went back to their original divisions. Those who were posted back to 54 Division were formed into a small intelligence unit called *Kusunoki Tai,* named, like several Japanese organizations, after the mediaeval warrior hero Kusunoki Masashige.   Of those posted back to 55 Division about half went off to join the main body of the division (Chū Force) under Hanaya at Pyinmana, as it attempted to block the southward drive of the British IV Corps.   The rest joined Shimbu Force and became the nucleus of a unit called *Shimpū Tai,* which carried out reconnaissance for the division in June and July of 1945. Casualty rates for *Hayate Tai* were high: by the time the unit disbanded in Moulmein in August 1945 its survivors numbered thirty-four.

The *Hayate Tai* recruiting procedure was supposed to be selective of the most courageous elements in 28 Army, those with most initiative.   But of course, as with any army, the reality was more prosaic. Very few commanding officers, when asked to despatch their best officers and N.C.O.s away from the unit for an unpredictable length of time, and with no certain guarantee they will ever come back, are likely to release them.   The actual process of selection must have been most often like that described by Sergeant-Major Ozaki, who was in the III Machine Gun Company, 3 Battalion, 121 Infantry Regiment. Ozaki is now head of the central broadcasting office in Hiroshima of the Japan Broadcasting Corporation (N.H.K.).   He kept a diary in Burma, and he recalls that in October 1944 he was on Ramree Island, off the coast of the Arakan, living in a little *basha* made of bamboo and palm-leaves, awaiting the next British onslaught on the Japanese positions. He was vaguely applying himself to learning about a new mortar when one evening his unit commander, Lieutenant Inaba, called into his hut and said, '28 Army's starting a thing called *Hayate Tai*, and I've nominated you for it.' Nothing could have been more unexpected, as far as Ozaki was concerned, and when he asked what sort of unit it was he was told it was 'one of those special duties sections *(tokumu han)',* and that he would be sent away for six months' training and then returned to the regiment afterwards for secret duties.

In the end three men were sent from 121 Infantry Regiment of 54 Division, and at 28 Army Ozaki found that about forty officers and men were living in barracks in Rangoon ready to start the special training, which was to be carried on in conjunction with the *Kempei,* Japan's tough and ruthless military police organization. Training was not likely to worry men like Ozaki—hard and difficult marches were, after all, an inseparable part of Japanese infantry training—but what they were instructed in was far more exciting than a route march. Karate exercises began the morning, followed by lessons in reading and writing Burmese, then the study of climate, then a cram course on Burmese customs. These were regarded as the basic groundwork for the secret operations the *Hayate Tai* men were likely to have to undertake—in how distant a future? None of them knew. Ozaki had a flair for languages and took to Burmese quickly. To some extent, he managed to communicate with the Burmese in their own language before he had finished. Language training was the focal point as far as the instructors were concerned, and this was to be one of the distinguishing features of *Hayate Tai* operatives. Two or three examinations in Burmese were carried out during the course.

Classroom proficiency was one thing, contact with the

Burmese another. Going into a village and trying to start a conversation with the villagers, they felt that the Burmese found their attempts at speaking Burmese childish, and their accent conspicuous—which meant they still had a long way to go before they reached that stage which *Hayate Tai* required. They did not quarrel with this: their work, as Hachisuka explained to them, would often involve the employment of Burmese spies to go into British camps and installations and send intelligence back to their units. To do this properly, they would have to penetrate the British lines themselves and it would be desperately dangerous work. Hence the total effect of 'Burmanization' aimed at. The Japanese soldier (and officer) often wears his head shaved almost bald, like that of a Buddhist monk, a *maru bōzu* or 'real bonze' style. But these officers and N.C.O.s were encouraged to wear their hair as long as they liked, and to wear *engyis* and *longyis* (the Burmese shirt and sarong-type skirt) and to walk barefoot or with Burmese sandals.

The hardest to bear was the fact that their legs, below the edge of the *longyi,* were often hairier than those of the Burmese. To complete the transformation, these hairs had to be plucked out one by one with great pain and difficulty, until smooth legs like those of Burmese men were achieved.

Against this background of endless effort, the one bright spot in the training was the daily visit to a Burmese village, during which they practised conversation with the polite and charming girls. At the time the people of Burma as a whole were still fairly co-operative towards the Japanese, and the lessons ended very often in a lavish meal in a pleasantly welcoming and humorous atmosphere. As far as Ozaki was concerned, the six months' training passed very quickly, and most of the candidates were sent back to their divisions. But they had by then developed a *Hayate Tai esprit de corps,* symbolized by the unit song. Ozaki remembers very well the sadness with which that song was sung when those who had worked hard and consistently together for half a year met for their last farewell—he doesn't recall the whole song, but one verse still stands out in his mind:

> *dare mo inai*
> *hitoribotchi no areno no hate ni*
> *na no nai hana ga chitte iku*
>
> in the desolate wilderness
> where not a single soul may stray
> a nameless flower blows awhile
> blows awhile, and blows away

The sadness and loneliness of the words were not inappropriate. The men of *Hayate Tai* would indeed often have to work alone, without the support of friendly comradeship in moments of danger and despair. With six others, Ozaki was transferred to 28 Army headquarters once his training was over, and they were sent out at once to investigate conditions on the frontier between Thailand and Burma, under the leadership of the *Hayate Tai* commander himself, Major Hachisuka, and accompanied by a number of Burmese. The journey into the Shan Hills, the frontier mountains, was a long one, and on the way back they made their way down the Salween River. In every village they came across the dead bodies of *Kempei* (Military and Security Police). Clearly the war was coming closer even to those distant Karen villages.

By the time they returned to unit headquarters in Rangoon they learned that the 28 Army commander and his staff had already begun to move into the Pegu Yomas. Taking with them all the food they could they piled into a lorry and made for Pegu as fast as possible. Pegu was at the time under heavy artillery fire from British guns, and they found their path cut and the Japanese Army in a panic.

During the monsoon movement in the Pegu Yomas was hell on earth for man and beast, says Ozaki. His last memory of Burma is of swapping his pistol with a village headman for ten chickens, rather than having to hand it over to the British when the Japanese surrendered.

The Burma National Army

Sakurai's men had more to contend with than a merely military situation and the hazards of jungle and river in a tropical climate. They were faced with a political problem which altered the situation as far as living off the land and feeling secure in the rear communications and forward exploration were concerned. The Burma National Army, which was a Japanese creation, trained and munitioned by the Japanese, had turned against them in the spring of 1945. This came as no surprise to certain members of the staff of 28 Army, though some officers of Burma Area Army headquarters seem to have been caught completely napping when the Burmese forces lined themselves up for a parade in Rangoon, supposedly before setting off for the front, and then calmly made their way out of the city and went over to the British.

The 55 Division infantry group commander, Major-General Sakurai Tokutaro, had continually emphasized to his staff that their control over the loyalties of the Burmese depended directly on their ability to keep the British a good distance north of Mandalay. 'The line which runs from east to west with Mandalay as its centre', he impressed on them, 'is the line of change of the public mind. Once the British-Indian Army crosses that line, the mind of the Burmese people will change overnight. If and when that happens, our job will be to begin guerrilla warfare, with our headquarters in the Shan States, and a contingent left behind in the Pegu Yomas.' That Sakurai could even be forced to envisage this possibility was a sad reflection on the way things had turned out for that much heralded friendship between Japan and the people of Burma which had been a constant theme of Japanese propaganda in East Asia for the past three years. The Japanese were always convinced that there was a special feeling of sympathy between themselves and the Burmese, and that the latter would always recognize that it was the Japanese who had freed them from the British tutelage and granted them political independence. And those who ruled Burma were, by and large, their pupils.

It had begun in 1940, when a Japanese colonel attached to the General Staff, Suzuki Keiji, visited Burma disguised as a journalist and contacted some of the young anti-British 'Thakins'. The word *'thakin'* means 'master' and a number of young Burmese graduates of Rangoon University had adopted the term to show they were the equals of the Europeans who ruled their country. Suzuki believed in encouraging Burmese independence from Britain, but he also intended to serve Japan's cause by hindering the flow of supplies to Chiang Kai-shek. These supplies went through the port of Rangoon and up the Burma Road to Kunming, and Suzuki thought he could use the Thakins to stir up trouble in Burma and make the Burma Road unusable. Thirty Thakins, under their leader Aung San, escaped British vigilance and received military training from the Japanese on Hainan Island in 1941. When war broke out, they acted as guides for the Japanese columns invading Burma, and began to collect the nucleus of a Burma Independence Army in the wake of the invaders. This army was placed under the control of Suzuki's *Minami Kikan* ('South Organization'), but differences of opinion soon arose between Suzuki and the Japanese army commander, Lieutenant-General Iida. There seems little doubt that Suzuki was a genuine advocate of immediate independence for Burma, and encouraged the Thakins to think along these lines. This did not suit the Japanese higher command in South-East Asia. The original Japanese plans for the invasion of Burma had only envisaged the seizure of Rangoon and an area in Lower Burma adequate for the establishment of air bases to act as the outer shield of the Greater East Asia Co-Prosperity Sphere. The comparative ease with which far larger areas of Burma were rapidly taken from the British made the Japanese think again, and it was not long before Suzuki and his Burmese friends were struggling with 15 Army to put an end to military government and grant the independence Aung San had been promised. Suzuki had in fact promised far more than the Japanese Army was willing to concede, and before Burma was finally granted independence under Japanese suzerainty in 1943, with Dr Ba Maw as premier, the *Minami Kikan* had been dissolved and Suzuki sent back to Japan.

Looking back on the achievements of that time, Dr Ba Maw in his memoirs unhesitatingly attributes to Japan the final liberation of the Burmese people from the yoke of colonial rule, and he affirms, too, the part played by the amateurish Burma National Army in that struggle: 'Notwithstanding all the evil done by many in it this spirit shone most fiercely in that ragtag army in the making. Nothing could wholly obliterate that army's role and significance in the revolutionary struggle which took place in Burma.'[2]

Ba Maw had no love for Japanese militarism; but he also felt that it was foolish to condemn *en bloc* all those who served in the Japanese army, and that it was essential to see how greatly their individual qualities differed. Of the first army commander in Burma, he writes:

Fortunately my relations with General Shojiro Iida, the Commander-in-Chief, had become close and warm. I had found him to be a unique type of Japanese soldier, human, fatherly, and very understanding, a militarist on the surface, but not altogether so deeper down; at least he always tried to see things your way too, which was what made him different from the other militarists. It gave him a good deal of inner perception, particularly of the fact that a war can be won or lost in many ways and for many reasons, one of the surest ways to lose it being to rouse the hostility and resistance of a whole people. The general was a *samurai* in his almost mystical devotion to his emperor, his warrior caste and code, and his country, but this very devotion which consumed him made him understand the devotion of others to their own gods. It was this rare, unmilitaristic quality which made him great in our eyes.[3]

Relations of this kind were duplicated at many lower levels, and this makes less surprising the experience of a Japanese engineer returning to Burma in 1955 and going out for a walk at night in the streets of Rangoon, to find himself addressed with affection and delight as 'Japan Master'. Aung San himself, who commanded the Burmese forces under the Japanese, went over to the British in 1945 not out of a belief in the superior virtues of the returning armies but as an inevitable gesture towards those who had come back to seize power again, and in the hopes of ensuring that what had been gained from the Japanese should not be dissipated under the British. Captain Takahashi Hachiro, who had been Aung San's constant companion and was attached to the Burma Army H.Q. as adviser, on hearing that Aung San was going to defect, followed his trail, starting out from Rangoon on 23 March, and finally met Aung San in Shwedaung, to the south of Prome. On 27 March, the whole of the Burma National Army came out in open rebellion against the Japanese, but Aung San made no move against Takahashi. They could still speak quite freely and openly to each other, and Takahashi asked him what he intended to do. 'To continue to collaborate with the Japanese from now on would mean the destruction of Burma,' Aung San answered. 'What sort of a deal have you done with the British?' Takahashi queried. Aung San, who had recently met General Slim, the XIV Army commander, and had discovered in him a blend of sympathy and toughness, said quite simply, 'Ideally, what we want is total independence for Burma. If that's not possible, then we shall accept being a self-governing dominion, and we're negotiating on that basis now. But if neither of these two things prove acceptable, I shall fight the British to the bitter end.'

Later still, in the early days of peace, Aung San contrived to pass a letter to Captain Izumi of the *Minami Kikan,* who was in Moulmein after the Japanese surrender. 'In order to preserve our independence,' Aung San wrote, 'we have had to co-operate with the British Army, but we still maintain our trust in our comrades of the *Minami Kikan*. The future of Burma may perhaps once again lie along the path of resistance, and it is not out of the question that we might need Japan's help once more.' When Izumi read this letter out to his fellow officers, he said, 'The war has been lost, but the devotion we have given to Burma will live for ever in the hearts of the Burmese people.'

So much for the vicissitudes of loyalty in war. At any rate, from the moment Aung San sounded the call to rebellion in March 1945 until the war came to an end in August (or in fact September in some parts of Burma), the Japanese lines of communication were vulnerable to attack by Burmese, villages ceased to be havens of rest for Japanese troops and became death-traps instead, and the collecting of accurate intelligence from local informants became more and more difficult. The fall of Rangoon finally convinced the Burmese officers of the Burma National Army that they had made the right decision.

CHAPTER TWO

THE FALL OF RANGOON
AND ITS AFTERMATH

The Japanese at the headquarters of Southern Area Army in Saigon were in no doubt as to what the fate of Rangoon should be. From their torridly vinous surroundings in that French provincial city transplanted into the tropical heat of Cochin-China, they decided that Rangoon should be held to the last man and the last round in true classical style. To let the British retake it was to let them punch a great hole in the defence buckler with which Field-Marshal Terauchi was hoping to protect the occupied territories of South-East Asia. They were already more or less cut off from Japan, by sea at any rate. Any ship coming from the southern harbours of Moji, Ujina, or Nagasaki had to run the gauntlet of American submarines and sweeps by reconnaissance aircraft, and reinforcements and supplies to the Southern Regions, as the Japanese called South-East Asia and the South-West Pacific, had been reduced to a negligible trickle by the spring of 1945. Mountbatten's South-East Asia Command was about to launch a vast military enterprise and retake Singapore and Malaya, and the assault on Rangoon was a necessary preliminary: it would provide sea and air cover well into Siam, and down the long coast of Malaya. From the British point of view, Rangoon simply had to be taken before the monsoon which was expected in the first week in May.

The advance south from Meiktila had gone well. On 26 April 1945, with five days to the deadline by which Rangoon had to be reached, 17 Indian Division was at Daiku, 60 miles north of the city. It then struck at the town of Pegu, which lies where the road northwards to Mandalay connects with the road eastwards to the Sittang River, Tenasserim, and the east. If the British held this junction, any Japanese left in Rangoon or the Irrawaddy Delta would be trapped. A scratch force of three Japanese brigades, consisting of the Rangoon Defence Force, hastily assembled sailors from the Naval Guard Units, businessmen, civil servants, and shopkeepers put up a fierce and bitter resistance in Pegu. But by 1 May, Cowan, the 17 Division commander, was in control of the town, apart from a few spots which had been mined and booby-trapped. It seemed as if the corporate will of 17 Indian Division, which had been beaten by the Japanese so thoroughly at this very spot in 1942, had focused in its commander and would now drive on to the capital. But the rains intervened.

1 May was the day the monsoon broke over Lower Burma in 1945. In no time at all the torrential rain had turned Pegu into a morass. Most dangerous of all, the airstrips began to be unusable, and they were vital for the continuous pumping of food, petrol, and ammunition into XIV Army's energetic vanguard. So in the end, knowing the intense disappointment he would cause to 17 Division, and in his heart reluctant to do it for that reason, Slim had a seaborne landing carried out by XV Corps on 2 May. This was the instrument by which Rangoon was captured, while the soldiers of 17 Division fumed at the weather-imposed halt on their movements, just over 40 miles north of the capital.

Militarily Rangoon was an almost empty city. A small group of Japanese put up a brief resistance to the Gurkha paratroops of 80 Parachute Brigade who had been dropped at Elephant Point. Then occurred one of those heart-lifting events which redeem some of the worst moments of war. An RAF pilot flying over the city saw a signal in English written in large letters on the roof of Rangoon Gaol. Not merely in English: in a style and vocabulary which was stamped with a telling authenticity–'Japs Gone. Extract digit.' Impressed by the lack of any sign at all of movement in the city, the resourceful RAF pilot decided to check for himself, crash-landed his Mosquito at Mingaladon airfield and walked into Rangoon from there. From the POWs who had been left behind in Rangoon Gaol he confirmed the fact that the Japanese had abandoned the city and then, with superb panache, commandeered a sampan in the harbour and sailed down the Rangoon River to meet the incoming flotilla of 26 Indian Division.

Of course Rangoon should not have fallen like this, almost without a shot, and that it did so is undoubtedly due not merely to the triumphant dash and energy of XIV Army but also to the nature of the Japanese Commander-in-Chief, Kimura Hyōtarō. A former Vice-Minister of War under General Tojo, Kimura had been made Commander-in-Chief Burma Area Army after the failure of the Imphal operation. Heads had rolled in all the Japanese formations involved from top to bottom, including the then Commander-in-Chief, Lieutenant-General Kawabe. Kimura was faced with the problem of defending Central Burma from the Allied armies, which had begun to move into it from all sides, and he made a skilful delaying job of it. On the other hand he was not a 'last-ditcher' by temperament. As far as Rangoon was concerned he felt it more important to hold Tenasserim District rather than retain a city which would be difficult to supply and hold against an enemy which covered every northern approach to it, though he was well aware of its political importance: it was not only the seat of the independent Burmese government under Dr Ba Maw, which collaborated with the Japanese, it was also an important centre for the Indian National Army, under the leadership of Subhas Chandra Bose.

In the city itself, as the British threat developed during April, there was total disagreement at the top. Kimura's Chief of Staff, Tanaka, was insistent that Rangoon should be held at all costs and fought for street by street if necessary. The Burmese Premier, Ba Maw, was in no doubt what this

would mean in terms of the destruction of lives and property.
Tanaka was for him the symbol of all that was worst in
Japanese militarism, and although he was deeply aware that
Burma owed her first taste of—highly qualified—independence
to the Japanese Army which had driven out the British in
1942, he had no wish to see that Army use a scorched earth
policy on a poor country that had already been ferociously
fought over. 'We have over a million troops in South-East
Asia,' Tanaka boasted to him, 'and we will throw every
soldier into the battle.' Japanese resolution was brought
home to him by the sight of the hill on which the Shwe
Dagon Pagoda was built being fortified and mined as part of a
last-ditch plan to hold Rangoon against the British. Explosives
were being buried under the big business blocks in the city,
which had once belonged to British firms—these were to be
blown up if the Japanese were forced to retreat.

Ba Maw's Minister of Information, U Nu, and some of
his colleagues learned that certain Japanese offices were
already being transferred to Bangkok, and that at Bassein,
in the Delta, telephone and barbed wire were being rolled
up.   This seemed to indicate that the Japanese were
contemplating withdrawal, but when asked about this the
Japanese authorities blandly asserted that these offices would
function more smoothly in Bangkok—it was merely a
question of administrative reorganization. Ba Maw himself
went to see General Kimura and warned him that if he used a
shrine so sacred in Burmese and Buddhist history as the
Shwe Dagon Pagoda for a series of gun emplacements, the
consequences would be catastrophic for Japan's hold on East
Asia.

Kimura heard him out and said little in reply, but Ba Maw
gathered an impression that the Commander-in-Chief, at any
rate, was by no means convinced that the kind of scorched
earth policy which had been followed in the Philippines—and
had succeeded in turning the Filipinos completely against the
Japanese—was appropriate to the Burmese situation. Ba Maw

took his case even higher. Later in 1944 he had been invited
to Tokyo to broadcast on the Japanese radio and meet
leading Japanese politicians. He now sought to impress on
Koiso, the Premier, and Field-Marshal Sugiyama, the Chief of
the General Staff, that no battle should be fought in
Rangoon and that Burmese administrators should not be
exposed to needless risk or reprisals in battle areas by being
abandoned to the British. Sugiyama assured him that Japan
would look after her supporters in Asia, and added that he
understood how Ba Maw felt about keeping the war away
from Burmese cities, particularly the Shwe Dagon Pagoda.
'We will do our utmost to spare your cities,' he promised,
'but I warn you that if, no matter how or through whom, the
enemy should come to suspect that we will not defend
Rangoon or any other big town we will fight anywhere
regardless of consequences.'

It was a clear indication to Ba Maw to keep his mouth
shut about the promise, and as good as told him that
Sugiyama had a shrewd idea that some members of Ba Maw's
government were already suspected of being in secret contact
with the British, and were only awaiting a suitable moment
to change sides.

Materially Rangoon had already suffered terribly from
British bombing in the spring of 1945. The railway station
had been wiped out and the big buildings in the centre were
so many shells. Bombing had destroyed the water supply;
there was no water in Rangoon from 22 March 1945, and
this had the ancillary effect of causing the sewerage system to
break down. The generating station had been bombed, there
was no electricity and no electric transport. And transport
by road was extremely hazardous. In the port 60 per cent of
the wharfage and 80 per cent of the covered accommodation
was destroyed.

Nonetheless, Southern Area Army needed to hold the city.
On 20 April Field-Marshal Terauchi wired Kimura from
Saigon to say it was imperative that Rangoon be held to the

last. 'I admired the sentiment expressed in the message,' Kimura later recalled with smooth irony, 'but I was at the same time astounded by the complete ignorance of the actual situation shown by the staff of Southern Army; it should have been clear to them that, at this juncture, in view of the phenomenally rapid advance of the British forces to the Sittang basin, Burma Area Army could not allow itself to be cut off and isolated in the Rangoon area. But the headquarters, both at Rangoon and Singapore, were so afraid of the prospect of Rangoon becoming the base of an all-out attack on Malaya that they were capable of issuing such fantastic orders as the one which instructed me to make Rangoon the graveyard of Burma Area Army. My decision to abandon Rangoon was and is eminently justifiable.'

This was so if his purpose was to conserve forces rather than to hold on to the capital city with its—by then—purely symbolic value. But, with complete inconsistency, after the order to evacuate was given on 24 April 1945, and Kimura himself had safely reached Moulmein, he at once began issuing orders for the recapture of the city.

The ordinary soldiers (and officers) who learned of their Commander-in-Chief's flight by plane to Moulmein while they were still fighting to save a desperate situation did not hesitate to express their disgust. Men from 18 Division who were defending the lower Sittang area ran out from their positions to beat with their fists the troops who came on foot in pursuit of the fleeing headquarters. And one Japanese private, Aida Yuji, now a professor of European history in the University of Kyoto, remembers marching through the streets of Rangoon early in 1944, when the city was still peaceful. Their squad met a car flying the General's yellow pennant coming from the opposite direction. They were young troops, new to Burma, and hoped to catch a glimpse of the general who commanded all the Japanese troops in the country. As the car drew level, all they saw in it were two or three Burmese comfort girls, dead drunk. It was a revelation to Aida of the way headquarters officers lived in Rangoon, and it made him listen sceptically to the words his platoon commander repeated to him after hearing a speech from General Kimura, welcoming new officers to Burma early in 1945.

'You've led a pretty sheltered life so far,' Kimura had said. 'Well, don't think the front line's going to be a pushover, it's not. If you're going to be of any use, you have to be ready, and you have to be resolute. Off you go. And see you die like men.' While he was in hospital, Aida was astounded to see a man without his right hand marked fit for service. The MO heard him whispering how monstrous it was to send an obvious cripple to the front, and burst out, 'He may not be able to fire a rifle, but he can still pull a horse's reins! Everyone is needed at the front, even those who are as little use as he is. Those are the General's orders.' With a surprising and unnecessary delicacy, Aida refuses to spell out the General's name in his book,[1] and calls him 'General K—' as he continues, 'This same General K—, when the enemy was drawing near to Rangoon, had all the civilians mobilized as a garrison while he himself got away by air. The Japanese who were left behind, civilians, nurses, everybody, were completely wiped out as the British Army enveloped the town.... After the words, "Die like men!", the general should have added, "Because I intend to escape to a safe spot by aeroplane." '

'It was indeed a great disgrace in the history of the Burma campaign', recalls a staff officer of 28 Army, 'that the Commander-in-Chief ran away with his staff officers, ignoring the fact that two or three weeks before he had boasted that, as far as Burma was concerned, Southern Army need have no fears, he would hold it.' The same officer criticized the army's failure to look after its comfort girls, to see to the security of Japanese civilians, to ensure that invaluable materials of war, clothing, equipment, weapons, were distributed to front-line units before the British closed in or the Burmese looted the warehouses. Two days before his retreat, in conversation with

Lieutenant-General Sakurai, when the plan for guerrilla warfare by 28 Army in Pegu Yomas was being unfolded, Kimura had told him, 'Don't worry, we will keep the line north of Toungoo till the end of the monsoon.'

The Japanese seem to have reached the decision to leave on 22 April, but the order was not issued until 24 April, and Tanaka's pressures on Kimura not to abandon the city—they almost came to blows when discussing the matter—had the disastrous effect of leaving the withdrawal until it was almost too late. And what might have been an orderly retreat from Rangoon was turned into a stampede for those who were less fortunate than Kimura and had to make their way overland to his new headquarters in Moulmein. 'Two huge armies,' wrote Ba Maw, 'Japanese and Indian, and two governments, Burmese and Indian, and an endless throng of vehicles in all sorts of conditions and moving at all sorts of speed choked the whole length of the narrow road to Pegu, and everything was just crawling along and even brought at times to a long halt, while a brilliant moon shone pitilessly showing up every object on the road.'

The refugees, for that was what they had become, were vulnerable to British air attack as they moved along in decrepit old buses or on foot—the Japanese refused to provide the members of the Burmese government with military transport. From the very first night of the retreat, 23 April, bombing and strafing of the slow column was continuous. Ba Maw was worried by domestic events as much as by international ones: his eldest daughter Tinsa was about to have her first child, which was in fact born at Kyaikto on the night of 28 April, after Tinsa had been driven nearly out of her mind by the rigours of the journey and the constant bombing and machine-gunning from the air.

The *Arzi Hukumat-i-Hind* ('Provisional Government of Free India') under Subhas Chandra Bose, was part of the same retreat, but with the signal difference that Bose himself refused motor transport at one stage of the journey and insisted on sharing the hardships of the march with his men. Bose had in fact wanted to stay on in Rangoon till the end, but his ministers persuaded him to make for Bangkok. He had women under his command, too, which added to his responsibilities: the girls of the Rani of Jhansi Regiment left in convoy—fifteen lorries, six cars—late in the evening of 24 April. Bose seems to have had more concern for Burma's capital than the Premier, Ba Maw, himself. There was no doubt it would be vulnerable to looting and pillage on a grand scale once the Japanese left, and since he felt a grave responsibility towards the large Indian population of the city, Bose instructed Major-General Loganathan to stay behind in command of 5,000 troops of the Indian National Army to maintain order until the British arrived and began their new administration.

In this way Japan's rule over Burma's capital city and her two puppet governments came to an end. In Rangoon itself the interregnum between the departure of Kimura and the arrival of the British, a period of about ten days, was a time of anarchy, looting and pillage. Little attention had been paid to the problems of the population. In fact some of the Japanese themselves were not aware that Burma Area Army headquarters had abandoned the city. Major-General Matsui, Commander-in-Chief of the hastily assembled Rangoon Defence Force (105 Independent Mixed Brigade), carried out the final conscription of Japanese residents in Rangoon on 26 April, the same day that most of the headquarters staff left by car. In theory he should have incorporated also 500 casualties from the Lines of Communication Hospital and in fact made up a battalion out of them, but they were so obviously useless as a fighting force that he finally shipped them off to Moulmein by boat. But what is interesting is that Matsui did not know, at the time, that his Commander-in-Chief, with a headquarters in the same city as himself, had decided to leave by plane on the evening of 23 April. He only found out later. When the news did come through Matsui at once sent a squad of the garrison defence force to the headquarters buildings. All they found was a chaos of documents, including nominal rolls of awards for merit which were lying about on office floors. Boxes of cigarettes intended for the troops had been rifled by Burmese who had broken into the building, and not a single one was left.

When the squad returned to report this, Matsui was speechless with fury. 'I'm the Rangoon garrison commander', he raged inwardly, 'and they've skipped out without saying a word!' Then he turned his attention to the matter of the prisoners in Rangoon Gaol. The Central Gaol held British and Indian prisoners-of-war, and he told Captain Sumida, commandant of the POW section, to collect the fit prisoners —there were about 300 judged to be in this condition—and march them out in the wake of the retreating headquarters to Moulmein. They had reached Waw, east of Pegu, when the column came under fire from Allied bombers, and Sumida decided to act on the instructions Matsui had secretly given him before he left: to release the prisoners if the situation demanded it. Similar instructions were conveyed regarding those who were not considered fit to be moved from the gaol. 'From tomorrow, 30 April,' Matsui notified them, 'you are free to move as you wish. Enough food and medical supplies have been left behind for you. The British-Indian forces will soon be in Rangoon and you can wait for them or not as you choose.' This was conveyed by a message pinned, in English, to the main gate of Rangoon Gaol after the Japanese guards had been withdrawn after dark on 29 April. Matsui had done the sensible thing as far as the 1,400 POWs in the gaol were concerned, and he turned his attention now to fighting. His unit had been formed as garrison for a city which his superior officer had then abandoned without so much as informing him. But the British had not yet arrived, and there was likely to be some point in delaying their resistance wherever possible, at Pegu, say—so Matsui put the Rangoon Defence

Force into the battle at Pegu. The order had been to destroy all port installations before leaving, but explosives were scarce and all that could be done was to blow up part of a bridge.

The women and children had mostly been evacuated to the rear as the Allied armies approached down the Mandalay Road axis, but there were still about a hundred left at the very end. Colonel Aoki, the Senior Staff Officer, ordered them to accompany units of troops withdrawing, but as they would not be able to keep up with the pace of the marching soldiers, the adjutant of No. 73 L of C Area Unit, Captain Shirasawa, went down to the harbour to find a boat for them. He commandeered the only wooden boat available and put the women in, together with the boxes of ashes of men who had been killed in the recent campaign. These had been stored in Rangoon awaiting shipment back to the Yasukuni Shrine in Tokyo. There were about 40,000 of these boxes. Shirasawa did not go with the boat himself, but went back into the city and made his way to Moulmein overland. Unlike some boats which tried the sea crossing, this one was not attacked by Allied planes and reached Moulmein without a hitch.

Lieutenant-General Sakurai, hearing that Burma Area Army was retreating from Rangoon, rang up from his headquarters to enquire what its intentions were in relation to the future movements of 28 Army. He was told that orders would be issued after Kimura reached Moulmein. His opinion of Kimura, never very high, fell to zero when this news came through. He knew perfectly well the disastrous effect on morale the Commander-in-Chief's flight was likely to have. The way rumours circulated in armies almost guaranteed this: the news spread round front-line units with terrific speed, and what annoyed Sakurai was the confusion in the men's minds about who exactly had run away. 'Army H.Q.'s moved to Moulmein' was how it was passed on, and that could be taken as '28 Army H.Q.', an ambiguity quite likely to wreck discipline among those who misunderstood it. And there was the business of stores, too. The withdrawal to Moulmein came so suddenly that large stocks of stores, weapons and ammunition were abandoned as they stood, without being passed on to the forward units. Sakurai's liaison officer with Burma Area Army decided to take matters into his own hands, and, as Sakurai put it, 'developed a taste for taking a car into Rangoon and returning with it loaded with trench mortars and ammunition.' He spent a day doing this and organized a squad for collecting *matériel* the following day, but it was already too late: the Burmese had been in and the stockpiles had almost totally disappeared.

Every kind of installation was uprooted and stolen by bands of roaming dacoits. Fittings of all kinds were wrenched away from the beautiful houses on the shores of Rangoon's lakes; taps and valves, switches, lamps, everything was ripped out or torn off. Cast-iron manhole covers were removed from the roads, vital records carelessly scattered or destroyed, vital parts taken from cars and lorries. The streets were clogged with great heaps of debris, the alleys with night soil. In places the streets were carpeted with millions of Japanese occupation currency notes, attractively designed in green and red but now worth only their value as paper. The roads were broken, with enormous potholes everywhere filled with water and mud. In May 1945 the abandoned city of Rangoon was a city in its death throes.

CHAPTER THREE

A LITTLE HELP FROM OUR FRIENDS: SUPPORTING 28 ARMY'S BREAK-OUT

When the British-Indian forces of XIV Army sliced the Japanese in two at the end of April 1945, one army, 28, was left in the Arakan and Irrawaddy Valley, and two others, 15 and 33, were left scattered to the east of the Rangoon-Mandalay Road or retreating south through the Shan Hills towards Tenasserim. 15 Army was never to recover from the thrashing it had received between the Chindwin and Manipur when its 'March on Delhi' was transformed into an agonizing, heartbreaking retreat of starving and sick men. 33 Army had withdrawn from its fight against the Chinese in the north of Burma to halt the British advance south from Meiktila, and had been harried and pursued by IV Corps from town to town until it was finally brushed away into the hills east of Toungoo and the flat marshlands of the Sittang Bend by 5 and 17 Indian Divisions as they thrust triumphantly towards Rangoon.

Once it had retreated into Tenasserim after the fall of Rangoon and had re-established itself in the town of Moulmein, the overall command in Burma, Burma Area Army, began a hasty redistribution of its forces. 28 Army had to be rescued from its encirclement and the British had to be prevented from penetrating into Tenasserim once they had secured Rangoon. Kimura realized from the mood of Southern Area Army's reaction to his abandonment of Rangoon that he would have to hold on to the south-east corner of Burma as long and as tenaciously as he could, since it would act as a deterrent to a British move down the southern tongue of Burma into Malaya, or across into Siam

by way of the invasion routes the Japanese had used
themselves in 1942. Japan's supply route to Burma was
threatened, too: the Siam-Burma Railway, which had been
built at such a great price in human lives, was regarded
by . the Japanese themselves as a tremendous engineering
achievement in terms of the difficulties of terrain overcome
and the hazards of supplying material so far from Japan,
when every ship ran the gauntlet of enemy submarines. Since
October 1943 the railway had fed troops and ammunition
and supplies into Burma, and Kimura intended to keep that
line open at all costs. It was vulnerable to assault from the sea
as much as overland, and there were many points on the
Tenasserim coast which could have been used for a seaborne
landing of the kind the British had made during the last act
of the Arakan campaign. Where the railway line between
Moulmein and Tavoy linked with the Burma-Siam Railway at
Thanbyuzayat, Burma Area Army established 24 Independent
Mixed Brigade to act as garrison, particularly against seaborne
landings. Needless to say, Kimura knew he could not rely
on a single brigade to repel a determined British force, and
33 Army was ordered to set up its headquarters at Moulmein
and ensure that 31 and 33 Divisions reinforced 24 Independent
Mixed Brigade. The road that led into Siam from Martaban,
through Kawkareik and Rahaeng, would be guarded by 31
Division, while 33 Division covered Moulmein and Mudon.
Further north, in the lower Sittang Valley, reading from
north to south, 53 Division, 18 Division and 49 Division
would hold the line of the Sittang and act aggressively across
it when the time came to support 28 Army's move out of
the Yomas.

Then there was the situation further north. At right angles,
almost, to the main axis of the Rangoon-Mandalay Road, a
number of roads ran into the Karenni and the Shan Hills to
the Salween River and so into Siam. One of these wound
from Meiktila through Thazi up into the delightful summer
hill stations of Kalaw and Taunggyi, beyond which the road

forked north into China, south to the Salween. At Toungoo another road ran east to the mines at Mawchi and the town of Kemapyu, from which—with difficulty—it was possible to reach Chiengmai in northern Siam. A newly-named formation, the Army Group Phoenix *(Ōtori Shūdan),* consisting of 56 Division and the remnants of 15 Army and 15 Division in its area, was to hold the area east of Toungoo, and block this road to Mawchi and the Salween against 19 Indian Division, which began probing up into the hills once it had set itself up in Toungoo. In fact the use of the term 'Army Group' was quite absurd, since almost immediately it was decided to transfer 15 Army and 15 Division out of Burma into Siam, leaving 56 Division on its own. These transfers were no new thing: in the height of the fighting on the Irrawaddy, 2 Division had been withdrawn from Burma and sent to Indo-China, where the Japanese were about to take over from the French administration by a *coup de force* on 9 March. This was intended to ensure that the inner bastion in South-East Asia was held, whatever might crumble on the periphery. 55 Division's main body was transferred to Indo-China after its unsuccessful attempt under the command of 33 Army to hold the Rangoon-Mandalay axis against IV Corps. Militarily these moves made no sense at all if the situation was seen to be one of holding on to Burma at all costs. But Southern Area Army, with a wider view, was clearly aware of the political rumblings in South-East Asia as it became more and more evident that the Allies were pressing in from Burma in the west to the Philippines in the east. The French resistance movements in Indo-China were, the Japanese knew, being supplied with arms flown in from China. In the north, a Communist revolutionary Ho Chi Minh was installed in the province of Cao Bang just north of Hanoi, fed with weapons and encouragement from the American O.S.S. detachments operating from Yunnan. Emissaries from General de Gaulle had made contact with units of the French army in Saigon and Hanoi, and were making ready to rise against the Japanese if the Americans landed on the coast of Indo-China. The Japanese knew that sooner or later their continued political and economic pressure on French Indo-China would have to be transformed into military pressure and decided to act first. On 9 March 1945, they took over every major installation, imprisoned the French army in its barracks, and massacred those units which resisted. Only one, under General Alessandri, managed to fight its way to safety across the border into China.

Siam was less restive, but the Japanese were not fooled. The *Kempei* had an excellent spy system working in the occupied countries, and it was known that certain highly placed Siamese had already made contact with Mountbatten's headquarters. But how extensive this contact was and how mature the plans were for a revolt to coincide with an Allied penetration into Siam, the Japanese did not know. At any rate they made no move against the Siamese government parallel to their move against the French.

Thus in Burma and the rest of South-East Asia collaboration with the Japanese was beginning to turn into indifference or positive resistance. The Japanese could no longer be sure that they had only the British-Indian forces to deal with and that the occupied countries would act as a cushion behind them. Throughout the area of the Shan States and the Karenni the British were beginning to send in groups of officers and wireless operators to receive parachuted drops of arms in readiness for the rising which was bound to come once the military hold of the Japanese was shaken by Allied victories elsewhere in Burma. In the Karenni, particularly, the British had friends. One British officer, Major Hugh Seagrim of the Burma Rifles, had stayed behind in the Karen Hills when the British Army retreated in 1942, and had succeeded in hiding from the Japanese and in keeping alive the flame of loyalty to the British cause. He had done more than this. When the Japanese sent a *tōbatsu,* or 'punitive expedition', into the Karenni to suppress Seagrim's core of resistance he refused to allow his friends to be tortured by the Japanese to reveal his whereabouts. To prevent this, he gave himself up freely and was executed in Rangoon in the autumn of 1944.

There were complications, inevitably, in sending in arms to guerrillas, whether they were the Karen levies raised by Seagrim's successors or the Shans and Burmese used by Force 136. Force 136 was the clandestine organization in South-East Asia corresponding to the Special Operations Executive (SOE) in Europe, and it had succeeded in forming a guerrilla movement behind the Japanese lines in Burma by co-operating with the political party called the Anti-Fascist Organization (later the Anti-Fascist Peoples' Freedom League). Arming an organization of this kind was, in the view of the Burmese government-in-exile in Simla, storing up trouble for the day when Burma would be free of military rule, as many British officers in the higher commands agreed. But military needs overrode political hesitation, and by the summer of 1945 these guerrilla units were operating up and down the Sittang Valley and in the Shan Hills.

Their work was two-fold: they harassed the Japanese lines of communication on the ground; and they gave the RAF ground information which aerial reconnaissance would never have uncovered. Japanese headquarters and supply dumps, fondly thought to be cloaked from discovery by surrounding jungle, suddenly found themselves the target of relentless bombing attacks on pinpointed positions.

The individual Japanese soldier felt the impact of the guerrillas in other ways. The entire area towards which 28 Army was making its break-out from the Pegu Yomas had become not a haven of rest for the starving and exhausted Japanese but a hostile inferno of ambush and slaughter. The troops of the battered 15 and 33 Armies found this out first, long before the break-out began. The experience of these men can be concentrated in the vivid description of one episode by a soldier of the 53 Division as he made his way south through the Shan Hills. His division had been ordered to make for Tenasserim after being defeated at Meiktila. It was later to act as a shield on the lower Sittang to ensure the safe crossing of 28 Army.

At the end of April 1945, a month after the guerrilla risings and the B.N.A. rebellion, the soldier Aida Yuji and a lieutenant were making their way south through the Shan States, charged with the duty of collecting the stragglers from their regiment. They had in fact known each other before their army days, and Aida, an intellectual in uniform, was delighted to be away from the bullying old sweats of the battalion and in civilized company—the lieutenant was a university graduate like himself. They set out a little while after the main body and let the distance grow gradually greater until they were a full four days' march behind. Almost at once they began to come across the corpses of Japanese soldiers and, lying here and there beside the jungle tracks, men who could not move for sickness or wounds. They tried to cheer them up and persuade them to move on, but there was no response. There were some who cried out to be helped along, but if they could not walk it was hopeless, because by this time neither Aida nor his lieutenant had the strength to lift anyone.

Several days before they reached the appointed rendezvous with their unit they came to a spot where two or three units seemed to have passed through. It was not easy to make out the tracks of their comrades, so they decided to spend the night there and look around in daylight. It was not a particularly pleasant place, being overgrown with prickly shrubs and cactus, but Aida was very taken with the colours and movement of the swarms of fireflies in the dusk and the tiny rivulets which had begun to gurgle in the hollows —the rainy season had not yet arrived, but there had been some monitory showers. The thick, dense green foliage hid them from marauding enemy aircraft, and they felt reasonably safe. Safe, and yet uneasy; for the place was, to all intents and purposes, a graveyard. It was a spot where many Japanese troops, moving south, had decided to spend the night, often so far gone in sickness that they could go no further, and lingered here to die. There were many such dead about, corpses almost incinerated by the torrid Burmese heat, picked at by vultures, and now exuding a terrible smell of decaying flesh.

There were the living, too—or barely living. A couple of soldiers lay underneath an awning they had fixed up for themselves about 40 yards farther on. They were very far gone indeed. One of them could just about open his eyes but was staring sightlessly into space, and he did not seem to hear what was said when Aida spoke to him. His friend answered that they were from 56 Division. A mess-tin lay beside them, with rotting rice in it which gave off a foul smell. Aida gave them water when they asked for it, but this was wasted; they were so near death that they could not swallow, and the liquid trickled down their chins.

Aida and the lieutenant went back to their own position, and after making a scratch meal decided to doss down for the night, choosing a spot as far from the clumps of corpses as they could. They were drowsing off when suddenly Aida sprang awake. He had heard a strange choked scream. The lieutenant had heard it too, and was wide awake, clutching his revolver. Aida slipped the safety catch off his carbine, and they both crawled slowly forward to peer through the quickly fading light. They made out, some yards away, a group of some fifty or sixty Burmese men, women, and children. They were raiding the corpses, Aida presumed, but could not understand why they should bother, since most of the Japanese were nearly naked and had nothing left save an occasional wrist-watch, carried in a condom for protection against the damp.

Or was there something else? As he watched, Aida's blood ran cold. He had heard rumours of what happened to stray Japanese soldiers caught unawares in Burmese villages, but now it was happening in front of his own eyes. He started

Above: pre-war portraits of (*left*)
Sakurai Shōzō, who as GOC 28
Army was overall commander of
the Japanese forces involved in
the breakout, and (*right*) Tsuchiya
Eiichi, chief staff officer of 28
Army

Right: Major-General Aung
San, commander-in-chief of the
Japanese-trained Burma National
Army

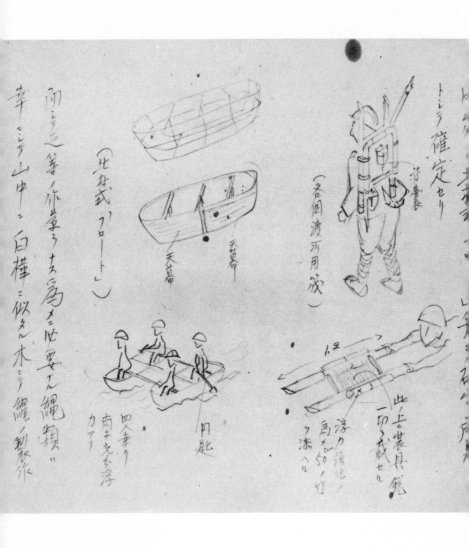

Above: these drawings by Lieutenant-Colonel Saito Hiroo show
the careful detail typical of all his planning

back in bewilderment, horror and disgust. The Burmese were taking out the teeth from the mouths of the dead Japanese. And not only the dead. Or rather, they had a way of dealing with those who were not quite dead. He watched as they placed a corpse's head on a rock, dropped a huge stone on it and broke open the face. They seemed to have something like a claw hammer with them, and once the face was broken open they began to pull out the teeth from the dead mouth. Why the screams, then? Aida understood. The two dying soldiers they had tried to talk to some hours before had been killed by having their heads smashed open in this way, and the stifled screams he had heard were the last expelling of breath from their throats. Fear in him was mixed with anger; neither he nor the lieutenant could do anything effective against a group so numerous; they only had thirty rounds between them, and the Burmese had set up a watch on the area, sentries armed with rifles. So they waited, in unbearable tension, until the tropical night came down and shrouded the whole scene in darkness. They heard the Burmese soon move off, and took turns keeping vigil until dawn. At first light, when the fireflies were still flitting here and there, Aida and the lieutenant left the place after praying for the souls of the men who had died there.

Aida's experience was repeated time and time again, both before the break-out and then, increasingly, after it, as the hapless Japanese wandered, often delirious with sickness, into a Burmese village looking for rice and shelter, only to find sudden death. Major-General Sakurai Tokutaro was perfectly right when he had said that once the British were past a line running across Central Burma through Mandalay the line would be transformed from a geographical one to a psychological one; it would be the line of rejection of the Japanese Army by the people of Burma. And so, approaching the banks of the Sittang or crossing it in bamboo rafts or stumbling through the swamp on the opposite bank, those Japanese of 28 Army who thought they had at last reached the safety they had so longed for on the heights of the Yomas when they had looked across in the evening towards the plain and seen the watery land glisten under the last light, found instead that the friendship of the Burmese had become a hail of bullets from a jungle thicket, or a chop from a *dah* (the chopping knife most Burmese carry with them for cutting their way through undergrowth) in the night.

The men Aida had seen murdered were presumably the remnants of a fight into which some isolated unit of 56 Division had been drawn in its attempt to bring pressure to bear upon the town of Toungoo. The division was used to moving in mountainous terrain after its experiences on the Yunnan border, and it had already made 19 Indian Division pay dearly for the attempt to move along the road to Kalaw and Taunggyi from Thazi. Unlike some of the other Japanese divisions now in the Shan States and Karenni it was still fairly resilient, and its men retained a battle initiative which had been drained from 15 Army. This was particularly evident in 56 Division's attempt to find out what was happening to the British formations along its front.

When 28 Army was just beginning its move into the Pegu Yomas, 56 Division determined to reconnoitre the strength of the British forces around Mandalay. At the beginning of May 1945, a patrol of six men under a sergeant-major left Kalaw. Each man spoke a little Burmese, wore Burmese dress, and carried a revolver in the usual little Burmese bag—though none of them had had a training as thorough as that provided by the *Hayate Tai*. The patrol marched as far as Mandalay, which had been in British hands for six weeks, and entered the city without difficulty. With imperturbable cheek they not only lingered for four days in the city but managed to get jobs as coolies working on the RAF airfield. After spending a few days profitably counting the sorties of British aircraft they moved off to Maymyo to make a rough count of the British troops there. From Maymyo they returned to Mandalay and hitch-hiked on to Thazi in a Field Bakery lorry driven by an unsuspecting Indian sepoy. After four weeks wandering around the British lines of communication they were safely back in Kalaw. They had estimated British strength on the Kalaw Road as one brigade (of 36 Division), 1,500 'lines of communications' troops in Mandalay, and a much smaller body in Maymyo. Meiktila airfield, they learned from a Burmese merchant at Thazi, had only half a dozen fighter planes, no bombers, and a few transport aircraft. By and large they concluded that the British were not going to employ a large force against Kalaw, and that the Japanese would be able to hold it quite adequately with a single Japanese infantry regiment.

Further south, on the road leading from Toungoo through Mawchi to Kemapyu, successive bodies of Japanese troops had fought delaying actions against 19 Indian Division as it tried to edge its way into their positions: *Yoshida Butai*—the remnants of the main body of 55 Division—until it was ordered to evacuate south from near Milestone 31; 15 Division, until 56 Division took over; then 56 Division itself. During the British dash for Rangoon, even though the Japanese had been forced out of Toungoo they still hoped they might make it untenable either by an attack in force from the east or by constant shelling, which would make traffic down the road impossible. The British Army commander himself found the Japanese shelling unpleasantly close when he drove down the main road to 19 Division headquarters after flying into Toungoo airstrip on 30 April. And this pressure was kept up throughout the summer months.

The actions along both the Kalaw Road and the Mawchi Road, however, would not of themselves have done anything to divert British strength from the cordon around the Yomas and the Sittang crossings. Much more serious was the attempt made by 33 Army to come forward from its positions on the Lower Sittang and constitute an active threat in the Sittang Bend area in the direction of Pegu. Here the fighting was bitter, taking place in impossible conditions, and the Japanese

pulled off a limited and temporary success which might have
had serious consequences had the offensive been mounted
a few weeks later to coincide properly with Sakurai's
movement out of the Yomas. Burma Area Army had
prescribed the starting period of 33 Army's offensive and,
overestimating the speed with which Sakurai could get his
units into the Yomas from the Irrawaddy and then out
across the Sittang, put the date down as the latter part of
June. 54 Division was still involved in fierce fighting in the
Paukkaung area in mid-June and could hardly be in a position
to leave the Yomas a week or so later. If the arrival of
54 Division was a condition of the break-out in force, then
the end of July would naturally have been a more sensible
proposition. Sakurai was well aware that to prolong his stay
in the Yomas by a month would create immense problems of
food supply and all the other problems that would arise when
the monsoon began in its full force, but he insisted on
ensuring that all units were fully under his control before he
was prepared to move.

On the other hand, if 33 Army observed similar reasons
to delay *its* actions, the effectiveness of its riposte against
the British-Indian forces might dwindle to nothingness.
This was because of the nature of the terrain over which
Lieutenant-General Honda, Commander-in-Chief 33 Army,
would have to operate. On 23 June he wired an appreciation
to Kimura in Moulmein, in which he pointed out that the
area of the Pegu road was submerged to such an extent that
it was difficult to move units of more than ten men
through it, and that patrols sent out had returned with the
lower half of their bodies covered with swellings as a result of
over-immersion in the water. Operations by large units were
therefore judged out of the question from mid-July onwards.
The first Sittang offensive was expected to begin early in July,
he concluded, and on 10 June he issued his battle plan.

Part of his force—he had around 7,000 men available—was
to be responsible for defending the area east of the Sittang.

The main body was to take the offensive and do everything in its power to harass the British along the Mandalay Road as they strove to block the exit from the Yomas of 28 Army and 105 Independent Mixed Brigade. The main area of the offensive would be the Pegu road area and the time the latter part of June, a date which was later revised to the early part of July.

The help was not to be confined to attacks on the British forces. At various points along what was expected to be 28 Army's route supplies were to be provided, and 33 Army was made responsible for this. At Salugyaung, on the east bank of the Sittang just below Shwegyin, 60 tons of food were to be stored, together with spare uniforms, enough medical supplies for 3,000 men for a month, and a month's supply of electric batteries and wireless valves. Food was to be left elsewhere, too: at Zibyaung (east of the ferry at Okpo) 60 tons; at Kyaikto (south-east of Mokpalin) 90 tons; at Paan (south-east of Bilin) 60 tons; at Thaton (south-east of Paan) 120 tons. The collection and storage were to be completed by 20 July.

This material help was to prove far less difficult than the military operations, largely because of the alteration of the landscape resulting from the heavy monsoon rains. It is fairly rich countryside on the lower reaches of the Sittang and there are a number of populous villages and small towns. The land between the road running from Daiku to Pegu and the line of the Sittang is intersected by canals, by a railway line (Pegu—Waw—Abya—Nyaungkashe—Mokpalin) and a number of roads, and contains a huge reservoir, the Moyingyi Reservoir. The railway crossed the Sittang River at the village called Sittang, where the bridge had been blown in 1942. All this land is very low-lying, and the maps mark many parts of it with the warning 'Usually flooded from June to October'. The warning was particularly apt in the summer of 1945. A combination of monsoon rain directly on the paddy fields and the overflowing of rivers and *chaungs* had turned the

terrain east of Waw up to the line of the river into what was
in effect a large shallow lake. It was possible to get from place
to place by using country boats, of course, or by moving
along the railway embankment, which was built up. But the
flooding of the terrain made infantry patrolling extremely
difficult and intensely uncomfortable; and although the
Japanese operating in the area were every bit as badly off as
the Indians and Gurkhas of 5 and 7 Indian Divisions (who
succeeded each other in control of the area), those Japanese
on the east bank who were on heights rising from
the river found it a relatively simple task to observe troop
movements on the flooded west bank.

7 Indian Division had taken over completely from 5
Division by the end of June, and on 3 July found itself faced
by the artillery and infantry assault of a determined 33 Army.
The weakened 53 Division—about 2,000 men in all—attacked
towards Myitkyo, and 18 Division, a tough and experienced
unit from Kyushu, Japan's southernmost island, with perhaps
another 1,000 men, attacked Nyaungkashe and Abya. The
British positions were held by Gurkha troops (4/8 Gurkhas)
belonging to 89 Brigade of 7 Indian Division. Both the
Gurkhas and the Japanese are of a height below the normal
European and Indian average, and in some places the flooding
was so deep that it exceeded 2 or 3 feet and became, as
7 Division reported, 'too deep for Gurkhas to operate'.
The   Japanese managed to cut communications round
Nyaungkashe, and soon the Gurkhas were in great difficulties.
They could be supplied by air but the dropping zone was
under fire and only half-plane loads could be risked. The
Japanese cut the railway line and the canal and gradually
tightened their hold round the village until they were
three-quarters of the way round it.   Directed from a
commanding height on to a small area the Japanese shelling
soon became intolerable and the Gurkhas began to suffer
heavy casualties. The regimental aid post was under so
merciless a fire that after a while every officer and man in it

had been killed or wounded.

The brigadier in temporary command of 7 Indian Division was extremely perturbed when he saw his Gurkhas about to be picked off like ripe fruit, with his own men powerless to reach them. He conferred with the Brigade commander, and a decision was reached to withdraw the Gurkhas from Nyaungkashe. The order was signalled at 2.30 on the afternoon of 7 July, and after nightfall the Gurkhas came out of Nyaungkashe along a corridor established by 4/15 Punjab and another Gurkha company holding the village of Satthwagyon. It was a difficult withdrawal because many wounded had to be brought out on stretchers. The Gurkhas had been told to destroy guns and equipment, but they came out in a hollow square with their wounded, mortars, and wireless in the middle. The difficulty arose from the terrain and not from the Japanese who, to the Gurkhas' surprise, did not react to the evacuation.

And for a very good reason. They were doing the same thing. Although they had achieved their object they too were finding the ground impossibly difficult to fight over. When RAF planes flew low over the village and over Laya to the north-west along the railway line they could see no sign of Japanese troops, and they came as low as 100 feet. The village of Myitkyo was also considered too expensive to hold, and was evacuated by 89 Brigade. The Japanese moved in on 9 July but constant harassing attacks by the RAF scattered them into the periphery of the village, and though sporadic fighting occurred in the area for a week or so, no serious offensive thrust developed. The Japanese did in fact begin later to attack the village of Letpanthonbin in the Sittang Bend, west of the Sittang Bridge, as if to tempt 7 Indian Division into a fresh displacement of its forces. But the combination of weather conditions and the determined aggressive defence put up by the Gurkhas made the Japanese realize they were not easily going to take Waw, which had been a principal objective. They too were having to struggle through mud and flooded paddy, with reeds growing to chest height and occasionally submerging the entire body. They too had found that the area was impossible even for bullock carts and were having to move by boat. Deployment of large groups of men was out of the question.

On one occasion at the height of the battle in the Nyaungkashe area, Lieutenant-General Naka, the GOC 18 Division, determined to find out for himself what the situation was like on his left flank and went off through the rain and darkness to visit one of his regimental commanders. The path went through mud and pools of water, which rapidly grew deeper, so that it took him over two hours to traverse a distance of 2,200 yards and reach the regimental headquarters—if such they could be called. The regimental commander and his staff were in the middle of a stretch of flooded paddy field, without a tent, without torches, without anything to sit on. Naka could not fail to notice the extreme state of fatigue of the men of the regimental headquarters, and his own difficulties in reaching them quickly gave him a realistic view of the kind of demands he could make. At this point the Sittang itself, across which they had to supply their troops, was becoming an increasingly fierce obstacle. South of the village of Kaywe (north of the town of Sittang and roughly level with Myitkyo) the river at this time of the year is from 1,650 to 2,200 yards wide, the narrowest point being at the railway bridge, where it is 880 yards across and over 12 feet deep, though sandbanks are dotted about in the middle. Near Mokpalin the tidal difference is around 6 feet and the change comes swiftly and with an overpowering noise of waters. It can be awesomely difficult to cross, and anyone unskilled in handling the Burmese country boats or generally unwary can soon find himself capsized and plucked to a swift death by the turbulent waters.

Movement by water became very important for the Japanese of 33 Army in this attempt to divert British attention from the Pegu Yomas. For one thing the unsatisfactory condition of wireless sets and their batteries had made it imperative to increase the number of officer patrols on liaison and reconnaissance duties. Liaison by wireless between Burma Area Army and 28 Army was down by this time to one transmission a week and between 28 Army and 33 Army it was non-existent. But both Honda and Sakurai needed to know how the other was reacting, and Honda decided he would have to send officer patrols to locate Sakurai's headquarters in the Pegu Yomas and bring back some account of his condition and the nature of the expected break-out.

Captain Mikuria and W. O. Fujimoto were put in charge of a patrol which managed to reach 28 Army after weeks of difficult marching. They were the first real source of up-to-date information which Honda had on his colleague's plans, and in his memoirs he speaks with affection of the bravery of men like Mikuria—usually subalterns who, whether they were comparatively green young conscripts or men with military school training, gave proof of soldierly character and a gift for special operations which he could never forget. He knew only too well that to send them on these expeditions was in some cases to ask them to undertake patrols from which they would never return. The reason was that Honda's area was itself no longer safe, even though the Japanese Army was in occupation of it. In the hills to the east British guerrilla bases were being established, and the men of 33 Army could see RAF planes going over to the supply drop points. Honda put some effort into propaganda among the local Burmese, but the situation had turned too radically against the Japanese for propaganda to be of much value. Even his own headquarters was unsafe. At first he had used a temple in a street on the north side of Bilin. It had remained relatively immune from air attack and a good number of Burmese still lived in the area, but soon after the headquarters was set up in that temple the Japanese noticed the Burmese beginning to drift away. Then about a score of

Allied bombers came over one day and plastered the area. It was quite obvious that the whereabouts of Honda himself and his 33 Army headquarters were being notified back to the British almost as soon as the moves had been made. That this represented a real danger was shown by the bombing attack. The temple went up in flames, the staff operations room was destroyed, and a number of headquarters staff were killed or wounded. And the roads had become very insecure. Colonel Tsuji Masanobu, one of the most eminent and idiosyncratic members of Honda's staff, was ambushed by a guerrilla unit after he had been summoned to headquarters Southern Area Army in Saigon. He was making his way to French Indo-China from Burma to report and was using the crossing point of the Salween at Bilin, when he was attacked by guerrillas and severely wounded. Tsuji returned to 33 Army headquarters covered in blood. The main road to Moulmein, the road connecting 33 Army with the freshly re-established Burma Area Army headquarters, was unsafe for single vehicles not travelling in convoy.

Given this daily situation in areas supposedly held in strength by the Japanese Army, it is not surprising that Honda realized that the patrols he sent out were likely to undergo even greater hazards in Burmese villages where the Japanese writ no longer ran. In spite of this Mikuria got through, and Sakurai told him to tell Honda that he would take advantage of the diversion provided by 33 Army's offensive on the west bank of the Sittang, and that he intended to break out across the Mandalay Road on 20 July. Honda's order of 25 June, putting into effect the plans for the forays out towards the Pegu road, was issued after the return of this information from 28 Army, but it remains surprising that Honda made his own Army 'X-Day' 3 July. By the time he had set up his headquarters in Bilin, Honda was a sick man. He had had a hectic few months organizing a fighting retreat against IV Corps and had nearly been caught napping several times. It is possible he thought an early attack might draw IV Corps forces down into the Sittang Bend area long enough for Sakurai to profit from the switch. But the crucial fighting in the Bend took only about a week, with sporadic outbursts after that. Even if IV Corps had panicked and decided to shift its weight from the Mandalay Road against 33 Army, it would have had ample time—ten days—in which to rectify any such move. As it was, only 7 Indian Division was involved, and as a diversion of British forces Honda's move decisively failed. Had it been timed for 20 July, at the moment Sakurai's crossing actually began, the effect might have been different, though it is unlikely that the final result would have been altered in any crucial way. As it was, 33 Army had spent its offensive too early.

18 Division's guerrilla offensive had no more success in damaging British installations in the Pegu area. What the Japanese envisaged as strategic guerrilla attacks, namely the formation of four groups of fifteen men to be sent against military installations, were frustrated by the cordons of 'Patriotic Burmese Forces', as the Burma National Army in its new role as collaborator with the British was called. Only one of the groups managed to infiltrate this cordon and did little damage, so tight was British security near Pegu. 'Tactical guerrilla warfare' was what the Japanese called attacks on lines of communication, and several attempts along these lines were made by groups sent out to the areas of Abya, Payabyo, and Waw, with the object of disrupting British supply traffic, but with one or two exceptions they returned to the division without success. Later in July, when it was decided to mount one or two small diversionary attacks during 28 Army's break-out, 18 Division put in a battalion attack against British positions at Satthwagyon and the railway bridge east of Abya, successfully occupying them.

That was on the night of 26 July. Four days later, at one o'clock in the morning of 30 July, observers saw a huge conflagration at the southern end of Abya, and then fingers of flame began to rise up in the station area, up into the night

sky, finally spreading to the whole of the village. At dawn a
message came in from the Japanese battalion commander,
'Attack successful. More than half village in flames. Main
body completed concentration in area south-east of railway
bridge east of Abya by dawn. No casualties. About one
company left at east end of Abya.' Effective as these attacks
were on the limited objective of an individual village, they
did not succeed in distracting the British-Indian divisions
from their stranglehold on Sakurai's forces. And although
that battalion was lucky in its raid on Abya, the Sittang Bend
operations did cause casualties—though not heavy ones in
comparison with what was about to happen elsewhere. The
Japanese official history puts the figures of killed and
wounded at 320.[1]

Further north, up the east bank of the Sittang as far as the
Shwegyin Chaung, 53 Division was attempting to secure a
passage area for 28 Army. The division had left Toungoo on
29 April at sunset and had taken the road south along the
Sittang, with 18 Division, while the British-Indian armoured
column pierced down the road to Rangoon parallel with
them. They were on the south bank of the Shwegyin Chaung
by 7 May and spent ten days securing that area, which was
left in the control of the second battalion of 119 Infantry
Regiment, while the main body of the division stayed south
of Kunzeik. The term 'main body' is perhaps misleading.
Unlike 18 Division, 53 Division was recruited largely from a
city area. 119 Infantry Regiment had been raised in Fukui,
128 Regiment in Kyoto, and 151 Regiment in Tsu. The men
were not peasants but city workers and less willing to accept
the hardships of life in Burma. They had had the life battered
out of them in the fighting in Central Burma and were only
too glad to reach the comparative safety of the Lower Sittang.
When this safety turned into a highly dangerous combat area,
their reactions were not like the highly aggressive reaction of
18 Division. Aida Yuji was a private in II Battalion of the
Kyoto 128 Regiment, and his 300-strong company was

reduced to ten men in the defence of the Sittang area, under a company commander and a second lieutenant, a recent graduate from Keiō University, whose days as an officer cadet were only just over. He recalls:

We were divided between the two officers, and the company commander crossed the river, leaving the second lieutenant in charge on the east bank. Both groups took cover in deserted villages. Our weapons consisted of nothing more than one light machine gun and some rifles. We had only a few hundred rounds for the machine gun, and if we fired it for more than a couple of minutes we would be lucky if it did not jam—we had no oil for it, and had to use pig's fat. The other ammunition was already used up and everything seemed to be coming to an end. No more supplies of arms or ammunition were coming through, and in this state we were supposed to guard several thousand yards of front-line.[2]

Officers like the young second lieutenant were by this time becoming something of a burden to the old sweats of the regiment. One of these, Corporal Ino, told Aida in prison camp after the war that he and the young officer from Keiō University—who, unlike the men, was strong and fit, had never had an attack of malaria in his life, and spent his spare time hunting for chickens and pigs—were part of a company attack on an enemy gun site on what was, in effect, an island position, completely surrounded by flood waters. He told Aida:[3]

When we got out of the boats, the island was so swampy we almost sank up to our waists in the mud. The British troops, who had never imagined the Japanese would come, got the wind up and fled, leaving their guns behind and allowing us to eat up all the tinned food thoughtfully provided by Churchill, ration packets, chicken and pork, all of which we had not seen for a long, long time. They lost their heads. At night, the British counterattacked and we had no ammo left. They came up unusually close and we couldn't stand up to their M.G. fire which never stopped. They were British troops, and we could hear them count out, as they threw their grenades, 'One, two, three! One, two, three!' The platoon commander kept shouting to us, 'Die, die in battle! Attack, attack!'—you'd have thought he was quite round the bend.

'Don't talk a lot of cock, sir,' I said to him. 'We're still in one piece. Let's get out of here while we can.' He looked as if he'd never heard me, so I had to grab his arms and legs and pull him back with me.

They left the position so quickly they even forgot to destroy the guns, which irked some of the more professional veterans —but there was no doubt about their views on the young greenhorn of a lieutenant.

Aida's regiment had been detached from 53 Division several times in the past few months. After the division as a whole was concentrated south of Kunzeik, Burma Area Army gave it the job of collecting river-crossing materials for 28 Army. The division was moderately successful in this: ten outboard motors were assembled, eight collapsible dinghies, and a variety of other boats of all shapes and sizes. In addition, there were *chaungs* to be bridged.

Aida Yuji describes what happened when an attempt was made to transport supplies across one such improvised bridge.[4] He and his comrades had been living for some days in a Burmese *kyaung,* or temple, and it was intended to build some kind of bridge across the river at this point, so that the depleted stocks of 53 Division could be brought up to date. Everything that they had brought with them from Central Burma was unusable: shirts, boots, mess-tin, water-bottle, socks, rifle, belt, tent, packs, all were rusting or rotten. Aida went off to collect stores with some friends and on the way back they found that the crossing to their temple had altered even in the short time since they had left. The small bridge which had been built across the *chaung* had been swept away by a fierce downpour of rain and a detachment of engineers was trying to repair it. Until the repair was completed the engineers were trying to ferry men across by means of a steel wire slung over to the opposite bank. The current was very strong and very fast but the water was only chest-high, so the theory was that by clinging hard enough to the wire one could gradually pull oneself to the other side. There were occasional warnings, though, of dangers ahead. Now and then a house roof or a large log would be swept by and on one occasion Aida saw a group of half a dozen Burmese men and women being carried helplessly downstream in a canoe, screaming like madmen as the river bore them southwards, seawards. 'Were they crying for help,' Aida wondered, 'or shouting to us not to fire on them? At the speed they were going, they couldn't steer the boat at all, and they couldn't last much longer in a river flowing with such tremendous force. But there was nothing we could do, and in a flash the canoe disappeared into the muddy waters.' The death of the Burmese in the canoe shook Aida and his friends so much that they lost the courage to go on with their own crossing operation. But they were carrying supplies, and there was no question of awaiting the uncertain completion of the engineers' bridge. The main weight of the supplies lay in the new stock of boots, and some raw recruits had been given the job of getting these across. The more experienced old soldiers had already crossed the wire carrying their own packs and little else. There were no bags, but the Japanese made containers out of the tents they were carrying and put sixty pairs of boots in each. It was a clumsy piece of packaging, but better than nothing—or so it seemed. Who was to go first? A young ex-student called Yoshimura, from Wakayama, who had shared Aida's intellectual interests and become friendly with him, volunteered first. Yoshimura had been dozing by the bank, and Aida wondered whether he had seen what had happened to the canoe.

Quite unconcerned, Yoshimura plunged straight into the river, while his lieutenant and the engineer bridging squad looked on. He had moved about ten paces into the centre of the stream, with great ease and confidence, when suddenly he came to a stop. 'It looked as if the river had suddenly gone deeper near where he was,' says Aida, 'and the brown torrent was swirling up to his chest. The water began to seep into the tent on his back, and made it swell up like a balloon. He couldn't budge an inch. For what seemed a very long time

Yoshimura gripped the steel wire in desperation and withstood the pressure of the water. Then in a split second he was on his back, his feet floating. I shall never forget how he looked as he stared at us straight in the eyes. He made no sound, but his eyes held ours, in a look of despair, pleading for help. We all turned pale.' The engineers began to shout advice to Yoshimura and two or three of them tried to string themselves out along the wire to him, but it was too late. The tents had been strapped to the soldiers' backs, and it was impossible to undo the knots in time. 'The next instant, Yoshimura's hand let go, and he was in the maelstrom of waters. He seemed to somersault a dozen yards downstream, and his feet whirled in the air. That was the last we saw of him. We swallowed, and looked at one another.'

No one attempted to use the wire after that. The engineers rigged up another wire, lashed a raft together to load the kit on, and Aida and the rest of his friends crossed by raft. Aida became obsessed by Yoshimura's death: in the last few seconds before he was swept away Yoshimura had gazed at him quite clearly across the thundering waters, but Aida could do nothing other than yell meaninglessly at him. Then, in a matter of an instant or two, Yoshimura had become no more than a few strokes of the pen in an army paybook. But this was hardly exceptional. 53 Division, like all the other Japanese units supporting or involved in the break-out, soon grew terribly used to the notion of death by water.

Part 2 The Break-out

CHAPTER FOUR

28 ARMY HEADQUARTERS IN THE YOMAS AND OVER THE SITTANG

By the end of May 1945, Sakurai's attempt to hold the Burmese oilfields against the British advance from Central Burma was over and done with. By putting forward provisional regroupings of troops drawn from 55 Division, at this time thoroughly milked of men, Sakurai had hoped to hold a barrier against the British-Indian XXXIII Corps to prevent it thrusting south to Rangoon down the left bank of the Irrawaddy. The barrier stretched from Mount Popa to Yenangyaung and Magwe, and the units which were to be his buckler were 72 Independent Mixed Brigade (Kantetsu Force) under Major-General Yamamoto, Kanjō Force (112 Infantry Regiment less 3 Battalion from 55 Division) under Colonel Furuya, and *Shini Butai* (chiefly 55 Cavalry Regiment from 55 Division). Sakurai planned to move the rest of his command out of the Arakan, across the Irrawaddy, and then into the shelter of the Pegu Yomas. From those hills he intended, at first, to send out guerrilla forces to harass the British-Indian divisions on either side of the Yomas, and then move across the Sittang Valley into Tenasserim, in the south-eastern corner of Burma, once his position in the Pegu Yomas had become untenable. The whole of the plan was termed Operation MAI and was to begin in May 1945. It is described in all its phases later in the chapter.

A number of things went wrong almost from the start. The British broke through from Central Burma much more rapidly than had been foreseen. The move of 54 Division out of the Arakan was slower than it should have been. As a result, its commander, Lieutenant-General Miyazaki, had to fight his

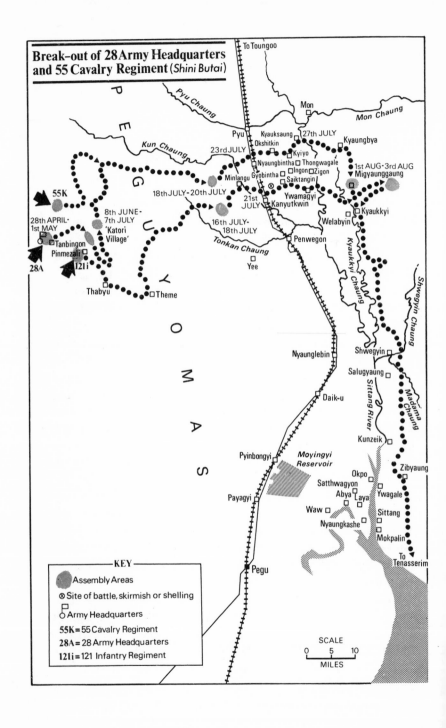

Break-out of 28 Army Headquarters
and 55 Cavalry Regiment (*Shini Butai*)

KEY

Assembly Areas

⊗ Site of battle, skirmish or shelling

⌂ Army Headquarters

55K = 55 Cavalry Regiment

28A = 28 Army Headquarters

121i = 121 Infantry Regiment

SCALE

0   5   10
MILES

way across the Irrawaddy at Kama and then engage in a
rearguard action at Paukkaung before he reached the shelter
of the Yomas. So disorganized did the 'shield' units of
28 Army become that they lost all touch with army
headquarters, and Kantetsu and Kanjō Forces moved into the
Yomas and out again across the Sittang long before the main
body of 28 Army, thinking that the rest of Sakurai's forces
had in fact already broken out ahead of them.

In Sakurai's plan, *Shini Butai* was to move ahead of him
into the Yomas and then act as the vanguard of the group
consisting of 28 Army headquarters and attached units. This
composite body is referred to as '28 Army' in the text, since
we shall consider in separate narratives the fate of 54 Division,
55 Division Infantry Group, and 105 Independent Mixed
Brigade, though they were under the overall command of
28 Army throughout.

Once in the Yomas, Sakurai's task was to establish contact
with his subordinate formations which were, from north to
south, 54 Division, 55 Division Infantry Group (Shimbu
Force), and 105 Independent Mixed Brigade (Kani Force).
He had to arrange for their training and foraging until 'X-day',
the day of the break-out, and then see to it that his entire
army, over 27,000 strong in June 1945, was brought safely
through the cordon of British-Indian troops which locked
him in on either side of the Pegu Yomas. Once through that
cordon, they had to cross the hazards of swamp, river, and
Burmese guerrilla ambush, into the last corner of Burma still
in Japanese hands.

Sakurai had been obsessed by one particular problem.
Given the operational objective—crossing the Sittang—and the
fact that further duties for his army lay ahead, he knew that
the only way to bring it across successfully and ensure that
it survived as an intact force was to bring it firmly under his
single operational control. Liaison was vital for this, and
liaison was the most difficult factor in his present situation.
As he had seen it, the Pegu Yomas was the obvious place in

which to concentrate his army once the Irrawaddy battles were over. They had a geographical unity, and could provide shelter, whereas to split up his units to north and south of the Yomas and try to force them through the British, say, just north of Rangoon and just south of Meiktila, would have been a sheer impossibility in terms of control, apart from any other considerations. A long time before he had sent patrols into the Yomas to investigate the terrain, the availability of raw materials for food supply and river crossing, and the state of the paths.

The Yomas ran roughly for 75 miles from north to south, and were less than 30 miles from east to west. They were not a high mountain range, by any means. Most of the hills averaged 1,600 to 2,000 feet in height, and some of them from 2,600 to 3,000 feet. The paths through them were mainly elephant tracks, narrow mountain paths through the dense jungle and bamboo forest. Sakurai was a shrewd general and once he began to observe the rapid deterioration of the overall military situation, and to suspect this would lead to political changes for the worse, he began to create dumps of food and ammunition at a number of suitable sites. In normal circumstances this would have been a preparation covering a considerable amount of time, but the British advance and the rebellion of the Burma National Army early in 1945 made him look to the actual move of his men into the mountains, and the careful siting of dumps had perforce to come to a halt.

As he envisaged the concentration, it was to run from north to south in the following sequence: 54 Division, Kantetsu Force (72 Independent Mixed Brigade), *Shini Butai,* units under direct army command, Shimbu Force (about one-third of 55 Division under Colonel Nagazawa Kanichi). When Kanjō Force arrived, during its retreat from Mount Popa under Colonel Furuya, he arranged for it to come under the command of Shimbu Force. The Rangoon Defence Force (105 Independent Mixed Brigade) had been put under

Sakurai's command, but he had no idea where it was concentrated, so patrols had to be sent out to find it. A reconnaissance found it confronting the British in a position to the north-west of Pegu, and Sakurai saw there was no point in bringing it further north into the Yomas, so he arranged for it to occupy the southernmost position for the break-out.

This did not put an end to the problems of concentration of forces. There were oddments still in the course of retreat from Rangoon—occasional civilians, technicians from the Southern Area Fuel Depot who had been up in the oilfield area round Yenangyaung, and so forth. They complicated the situation tremendously, as did the women. All of them, Sakurai decided, should be technically incorporated in some way into the Japanese Army, and they became *gunzoku* (civilians serving with the forces) and all the women were made to wear army uniforms. Far from being the hindrance he suspected they would be, the women were a great help and put up with the same hardships the men suffered with no less fortitude and courage. These were virtues which began to be necessary once the fringes of the Yomas were left behind. The Army had been in Tanbingon on 28 April, only a few miles east of the main Prome Road, still within sight of civilization. After a few days, headquarters moved east to Pinmezali and began a life which Sakurai refers to as 'the life of roving mountain nomads'.

He managed to make definite contact with most of his forces, but with the main body of Kantetsu Force and 54 Division no link was established. Kantetsu, he knew, would be retreating from Yenangyaung; Kanjō Force was bound to be withdrawing through the Yomas from Mount Popa—but there was no indication from either of them. Sakurai's whole effort was directed, therefore, towards the organization of officer patrols to reach the scattered formations.

On 18 June, a signal was received from Captain Tsukamoto, a 28 Army staff officer, who had been sent to look for 54 Division, to say that he had managed to make contact.

Two days later, Lieutenant Norinaga arrived from 54 Division itself, and spent a great deal of time with 28 Army staff explaining the division's situation. The main body of 54 Division could therefore be considered under control. This was a great relief to Sakurai, since its strength of close on 10,000 men constituted his largest single force. Liaison with other units was to come sporadically, later. A heavy artillery unit attached to Kanjō Force reported, and then a signal came from Burma Area Army headquarters to say that Kantetsu Force H.Q. and Sato Battalion (188 Independent Infantry Battalion) attached to it, had already moved east of the Sittang—so their crossing would not have to be supervised. The main body of Kanjō Force remained out of touch until the very end of the operation, as did the smaller units attached to Kantetsu Force.

In 28 Army's original planning, the project for the breakout was named 'MAI Operation'. *Mai* is a Japanese character meaning 'great', 'excelling', and 'to go', and it is part of a compound *maishin* meaning 'to dash forward'. The notions of excellence and rapid advance being combined in the character, it was thought to be a fitting one for such an operation which would demand alacrity and courage of a high order in all its phases. It was a resourceful notion, and it says a good deal for Sakurai's flexibility that while he and his staff were doing their desparate best to extricate their divisions from a British trap, they could devise plans for aggressive guerrilla warfare. The actual break-out operation over the Sittang was, as will be seen from the details of Operation MAI, only the third phase of what was anticipated. In the event, the guerrilla planning came to nought, and Phase Three entered history as the Battle of the Break-out.

The object of Operation MAI was outlined by Sakurai as follows:

Intention: The entire force of 28 Army is to concentrate with all speed in the southern end of the Pegu Yomas. With the Yomas as a base, guerrilla warfare is to be developed against the Pegu-Rangoon road and the Rangoon area. As future opportunity offers, the Sittang Plain will be crossed and after the western foothills of the Shan Hills have been reached the Army will proceed to the area of Bilin.

The operation was to be divided into four phases:

Phase One (from early to late May):   concentration in the Pegu Yomas. 54 Division will operate against the enemy in the northern sector, in an area extending from east of Allanmyo to east of Prome; Shimbu Force will operate in the area between Taikkyi and Letpadan against any enemy forces moving up from the Rangoon area. Military supplies will be collected and concentrated in the Yomas under the protection of these forces. The Army's entire force will then concentrate in the Yomas.

Phase Two (from the end of May to mid-June): preparations for operations after Phase Three and guerrilla operations.

Phase Three (end of June): break-out across the Sittang Plain. The break-out front will extend from north of Nyaunglebin to south of Toungoo. Units will move off simultaneously from the eastern foothills of the Pegu Yomas. The Mandalay Road and the Sittang River will be crossed in a short time and the area of the western foothills of the Shan Hills will be reached.

Phase Four (from end June to early July): move to Bilin area. Shimbu Force will be employed against the enemy in the area of Shwegyin to cover the move of the Army's main force. The Army's main force will proceed towards Bilin through the area along the western foothills of the Shan Hills in the following sequence: 105 Independent Mixed Brigade, units under direct Army command, 54 Division. Shimbu Force will continue its advance to the rear areas as the army's main force passes through the Shwegyin area.

Each Force *(heidan)* will form guerrilla units using the infantry regiment as a nucleus. Each unit is to have an independent guerrilla warfare capacity.

Phase Three, the break-out across the Sittang, presented security problems. Sakurai well knew that the more precise the knowledge of his intentions the enemy possessed, the more difficult it would be to bring his forces across the Sittang unscathed. He made it a special requirement, therefore, that any patrols sent out to the Sittang on reconnaissance should be selected from really efficient and trained men and their number was to be severely restricted. They should be disguised as Burmese to avoid detection. In addition, to mislead the British as to the Army's intentions, guerrilla warfare should be concentrated on the Pegu and Prome-Rangoon road areas, away from the strip of front across which the Army intended to break out.

This plan undoubtedly would have done two things: it would have gone some way to meeting Burma Area Army's requirement that 28 Army should harass the British-Indian forces in the Rangoon area and hinder their preparations for a future offensive; and it would have ensured that a fairly high proportion of 28 Army would have come through the British cordon, *if the time-table had been followed.*

Kimura had, of course, been prodded from above by Southern Area Army, which had been angered by the loss of Rangoon. Lieutenant-General Numata, Chief of Staff of Southern Area Army in Saigon, had sent a message to Kimura telling him to secure and stabilize the line Kemapyu-Toungoo-Lower Sittang River, and the Tenasserim area, and to occupy the Pegu Yomas and harass the British from there to prevent them mounting an offensive against Southern Malaya with Rangoon as a base. 'Can Southern Area Army really be demanding that we retake Rangoon?' Kimura had asked Tanaka, his Chief of Staff. 'I'm sure that's exactly what they mean,' Tanaka had replied. 'But isn't that a sheer impossibility?' Kimura retorted. 'Yes,' came the answer, 'but there are some factors to take into account: the monsoon has begun, and this will check movement by British armoured units. We could take advantage of this situation and paralyse the enemy's offensive preparations by guerrilla warfare. I think you should show Southern Area Army that your intentions are offensive and that you are determined to retake Rangoon.' It was under pressure of this kind from the forceful and aggressive Tanaka that Kimura had sent a signal to 28 Army on 9 May: 'Concentrate your forces in the area north-west of Rangoon, and retake the city when opportunity presents itself.'

That signal had caused great and grim hilarity in 28 Army headquarters, since on the day it was sent the main body of 54 Division was still on the west bank of the Irrawaddy, and there was considerable anxiety about whether it would be able to escape unharmed to the east bank. Sakurai and his entire staff had burst out laughing when the order to retake Rangoon was received, and he signalled back to Kimura what the real situation of his army was. To expect it to undertake an operation like the recapture of the city which Kimura himself had abandoned was to live in a world of fantasy. Other staff officers were less amused. To Saito, of 55 Division, the order was an act of 'shameless, impudent effrontery'.

28 Army reported to Burma Area Army on 25 May that it intended to start guerrilla warfare but nothing was said about retaking Rangoon, and the matter was tacitly dropped. On his intentions to move south across the Sittang to Bilin, Sakurai kept his cards close to his chest as far as Kimura was concerned. There were good reasons for this, as Major Fukudome explains:[1]

When Area Army left Rangoon in such a hurry, 28 Army enquired what its intentions were about future operations. We were told instructions would be forthcoming after Area Army reached Moulmein. We knew our operations were going to be very difficult, and representations were made that Burma Area Army should send us one of its staff officers, but no attention was paid to this request. After Area Army had moved to Moulmein, 28 Army was pretty dissatisfied with the operational guidance it received, and began to think of acting independently. This was the origin of Operation MAI, though the idea of starting guerrilla warfare from the Yomas had been in 28 Army Commander's mind for many months. The question now was, how long could we stay in the Yomas? They were not a very extensive range, not very wide from east to west, and they had no source of food supply to make us independent. So we could not support ourselves there or continue to fight from there for very long. We began to think more and more in terms of moving to the east bank of the Sittang before the next dry season.

Naturally, we said nothing of this to Burma Area Army, but began to plan independently. At the end of April, I spent a sleepless night with Major Yamaguchi Tatsuru, the staff officer responsible for lines of communication, drafting the plans for the operation, and presented it the following day to our Chief of Staff, Iwakuro, who promptly gave it his sanction. Based on this plan, all units under 28 Army's command were ordered to move into the Yomas on two days, 26 and 29 April. At this stage nothing was said about breaking out across the Sittang; the order was confined to the withdrawal into the Yomas.

From 28 April, 28 Army headquarters had moved from Taikkyi to Tanbingon, a village in the western foothills of the Pegu Yomas; but this was almost at the end of a motorable track leading from the main Rangoon-Prome road, near Okpo, and very vulnerable to British armoured penetration. It was decided, therefore, to move right into the Yomas, on the banks of the Mezali River. This is where the mountain life began in real earnest.

Soon the hillside of the new headquarters was covered with the bamboo huts or *bashas* that characterized the temporary encampment of both British and Japanese armies in Burma. As Colonel Tsuchiya remembers, 'One thing the Japanese army never forgot was how to plan and build elegant structures out of bamboo, even in moments of danger and difficulty.' He and three other staff officers of 28 Army shared a hut: a staff room, an office with a fireplace scooped out of the floor in true Japanese fashion, and a bedroom. He and the other three—Fukudome, Yamaguchi, Okudaira—had developed a close friendship which continued right into the post-war period. All four of them had done their military history at the Military Academy years before, in Japan, and the break-out operation they were planning for General Sakurai had echoes for them.

'It's exactly like the battle of Lodz in the First World War' —this was the obvious comparison—'when a German army corps was surrounded and had to break out through Russian encirclement.'

'Yes,' came the answer, 'but with a lot of differences, and they're not in our favour. The Germans had no restrictions of climate or landscape to cope with. Whereas, in addition to the enemy, we have the monsoon rain, an army in poor physical condition, waterlogged ground that will be a swamp by the time we're going through it, and lastly the Sittang itself. If we fail, it'll be a repeat performance of the annihilation of the Russians at Tannenberg. On the other hand, if we pull it off, it'll be the most conspicuous break-out operation in the history of war.'

The reference to Lodz was not, of course, unexpected. That bitter campaign in the icy winter of 1914, when thousands of sick and wounded men froze to death in the Polish wastes, was the result of Ludendorff's plan to crush the Russian armies which were threatening Silesia and Cracow. The Russian transport system was faulty. They were operating in an area devastated by a recent retreat, and therefore with poor rail communications. Their air power was minimal; and so the Germans risked transporting an entire army with 800 troop trains and got away without being discovered. Russian intelligence was terribly weak. Both sides undertook some incredible feats of marching; Mackensen's men covered 50 miles in four days over abominable roads and caught the Russian Second Army on the move while it was turning north-east to cover the city of Lodz. In the ensuing battle the Russians lost 25,000 prisoners and were forced back on Lodz in confusion. They managed to cover three sides of Lodz and the city's commander, Plehve, summoned up two corps to cover an exposed southern flank. They marched 70 miles in 48 hours and were then hurled into battle. Then the Russians turned the tables on the Germans, and, from being encircled themselves, bit off the German force which had been thrusting ahead and bade fair to annihilate it. Had the Russian general Rennenkampf not been so dilatory, he might have had

50,000 Germans in the bag. As it was, his delay left a gap between which the German commander, Schleffer, broke through a Siberian division and made a fighting retreat which has become a masterpiece for students of tactics. Schleffer brought out from the Russian ring not merely his own men but 10,000 prisoners and sixty guns as well.

The Japanese staff officers were, clearly, underrating Schleffer's problems when they said he had only the enemy to consider. Schleffer was fighting in the bitterest conditions of a Polish winter, and also against greater numbers than those British and Indian troops who were out to cut Sakurai's 28 Army to pieces in the summer of 1945.

At any rate, with Iwakuro to guide them, Tsuchiya and his staff officers worked endlessly on the plans for the break-out, under the ceaseless rain which beat on the bamboo and palm of the huts, turning the surrounding area into a quagmire, softening paper and making it rot, destroying the leather on boots. It was conditions like this which made it doubly hard to keep intact the liaison arrangements with subordinate units. For the last study conference of the operation it was essential to have representatives from every major unit under command. 54 Division in particular had been difficult to locate, and then on 18 June an officer patrol under the young Captain Tsukamoto made contact and sent a message in to say so. 54 Division itself had sent out officer patrols to find 28 Army and on 20 June Lieutenant Norinaga arrived at Army headquarters and gave a detailed report on the situation in the division. In this way, 28 Army gradually built up a picture, however inadequate, of the forces under its command, and by 25 June, it was judged appropriate to hold the last study conference on the operation in 'Katori Village'.[2]

Iwakuro presided as Chief of Staff. Others present included Colonel Sugimoto, commanding officer of *Shini Butai,* Major-General Sei, GOC 14 Transport Headquarters, Lieutenant-Colonel Saito, Chief Staff Officer of Shimbu

Force, Lieutenant-Colonel Murata of 54 Division staff, and Takeda, a staff officer of Kani Force, the brigade which had been made up from the Rangoon Defence Force. Both Murata and Takeda had taken a whole week to get to 'Katori Village' through the driving rain and lonely mountains, and were exhausted by the time the conference began. But in Murata's case energy had to be found from somewhere because his General had entrusted him with a series of arguments about the date and place of the break-out, on which the lives of thousands of his men might depend.

54 Division had broken off the fighting round Paukkaung on 17 June, and gradually withdrawn into the western foothills of the Pegu Yomas. The divisional commander, Miyazaki, had a number of possibilities in mind for the route his division should follow when the break-out was to be attempted: (i) they could break across the Mandalay Road north of Toungoo, and so reach the Shan Plateau; (ii) they could attack Toungoo, then march towards the Shan Plateau; (iii) they could wait for the beginning of the monsoon in the Pegu Yomas; and (iv) they could break out across the Road in the Pyu area, well to the south of Toungoo, and reach the Shan Plateau. The time of the break-out, from Miyazaki's point of view, should be the end of July onwards.

The case which he wanted Murata to make at the final study conference against breaking out *south* of Toungoo, was that the situation on the Sittang banks would be unfavourable to an army crossing—the river would be much wider, for one thing—they would have to abandon any guns larger than battalion guns, and concentrate simply on getting the men across. South of Toungoo, the division would have to accept a possible loss of two-thirds or more of its men. It was a gloomy prediction, but not unrealistic.

Murata left the divisional headquarters on 23 June, and reached Army H.Q. on 28 June, the second day of the conference. The Army staff listened to his points, but they were not enthusiastic at all about changing the general principles of their plan, whether these involved altering the routes or the timing. Murata had little choice but to accept the general decision to hold to the original plan. It was refused, in principle, that a part of the division, or even the main body, might cross the river north of Toungoo if the divisional commander so desired. No doubt it was right not to consider as too important the question of loss of artillery: given the nature of the break-out operation it was highly unlikely that any artillery which had been brought as far as the Mandalay Road would ever be carried farther to the banks of the Sittang, or transported across the river if it did. By the time they had moved from west to east across the Yomas, the division had already had to give up all its field guns over 75 mm calibre. They also had no wireless equipment to speak of, which had made it difficult for 28 Army to get in touch. The divisional signal unit had been attacked on 29 April by RAF planes north of Thayetmyo and all its sets smashed to pieces by bombing. So what was left was, basically, manpower, and there was some sense in ensuring that at least some of *that* should survive. Not that Miyazaki needed any persuading on this point: one of the things he had sworn to do was to get these troops to the Irrawaddy out of the Arakan without losing a single man, and he had already lost heavily at Kama.

His pessimism about the routes was based on a reminiscence of what had happened on Ramree Island to his 121 Infantry Regiment under Nagazawa earlier in the year. The Ramree garrison had been left too late and had been cut to pieces by the British as it tried to make its way across to the mainland in small boats. 'It'll be a repeat performance of the evacuation from Ramree,' he told Murata. 'We will lose most of our men.' But when Iwakuro asked why Miyazaki had this view of the conditions on the banks of the Sittang, Murata had to admit that it was based on a single officer reconnaissance report. A *Kempei* captain attached to the division had reconnoitred the area around Toungoo, and had reported that the river was flowing fast and was 220 yards across. 'Our

Above: a British patrol, muddied to the thighs, approaching a Burmese village

Below: Allied prisoners of war left behind in Rangoon by the retreating Japanese

Above: Shwegyin village on the banks of the Sittang River
Below: Japanese prisoners wade knee-deep through a flooded *chaung*

information is different,' Iwakuro said, 'and in addition we need 54 Division to act as a shield for the left flank of the main body of 28 Army.'

Murata was not the only one to bring objections to the conference. When the date scheduled for the operation was named as 20 July, there was general agreement, though many formations clearly thought it was an optimistically early start; but, 'If that is the Army's order, we will carry it out,' was the general response. Not Saito's. 'If possible, I would like the date to be 23 July.' In fact, the army commander himself did not feel an issue should be made of the selection of a particular day and told his staff to restudy the date. Colonel Okamura, an engineer who had become the senior staff officer of 28 Army and who, in Saito's view, had not much experience as a staff officer with front-line units, although he had been an instructor at the Military Academy, said, 'Everything has been decided; let's keep it as the 20th, it's a Friday'—this was said with some flippancy, which to Saito seemed grimly out of place. The next day the decision was handed down: 20 July. Saito's impression was that in a sense Sakurai was acting with Southern Army headquarters rather than Burma Area Army in mind.

When the Chief of Staff of Southern Area Army, Lieutenant-General Numata, had visited Burma, he had been told by General Kimura, the Commander-in-Chief of Burma Area Army, 'Don't worry about the situation in Burma; we shall hold on to what we have until the end of the monsoon.' 'What we have' included Rangoon, and it was only a month after making that statement that Kimura ordered his last-minute panic-stricken withdrawal from Rangoon to Moulmein.

Sakurai knew full well that Southern Area Army must have been stunned to learn of Kimura's abandonment of the city. Therefore, although he knew he could not retake it, he nonetheless felt he must use his forces to play an active role in the operations which were bound to develop in Tenasserim later in 1945, when a British offensive developed south of

Rangoon. He saw he had a duty to get his men out of the Yomas and across the Sittang Plain, in some kind of order, so that by the end of the monsoon they would be a real fighting force again. It was with this urgency in mind that he decided to opt for the initial date, and to overrule Murata's and Saito's objections.

There was something else, too. The Army was already on the C ration scale (about 400 grammes of rice a day) and the rice stored at a number of points in the western foothills of the Yomas was in territory now under the operational control of the British. This meant there was a limit to the likely continuance of any sort of reasonable ration and provided another reason for attempting to get across the Sittang without a moment's delay.

When Murata returned to 54 Division, Miyazaki listened to the way his ideas had been received and then said, 'We have no choice, then; we must move in accordance with the Army plan. Since they make it a matter of principle to hold on to the idea of moving south of Toungoo we shall have to make our divisional plan on that basis.' But it was with a heavy heart and a brooding knowledge of many casualties to come.

At Army headquarters, once the final decision had been taken, there was a certain relaxation of tension. It reminded Lieutenant-Colonel Tsuchiya of the pauses in the spring rain showers at home in Japan. The rain falls softly, softly, and then stops for a while. Similarly, even in the apparently ceaseless Burma monsoon, there were intervals. Most of the time the rain fell in sheets, so that the bamboo huts quite close to a track could not be seen through the barrier of rain. But now and then the skies called a halt. During intervals like this, the Army commander would take himself off to a *chaung* with a bamboo cane and line and sit fishing by the rushing waters. Like Montgomery after the final touches had been put to the battle plan, and after the general himself could do no more, he slept soundly. 'Do your best,' runs a Japanese saying, 'and then leave the rest to Providence.'

Iwakuro, his Chief of Staff, was of a like mind. He had brought into the Yomas with him a notebook in which he had jotted down an account of those feverishly exciting weeks early in 1942—how remote that triumph seemed now!—when he had led his Guards Regiment down the coast of Malaya and helped to take the supposedly impregnable British fortress of Singapore. Difficult as it was to keep the pages dry, he sat now correcting the text of what was later to become *The Assault on Singapore.*

After concentration of forces, food was the next most pressing problem, and it had been rendered even more serious by the delay of one month imposed by the slow liaison processes. It was bad enough arranging for the subsistence of an army in the plains once the people had turned against them. Up in the hills, with no villages to forage from and another month to go over and above the original date, the problems were increased tenfold. The responsibility for supplies was that of Staff Officer Yamaguchi, a 28 Army major in charge of lines of communications.[3] Yamaguchi knew that he was faced by alternatives both of which would be unacceptable under ideal conditions: he could rely on foraging—but there simply were not the village resources in the Yomas; or he could send his foraging units out into the flatter land between the Yomas and the Prome Road and take the risk of clashing with British troops who were continually patrolling the area and probing up the side roads to ensure that the Japanese were safely locked into the mountains. The upshot was that Yamaguchi recommended strict rationing and the use of bamboo shoots and field grasses to supplement the ration. Bamboo shoots were mixed with edible grasses and cooked together, with whatever rice was available. As a means of spinning out the ration it was quite successful but by the end of June when the amount of rice had dwindled daily and the quota of bamboo shoots was, of necessity, increased, even this method was no longer satisfactory.

The actual bringing of rations in bulk into the Yomas had been the job of 14 Field Transport headquarters under Major-General Sei, but 28 Army felt it was imperative that none of its units should rely on a central supply of this kind, but should be as nearly self-supporting as possible. Every officer and man who came into the hills was told to carry as much food as he could in his pack, or wherever else he could put it; and to ensure that this regulation was carried out, Sakurai put out an order that military police *(Kempei)* were to be stationed at the entrances to the paths into the mountains to check each man to see that as he left the plains he carried at any rate enough main rations to last for fifteen days.

By the middle of May 1945, about 5,000 men had assembled in the area around the headquarters camp, which meant that it became imperative to forage in the plains. The villages between the Yomas and the Prome Road were under the control of the Anti-Fascist Organization and the Burma National Army, and Japanese foraging units often had to fight for the rice they needed. In his original conception, Sakurai had not anticipated a long period of siege in the Yomas, but the delay of concentration, particularly of 54 Division, extended the siege conditions to two months instead of one, and the ration was forced down to 250 grammes per day.

The men began to show symptoms of salt shortage. When engaged in hard physical labour under tropical heat conditions the human body needs to have its salt replenished in greater quantities than would normally be thought necessary. If it does not get the salt it needs, heat exhaustion ensues, followed by heat cramps and dehydration. The Indian Army worked out once that for an average man with access to an unlimited water supply (this was *not* one of Sakurai's difficulties in the Yomas) and working hard enough to sweat at the rate of a litre an hour, about 2 grammes of salt per working hour were required to maintain what is called 'sodium chloride balance', plus ½ gramme of salt per hour of rest. In other words, a man working hard for eight hours daily would need about 24 grammes of salt a day. Had the Rangoon stocks been properly distributed before Burma Area Army fled the city, ample supplies could no doubt have been stored in the Yomas. But salt was one of the things that quickly began to run short. An ingenious attempt to palliate the difficulties arising from this was to obtain a sour sauce from mangoes and use it as a flavouring with the rice. The only thing which did not run short was bamboo. In fact, it was the best time of the year for picking the bamboo shoots, and a gruel of rice and bamboo shoots became 28 Army's standard diet, supplemented on occasion not only with wild plants but also snakes and lizards. Not surprisingly, more and more men began to go sick. But even the highest ranking officers were not spared this diet: at the end of the last operational study conference on 25 June, the colonels and generals dined together, and their farewell meal consisted of field rations and bamboo shoots.

In a sense, it was a very Japanese solution, as were the bamboo huts that Tsuchiya had had made for the headquarters encampment. Bamboo is one of the natural materials the Japanese know best. It has been part of their intellectual and spiritual life ever since they began to use Chinese characters in the sixth century AD. Bamboo tubes of all dimensions are used as writing brushes, or to make the little pots in which the brushes stand. Bamboo is a component of the distinctive style of Japanese architecture which employs wood perhaps more successfully than any other national architecture—the oldest and most beautiful wooden buildings in the world are the Hōryūji temple buildings at Nara. Bamboo figures as a symbol in Japanese painting, along with the cherry and the plum.

At first, clothing was less of a problem, though Lieutenant-Colonel Tsuchiya, who had moved rapidly across country for the past few weeks with only the clothes he stood up in, was in a sorry state by the time he rejoined headquarters. Taking pity on his sartorial destitution, Iwakuro gave him a coat, Fukudome some leather gaiters and a jacket, and he had a raincoat from Captain Sakurai. With some relief, he stripped off the garments he had worn since mid-April, and dressed himself in the oddments his colleagues provided.

Later, of course, when the rain had really been coming down for weeks at a stretch, clothing and boots began to disintegrate. Officers and men who marched day after day on slippery mountain tracks, sinking down into the sucking hold of the mud or churning it up with their tired strides, soon found that their feet were their most vulnerable part. 'Boots rotted in the long advance through the rains,' General Koba of 54 Division remembers, 'and because feet became soaked with water, and it was impossible ever to dry them out, they swelled up as if the soldier was suffering from dropsy. Then the swelling broke, the skin split, and flesh showed through. Every moment of the march became like walking up a hill of needles. Legs and feet swelled up, from ankles to thighs the men's legs became round, fat and huge so they were almost prevented from moving.'

Despair was not long in setting in for men in this condition. And the lack of matches and kindling, and the impossibility of their being used even if the men had them, meant that on the march it was impossible to cook the white rice they carried in their packs. Koba came across men wandering crazily down muddy paths, chewing away at handfuls of raw rice, and muttering insanely as they lost their way in the hills. The Japanese describe the Yomas as 'uninhabited' or 'almost uninhabited'. In fact, Koba occasionally came across tiny settlements of what he terms 'nomads'; he thinks they were Chins or Karens, not Burmese proper, and lived in little groups of four or five houses; but he could never get close enough to find out what they were, since they fled at the approach of the Japanese.

Training the men for the cruel operation which lay ahead had not been forgotten. Sakurai insisted that the troops under his command should be able to traverse 5 miles of mountain area a day, and training marches were carried out with this objective. There were, after all, 310 miles to cover between the army's present position and its ultimate station in Tenasserim. For women and wounded to cover this distance was going to impose tremendous stresses, even without the hazards of mountains and rivers, and lack of food. At the back of Sakurai's mind there was always the river. When the phrase 'operational preparations' was used by him, it was always 'river crossing' he had in mind, not, any longer, an offensive against the British. That might come later, but in the meanwhile the enemy was the Sittang.

Conditions along the river were being reconnoitred by his patrols. But one of his sources of information—sparingly used, because of the scarcity of dry batteries—was listening in to British wireless signals, and it was clear from this traffic that boats were being daily destroyed on the banks of the Sittang to prevent the Japanese using them. If country boats were not available, then the Army would have to cross in its own way, and that meant bamboo again. Bamboo had saved life in the Yomas, its shoots had filled the stomachs of starving men. It was to become a life-saver in another sense, now, since it was the only material 28 Army had from which to make rafts. Okamura, his Senior Staff Officer, Sakurai remembered, had been an engineer, and he promptly gave him the task of devising methods of binding bamboo lengths into rafts. As a result of Okamura's tests, it was found that 24 bamboo poles, each 16 feet long, would be buoyant enough to support ten men. Such poles were to be carried out of the Yomas at the rate of one pole for every two men. Every man was to carry three lengths of rope, each 13 feet long, to act as binding material. This was to be 28 Army's lifeline—bamboo and bark rope—to which it entrusted the life of its thousands of soldiers. It was an example of great resourcefulness on the part of the staff, this creation of a lifeline out of next to nothing. And even when it was found that the practice of two men carrying a 16-foot pole was extremely awkward on the march, and hindered progress considerably, the order was promptly changed. The poles were ordered to be sawn in half, and 8-foot lengths were to be carried by individual soldiers.

River-crossing units were specially created for the purpose of collecting these poles and ropes and quickly constructing rafts from them as the men arrived at the crossing points. Then other difficulties arose. Casualties from sickness—beri-beri, malaria, amoebic dysentery—increased, and the number of men capable of carrying the materials decreased, which meant that fewer rafts would be available; and it was found that although the rafts were adequate for the smaller *chaungs* and creeks of the Pegu Yomas, they might not prove viable for a river swollen so mightily as the Sittang. So it was decided to tell the men to load their weapons and equipment on the rafts and swim them across, clinging to the sides. Training for all this was carried out in the *chaungs,* and each formation was instructed to use its small engineer unit—28 Army was short of engineers—as a nucleus for its river-crossing party. Sakurai came more and more to realize just how much he would have to rely on the ingenuity of these crossing parties as patrol after patrol sent out to the Sittang failed to return. Almost none of those sent out from the beginning of the Army's concentration in the Yomas had come back with information, and the situation on the actual river banks of the Sittang was not at all clear in Sakurai's mind. A determined effort would have to be made to attempt reconnaissance once again, after the Army had moved into its starting position in the eastern foothills of the Yomas.

The Army headquarters and units under direct command divided temporarily into two columns to cross the Yomas from west to east. The left column was made up of the headquarters, *Shini Butai* and *Mukai Butai* (542 Independent Infantry Battalion and 543 Independent Infantry Battalion, both belonging to Kantetsu Force), the right column of *Sei*

Butai (14 Transport Unit) and *Baba Butai* (121 Infantry Regiment from 54 Division). In order to reconnoitre the enemy positions and the topography of the road and railway areas, and to provide for escorts when breaking across the road—if escorts proved necessary—a small unit was sent on ahead of the left column, consisting of forty men under Lieutenant-Colonel Tsuchiya, together with an infantry company. The columns moved off on 6 July, *Shini Butai* in front, followed by headquarters and *Mukai Butai* in sequence. The tracks through the Yomas were steep, narrow, and winding—they made what seemed a gratuitously unnecessary number of detours—and there were swampy areas on the tops of the hills which the incessant rain had turned into deep bogs. The casualties and sick who were at their last gasp before the march began found the going agonizingly hard, as they panted along, helped by sticks or the arms of their comrades. There was no way of transporting the serious casualties other than carrying them on a stretcher, and as the paths were simply not wide enough for two men to walk abreast carrying stretcher poles, the net result of attempting to bring them along was that the stretcher-bearers themselves constantly slipped and fell and were soon in a state of filth and fatigue little better than that of the men they were carrying to safety.

That was why, on the day they moved off, Lieutenant-Colonel Tsuchiya heard over and over again the sound of hand-grenades exploding in the shadow of the mountains, or down in the dark valleys; the mournful melancholy sound which indicated that some seriously wounded man realized he could not submit his friends any further to the intolerable burden of carrying him, and decided to take a quicker way out of his misery, destroying himself with a hand-grenade clutched to a retching stomach. The condition of the tracks was such that when the stretcher-bearers slipped—and this was very often—the effect on the wounded man on the stretcher was terrifying. He could be thrown into the mud and have to be pulled out again, or his weary, sick body was jolted and knocked until the pain became too much for the mind to tolerate. And constantly, mingling with the mud and rain, was the unceasing drip-drip of fresh blood from inadequately bandaged wounds, or newly opened ones.

Although those wounded by enemy air strikes were very few, the number of suicides grew and grew as the Army spun out across the defiles of the Yomas. Experienced and hardened in warfare as he was, and no stranger to sudden and violent death in the most hideous conditions, the constant repetition of the echoing grenade explosions in the dripping jungle began to bear heavily on General Sakurai's nerves. It was as if a hand was gripping his heart every time the sound ripped through the driving rain.

At last, Army headquarters reached Hill 1411, the objective of its west-to-east advance, in the eastern foothills of the Yomas. It came on to the hill, with the left column, on 16 July. About the same time, the right column came to the eastern edge of the hills at a point south-west of Kanyutkwin, and immediately contacted headquarters. There was liaison from another quarter too, hoped for but unexpected by this time—a heavy artillery battery from Kanjō Force, under Captain Nakajima, which had been retreating from Mount Popa and from whom there had been no news at all. Liaison was also made with I Battalion, 112 Infantry Regiment, from Kanjō Force, under Major Hosokawa. But there was no news whatever of the main body of Kanjō.

Without pausing for rest, 28 Army headquarters pressed on further to the eastern edge of the Yomas on 17 July. The exits from the mountains were, it was soon obvious, closely guarded by British-Indian forces. In order to avoid them, it would be absolutely essential to come down from the mountains by tracks not shown on the maps. The units moved along tracks inside the jungle, or opened up ways through it where necessary. Finally, burdened by their bamboo loads, the men of 28 Army came out from the mountains and on to the level plain on the night of 19 July. They began their last preparations, and took some rest—it was by no means certain when the next opportunity would be offered.

Tsuchiya's reconnaissance groups had already begun to send in reports. Some of the divisional patrols, too, had sent in information, though the divisional staffs were not always prepared to place great faith in it. A sergeant-major of the *Shimpū* or *Kamikaze Tai,* an intelligence group attached to Shimbu Force, had twice undertaken patrols out of the Yomas, once on 10 June and once again on 5 July. During this latter patrol, he reconnoitred the paths from Myogyaung up to Penwegon, and came into the village of Penwegon from the Yee road around midnight. He was spotted as a Japanese by a Burmese from whom he had something to eat, but the Burmese did not report him to the British, and he returned safely to Lieutenant-Colonel Saito at Shimbu headquarters, with the news that Penwegon was stuffed with British and Indian troops until it could hold no more. He thought there must be around 3,000 of them, British, Gurkhas, and Indians, with at least twelve big guns and twenty field or mountain artillery pieces and nearly a score of tanks. There was also an airstrip serving the village, he told headquarters, and it was defended by about 150 men.

28 Army's *Kusunoki Kikan* was also put to the task of reconnaissance, though its original aims had been rather more exalted.[4] Burma Area Army headquarters had ordered 28 Army to form this unit at the beginning of April 1945 with the object of getting in touch with the leaders of the rebellious Burma National Army and of persuading them to bring an end to hostilities against the Japanese in the Taikkyi, Letpadan, and Prome areas. Many of the officers of this organization had had training or experience with the *Hikari Kikan,* and were no strangers to political activity. These included its commanding officer, Major Kimawari, who was at one time attached to Burma Area Army, and the adjutant, Captain Kawaji. Agents of *Kusunoki Kikan* did in fact succeed

in contacting some of the officers of the Burma National
Army, but they failed to persuade them to renounce the
anti-Japanese policy they had adopted, and orders came from
Burma Area Army headquarters to return. There was no
question of going back to Rangoon by this time, as the
British had cut the *Kikan's* road of retreat, so Kimawari
decided to move into the Yomas with 28 Army, as the former
parent unit. They were a godsend to Sakurai who badly
needed trained intelligence patrols, and they were sent out to
check British positions and look for crossing points on the
Sittang. The idea was they should make a traverse from the
Yomas as far as Kyaukkyi, where they were to use wireless
sets in the hands of 144 Infantry Regiment and send reports
to Shimbu Force, under whose command they were placed
on 1 June. The reports were never sent, and for a very good
reason. Most of the patrols of *Kusunoki Kikan* were killed
before they reached the Sittang. One of them, for instance,
set out from the jungle round Hill 978, to bivouac in a group
of bamboo shacks about 6 miles west of Yee on the morning
of 4 July. They rested in the shacks until the morning of the
6th, then crossed the Tonkan Chaung about noon on the same
day. The following morning, around eleven o'clock, they were
attacked by a Gurkha patrol about forty or fifty strong. A
couple of officers were wounded, but none of their party was
killed (there were just over forty of them) and they retreated
into the edge of the Yomas. They tried the Mandalay Road
crossing again the following day and curved round north of a
village with a railway station (Tawgywe-in). It took them
about half an hour to reach the line of the railway, and then
they began to spread out. Major Kimawari, Lieutenant
Nishiyama, and a *Kempei* N.C.O., all of them walking with
difficulty because they were suffering from foot-rot, reached
the Kun Chaung[5] about noon. It was important to check the
crossing of this *chaung,* since 28 Army would certainly use
the route, and the three attempted it. The *Kempei* N.C.O.
made a scratch raft from bamboo, put his clothes and his

revolver on it, and swam across. He turned to watch the other two as he neared the opposite bank, and to his horror saw them go under and disappear in the stream.

He decided to push on alone, and came into a village with a *pongyi kyaung* (Buddhist temple) where two priests in their saffron robes came up to him and offered him food. They fed him well, and he thought it would be a good opportunity to dry his soaking clothes. He took them off, and, as he hung them up to dry, he noticed that the priests and some Burmese children who had gathered round to watch had suddenly disappeared. He looked out of the *kyaung,* and heard the noise of approaching footsteps. It was the priests returning, and in the company of troops of the Burma National Army. The *Kempei* grabbed his revolver, put his still wet clothes back on again with lightning speed, and fled. Early in the evening he climbed a tree to rest, and, as it grew dark, fell out of it again. He spent the whole of 9 July in the branches of a tree, and then marched on the following day, but was too weak to cover much ground. Soon he could walk no farther and went into a Burmese hut. The villagers gathered round him and gave him food. They told him to take his trousers off and wear Burmese clothes, which he did, exchanging his trousers for a somewhat tattered old *longyi.* He should have been on his guard by this time, but was too weak to resist when some of the village youths snatched his revolver away. The following day Burmese troops wearing red badges and white stars came into the village and hauled him off to British headquarters.

His story is not untypical of the fate of men of *Kusunoki Kikan* and the other patrols of 28 Army. They were trained men, but no longer fit, and the exertions they were called upon to perform demanded more than their bodies could cope with. Marching in particular, for men suffering from foot-rot and beri-beri, quickly became unspeakable agony. Since some of them were *Kempei,* their intelligence was a cut above that of the normal Japanese infantryman, and their knowledge of what was happening at home in Japan rather more extensive. In a sense, this made their morale more vulnerable—no news was coming through from Japan by this time, at least not at their level—and the last news they had heard was of the American air forces gradually coming closer and closer to the Japanese mainland and bombing their homes.

Kempei were also the nucleus of Tsuchiya's reconnaissance party, which left Mezali early in July to discover crossing points on the Mandalay Road. On 14 July, Tsuchiya split his men into groups of two, dressed in *longyis,* and carrying Burmese handbags containing their grenades and pistols. They checked the condition of crossing points on the Kun Chaung, and on the road and railway in the area of Kanyutkwin, where some of them were captured by Indian troops on patrol. Tsuchiya expected them to report back on 17 July —later groups were told to come back by the 19th, as Sakurai needed absolutely up-to-date information; the nature of the *chaungs* and their banks and the tracks leading to them was changing almost hour by hour. Like the groups of *Kamikaze Tai* and *Kusunoki Kikan,* Tsuchiya's *Kempei* reconnaissance suffered casualties from rivers, Burmese ambushes, and British patrols—some information did, however, trickle back. In Kanyutkwin, Indian forces were reckoned at around 900 men, and it was estimated that a battalion of Indian troops was in occupation of Pyu. Between these two villages, in Nyaungbintha, was an artillery post with five guns. Tanks kept up a regular patrol between the villages. On the Kun Chaung, Tsuchiya's men observed groups of Burmese acting as sentries and spotters—they appeared to be in telephone contact with British Army units too.

Once the reconnaissance patrols—at any rate those who survived—had returned, and before the columns moved off, Tsuchiya went to the spot where a track issues from Hill 1411. Stretching out below him he could see the watery gleaming levels of the Sittang Plain. The only road to life, he thought, lay in crossing that plain, with its surface turned into a sheet of water. Here and there the shining wet surface was broken by black dots, the shapes of dark islands on a sea—villages of the plain rising above the water. On the margin of the plain could be glimpsed the smoky purple line of the Shan Hills, and then, flashing here and there as it curved into a beam of sunlight, the river that everyone in the Army had seen in his dreams for months, the River Sittang. As Tsuchiya gazed at the low cloud cover over the plain, he saw formations of enemy fighters dive down and seem almost to skim the paddy fields as they flew south, searching for bodies of troops. 'They're keeping a close watch on us, they're waiting for us to come out,' thought Tsuchiya. He looked as the vanguard of *Shini Butai,* the Tsujimoto Battalion, began to come down the mountainside, each man carrying his two poles of green bamboo and wearing his rope around his middle. Judging from the flight of the British planes, Tsuchiya knew that these were not useless burdens. The bursts of gunfire from the aircraft as they swooped low over the distant Sittang were not aimed at men, necessarily; their target was often the rows of little country boats floating moored against the river bank, often some way up a tributary *chaung*, which the RAF was systematically destroying to prevent the Japanese using them. The men picked their way carefully, following the only guide they had, the sweating buttocks of the man in front—plastered on them was what Tsuchiya calls 'Burma's speciality', the green shining moss whose glow acted like a firefly for the marching men. The route lay across the Kun Chaung at one point. Suddenly, on this particular day, the *chaung* began to swell to unexpected proportions, and it was obviously quite impossible to ford it. The vanguard came to an abrupt halt on its banks. In this way, on the night of the first day of the movement from the starting line, the plan for crossing the Mandalay Road began to go awry. And from that night onwards, the sound of artillery in the Sittang Plain began to reverberate, endlessly—a sign, Tsuchiya believed, that every unit had begun to move off from its starting line simultaneously.

In the evening of 23 July, the left column of 28 Army, 4,500 strong, assembled near Milestone 137 on the Mandalay Road. On the very edge of the forest of green bamboo could be made out the faint silhouettes of three officers on horseback, Sakurai himself, Iwakuro, and Colonel Sugimoto, the commanding officer of *Shini Butai*. Tension was running high—all the ardours and suffering that had been the Army's lot in the Yomas were suddenly seen to be trivial in contrast with the risks that lay ahead of them, here on the first threshold of the way to the Sittang. The men felt this too, as they waited under the slanting sheets of rain. 'Tsuchiya! Tsuchiya!' The cry went up from the group under the trees. It was Iwakuro's voice, and Tsuchiya's reverie was left unfinished.

'You are to go ahead of the vanguard and come out on the Mandalay Road,' Iwakuro said urgently. 'When the column crosses, you will ensure its safe passage, if the enemy puts in an attack. Yamaguchi will go with you.' Tsuchiya picked two orderlies, Yasui and Morimoto, and set off at once. As he moved away, a green signal light shot up into the sky high above the Mandalay Road. 'That's it! The enemy's spotted us! They'll attack the column now!'—these thoughts flitted through Tsuchiya's mind as he watched the green light float and lazily go out. Soon he was joined by Yamaguchi, and they both made their way quickly up the embankment, and debouched on the Mandalay Road. The road was strangely quiet. Tsuchiya acted like a patrol leader on reconnaissance and sent the orderlies Yasui and Morimoto to either side of the crossing area, north and south, to act as sentries. He waited for the formations to come forward.

Then, in the night, the stillness altered. Like the sound of waves breaking, masses of men came out of the darkness of the Yomas and clambered up on to the road, up and over, over and across, and down the embankment on the other side.

It was more than the sound of marching men. There was the noise made by the bamboo poles as they rubbed and cracked together, and the shouts of encouragement to each other made by the men as they moved forward, the sort of shouts Japanese folk-songs have rendered immemorial as rhythms of work— *'Yoisho! Yoisho!'* 'At last we're on the road' was the thought going through the minds of nearly all the men as they climbed up the embankment and heaved themselves on to the road, with its solid feeling under the feet after weeks of pad-padding over soft marshy ground.

Fukudome came up to Tsuchiya: 'The enemy doesn't seem to have spotted us, you know.' 'Yes, it's gone well so far' was Tsuchiya's cautious reply. He was pleased, though, and both of them enjoyed a moment of self-congratulation as Sakurai and his Chief of Staff went by. The column accomplished its crossing smoothly enough, and Tsuchiya verified that the tail-end was over before he went down the embankment on the eastern side. The Senior Staff Officer, Colonel Okamura, brought up the rear, and stayed for a moment on the west side encouraging the stragglers and driving them on. When he came over, Tsuchiya and Fukudome realized that this part of their task was done. By three o'clock on the morning of 24 July, the headquarters column of 28 Army was safely across the Mandalay Road, undiscovered by the enemy.

Sakurai was rather less delighted than Tsuchiya had been. He had felt the vanguard come to a halt before it reached the road, and start to get bogged down very literally in the marshy ground; and the units from behind kept moving forward into those in front until the column was thrown into confusion, and there were screams and cries of distress from the women. Sakurai began to wonder if the units would ever get themselves sorted out, when Fukudome and Yamaguchi came over from the road to put some order into the chaos. Sakurai deliberated for a moment whether to hold up the advance until there was a better discipline of sequence, but decided against it and ordered the column to break out across the road immediately

even though its units were imperfectly under control.'Units–',
he thought, 'they're not units any more, they're more like a
mob', and he prayed that no enemy attack would come
pouring into this 'mob' as it streamed, vulnerably, across
the highway. But it was easier than he had feared at first and
the whole operation was over in twenty-five minutes.

Then, as the column kept going eastward in the wake of
the vanguard, there was another movement of dispersal.
Sakurai came forward to find out what was going on, and he
found units here and there breaking out of their line of march
to eat the sweet potatoes they had found in the fields.
Officers and men alike broke ranks and began to gnaw at the
raw vegetables. Sakurai could understand why. Men who had
just about kept body and soul together with a few handfuls
of rice and a pinch of salt for days on end were bound to see
the sweet potatoes as manna from heaven–but the disorder it
produced could have been serious, and the unit commanders
were told to round up their men and keep pushing them
eastwards.

Not a moment too soon. About 5 miles from the spot at
which they had crossed the road, the headquarters came
under heavy artillery fire which shrieked through the quiet
calm of the tropical night and made the column split asunder.
The men began to run to and fro heedless of direction,
heedless of water and sucking mud, anywhere to escape the
shelling. The staff officers, Iwakuro in particular, were almost
frantic with despair, but they did eventually manage to restore
some order where this had broken down. It was not easy,
though, and it took some time. Soon dawn was approaching
and then–perhaps as a result of his exertions–Iwakuro
collapsed. For a while, the column took refuge in the jungle,
while *Shini Butai* kept up its pace towards the Sittang. It
was not long before contact was lost with *Shini* altogether,
and after a while the headquarters column moved off
independently.

For hours Iwakuro had been moving up and down the

broken units of the column, yelling himself hoarse to get them moving in sequence and reunite the shattered remnants. Saito was right when he said that the staff officers of 28 Army never hesitated to go to the front line and share the life of the troops. In fact they often did more and, as the case of Hachisuka and Tsuchiya shows, were often involved behind the enemy lines as well as in front. On this occasion, whatever fever Iwakuro had been incubating was no doubt at first acting as a driving force, but it soon became evident that he could go on no longer. This was evident to his staff, but not to himself, and it finally became necessary for Fukudome, a big, burly figure, to force Iwakuro to calm down. Iwakuro resisted Fukudome's well-meant efforts, and the two men began to struggle. Fukudome pinioned the Chief of Staff in a wrestler's embrace, but with a real access of strength Iwakuro broke free and hurled Fukudome on his back, pressing him down into the monsoon-soaked earth. The men who were watching this stood aside at first, but, fascinating as this wrestling match between two senior staff officers no doubt was, it threatened to go too far. Several of them pulled the quivering Iwakuro off Fukudome, and Yano, a young medical officer, put a morphine injection into him. Before long, Iwakuro calmed down, and began to nod over into sleep. He was clearly suffering from a violent bout of malaria, as well as the extreme tension of responsibility for the Army's movements. Throughout the whole day of 24 July, Iwakuro slept on. By the end of the day he began to recover a little, and by sundown the headquarters column moved off once more. Sakurai called the staff together, in a clump of bushes: 'H.Q. will stay here until sunset, concealed from the enemy,' he told them,, 'but if the enemy does attack us, we will stick it out and defend ourselves on this spot. After sunset, we will begin to move east again. We must have absolute quiet during the day.' 'He looks very sad and drawn,' thought Tsuchiya, who realized better than most how much Sakurai had relied on Iwakuro's energy and judgement, and how he must have felt that he had placed too great a burden on him. Then Tsuchiya's own troubles began to impinge. From the day he had left 'Katori Village' in the Yomas, on 3 July, he had been marching through rain or on rain-soaked ground, and his feet had begun to swell. As if this were not enough, sand had filtered into his boots, the friction between skin and sand was producing great red blisters, and after the session with Sakurai he discovered that four great leeches as big as his thumb had clamped themselves to him.

Tsuchiya went back to his own clump of wet shrubbery, and began to chew at some cooked rice. Then what Sakurai feared took place—the sound of heavy artillery firing, over in the west. The strip of bush and shrubs which Tsuchiya, in the darkness of the previous night, had taken for jungle, was all at once a focus for a storm of shellfire. There was nowhere to hide from it, and all they could do was cram their steel helmets on their heads and fling themselves flat on the ground. In the intervals of firing, Tsuchiya thought he had better see what had become of the Army commander. Sakurai was unperturbed. He had a foxhole dug, into which the water was seeping, but he remained quite calm. The shelling stopped finally, and the casualties were counted: twenty. In the open as they were (comparatively speaking), it could have been a lot worse.

On this particular day, headquarters became vulnerable to other hazards, too. The sun showed its face for a change, but that brought out the enemy fighters. Both north and south, the sound of enemy artillery rolled along the Sittang Valley, In the afternoon, the noise of tanks patrolling the Mandalay Road made a counterpoint to the guns and Tsuchiya began to long for nightfall. Night was an ally, a screen of darkness behind which the eastward advance could go on, away from the prying eyes of RAF pilots and the binoculars of Burmese guerrilla groups.

Sunset finally came, and headquarters moved off, still in heavy rain. They passed through the villages of Okshitkin and Gyobintha and reached Kyiyo on the 26th. Kyiyo is two-thirds of the way from the Mandalay Road to the Sittang, and once there the Army headquarters began to put in hand preparations for the river crossing. The journey had provided another heavy blow for Sakurai—and for Tsuchiya too. Colonel Sugimoto, the officer commanding *Shini Butai,* and 55 Cavalry Regiment, had been killed in Okshitkin at three in the afternoon of the 23rd, in the course of a British artillery attack. His unit had acted as a very effective vanguard for the main body of the headquarters column, and most of the men in headquarters realized that in a sense Sugimoto had probably been the victim of an attack meant for them. Where was *Shini Butai* now, Sakurai wondered—they were not in Thongwagale, a village to the east of Kyiyo, which was where the main body of *Shini* had been expected to concentrate. Then news came that they were in a village called Aukwedo-Ingon[6] and Sakurai sent Colonel Okamura off to investigate and to report back on the situation of the terrain at the same time.

When Okamura returned, he told Sakurai that if *Shini Butai* carried out their crossing where it had been originally planned, they were quite likely to run into trouble from enemy ambushes on the banks of the Sittang. In addition, the track to the crossing point led through waterlogged paddy which was now so deep as to reach head-height, and he had drawn the conclusion that for the unit to cross in a single night would be quite impossible. Headquarters decided therefore to alter its crossing point, and to make for the Sittang at a place called Kyauksaung, north-east of Kyiyo. While the planners looked at this possibility, Kyiyo came under heavy shellfire, but Sakurai refused to be forced out of his position during daylight hours and the headquarters column grimly held on until sunset, at a cost of six killed and twenty wounded.

In the meantime the left column of 28 Army central group, with *Baba Butai* (121 Infantry Regiment) as its nucleus, had

left the concentration point in the Yomas at nine o'clock in
the morning of 19 July, and made for the highest point on
the eastern ridge overlooking the plain. When they came out
on the ridge they saw, as Tsuchiya did, the entire vista in
front of them transformed into a sheet of water, dark under
the monsoon clouds and then scintillating suddenly as a shaft
of sunlight shot through. They collected together their
river-crossing materials, and spent the last night before the
break-out in the pouring rain, listening to the rumble of
artillery in the area of Kanyutkwin through which, they
realized with heavy hearts, they were to pass the following
day.

Dawn on 20 July was around six o'clock, and the units set
off in four columns, came quickly down the slopes and out
into the level ground. At ten o'clock a report came in from
the river-crossing unit which had been sent to investigate the
Kun Chaung—an obstacle now in itself, long before the
Sittang had to be crossed—that the selected crossing point at
Minlangu, just downstream from where the Kun Chaung
debouches from the forest on the edge of the Yomas, was
now unfordable. The Regimental Commander, Colonel Baba,
ordered the columns to split up into smaller units, and each
of the columns, at five o'clock in the evening, assembled at a
point in the eastern foothills from which the break-out would
begin. Late that night, around eleven o'clock, the columns
made for the Kun Chaung, and began to cross. Then the
predictable began to happen: men who had been sent in
upstream by the river-crossing units there began to be swept
downstream by the fast current and mingle with the swimmers
further south. The concentration of the units became more
and more complicated, and the whole process of crossing and
concentration took far more time than was expected. By the
time everyone was ready to move off from the Kun Chaung
area, it was already four o'clock in the morning of 21 July.
The going was terribly hard, the fields through which their
path had been traced were deep acres of mud, and every

individual soldier began to get bogged down as he struggled on. With only three-and-a-half hours to go until dawn, they would be faced with the problem of crossing the Mandalay Road in broad daylight—an invitation to be massacred.

There was no question of imposing a fresh march discipline on the troops—officers and men were tired out, columns were mixed in with each other, and to attempt to put some order into them would have delayed the eastward march to the point where it became dangerous. Colonel Baba renounced it and let them march on. Soon heavy rain began to pour down, the surrounding fields grew dark, the units became more and more confused, and men began to drop out. There was no time to collect stragglers, and the columns pressed on through the sodden fields, using compasses as guides in the brief intervals of light which the approach of dawn opened in the rainy darkness.

Baba himself was in the van of the third column, with regimental H.Q. and a flag-party of seventeen men bearing the regimental flag. Soon they were at the Mandalay Road, at a point to the north of Kanyutkwin, and slipped swiftly across. The enemy did not spot them and they marched on without a pause until they had reached the line of a small stream some 2½ miles east of Kanyutkwin, by dawn on the 21st. Of the other three columns, the first brushed aside an enemy assault at nine in the morning of the 21st and pushed on to the village of Saikthangin, 3 miles north-east of Kanyutkwin; the fourth skirted around the north side of Kanyutkwin itself, and reached Ingwin by dawn on the 21st. The second column was not so lucky. Its advance to the road had been slower than that of the others, and as it tried to break across the road with its vanguard just after daybreak, it came under merciless fire from tanks and armoured cars lying in wait in prepared positions. The column broke, and retreated away from the road to wait for nightfall, but once elements of the British cordon had spotted them, they began to close in. Shelling ranged on the Japanese from Kanyutkwin, and planes came over and bombed them as they floundered desperately in the mud, attempting to get out of range of the guns on the road. They lost heavily that morning.

The other columns could not wait, and were not expected to. They had their own problems: the first column was shelled fiercely while harbouring in Saikthangin. The fourth moved on during the daylight hours of the 21st and halted for a moment at Ywamagyi, which it reached during the night of the 22nd. The Sittang was not far away by this time. Colonel Baba's contact was maintained with the first column, and he resumed full control of first and third columns by dawn on the 22nd. It was then a question of checking the Sittang crossing points. He decided to opt for a point south of Zigon. Halfway through the night of the 23rd, a report came in from Major Tanaka, the commander of the first battalion of the vanguard: the fourth column had decided to attempt the crossing on the night of the 23rd on its own, south of Zigon, and had been unable to land on the opposite bank, where a unit of rebel Burmese, 150 strong, was holding the crossing point. They were preparing to make another attempt.

It was not a British or Indian unit on the opposite bank, thought Baba—we might as well try and force a crossing. So he instructed Tanaka's battalion to give cover to another battalion—Yukō Battalion of the fourth column—which was to occupy the opposite bank by force. After the point was taken, Tanaka and his battalion were to cross at once, and occupy the area to let the main body pass unhindered. Baba himself was on the river bank at seven in the morning of 24 July and watched Yuko Battalion begin to cross. Suddenly the surface of the water was alive with a hail of bullets from the other side. Bathed in a fierce shower of fire, the men continued to push their rafts across, contending with the urgent current. The current pulled them away from the gunfire, on and on downstream, until they reached a point a mile south of the original crossing point, after swimming for about half an hour. They moved up on to the opposite bank, but it provided no haven. Here too the enemy was lying in wait for them, and poured fire into the battalion as it came up out of the water. Tanaka's battalion had better luck. By midday it had struggled across, and swept the Burmese out of their ambush. Tanaka held the area of the crossing point that night and Baba put the rest of his force across.

In the early hours of the morning of 28 July, Lieutenant-Colonel Tsuchiya stood with Sakurai on the banks of the Sittang. Sakurai gazed at the muscular waters rushing past in the darkness with feelings to which he could scarcely give voice: this was the same river he had crossed three years before, spearheading a victorious campaign which was to end with the British rulers of Burma being thrust out to the borders of India. He had planned and executed a conquering march, reaching out across this river, right to the capital of Burma and then up and up into the central plains and the old city of Mandalay. Three short years ago. The edifice of Japan's occupation of Burma was, in such a brief space, in ruins. And he stood now on the banks of the Sittang, commander of an army racked with disease and with a relentless enemy closing in on every side. It was a pleasant river, he remembered, in the dry season—but now! The waters thundered by, glittering now and then in the thick tropical night, with suddenly here and there a blacker spot in them as something was swept past—a tree-trunk perhaps, or ...? It looked about 220 yards across at this point, and was running fast. He could tell from its strength and speed that it was going to exact a host of living sacrifices from his army before it had finished with them.

They were not logs floating past, nor tree-trunks torn from the bank upstream. As he and Tsuchiya watched, a screaming voice came from the river, mingled with the roar of waters, *'Tsuwamono da! Tasukete kure!'* ('54 Division here! Help, for God's sake!') *'Tasukete kure! Oretachi wo misuteru ki ka!'*

('Help, help! Don't let us go!') The voices were full of agony and terror, but neither of the men on the bank could make out distinctly any human shape, just a deeper blackness here and there on the face of the water.

Men came up behind them and shouted out, helplessly, *'Gambarē! Gambarē!'* ('Hold on, hold on—you'll make it!') In a very real sense, they were encouraging themselves, because the fate each one feared for himself was happening under his very eyes. One by one, the raft teams got to work on the bamboo poles, twelve to a raft for six men. The men threw their equipment on the rafts and pushed out into the stream —this was the headquarters vanguard, Hosokawa Battalion— and began to swim the raft over to the other side. But the river was too strong for such an easy crossing, and the rafts were soon moving faster and faster downstream. *'Yoisho! Yoisho!'* the old cry of encouragement went up from the voices which were quickly choked by the gathering darkness, or drowned by the thundering river. There was no longer any point in pretending to keep the crossing secret from the Burmese guerrillas—there were occasional shots from the opposite bank, but the real enemy was not there at all: it was the swirling, liquid monster into whose arms each and every man had to lower himself, as it tore its way southwards with an irresistible energy and power.

The first attempt by headquarters had in fact been made just at midnight on 27 July, and was followed by a second and a third. The effort needed was immense, because the rafts were repeatedly swept back into the nearside bank and had to be pushed out again several times against the current. Once this difficulty had been overcome, the raft was in midstream and about to be plucked like a twig and hurled away downstream. There was little alternative, even for those who managed to cross in the few country boats which had been found in the Army's crossing area, undestroyed by the vigilant RAF. To choose a safe spot for the General's crossing, Major Yamaguchi sprinted along the embankment above the river, wearing nothing but his loin-cloth and sword, looking like a mediaeval warrior, checking points further downstream. Tsuchiya hobbled painfully along behind, and both of them came to a sudden halt when they heard a movement below them on the river bank. Suddenly a frightened voice called up to them in Japanese—'Hey, you there! Is this the near bank of the Sittang or the opposite bank?' Both Yamaguchi and Tsuchiya felt their tension vanish in an instant at the pained puzzlement of a raft-load of soldiers and burst out laughing. A little way further on they came to a cluster of huts. There were men moving about in them in the darkness, one of them a big man wearing only a loin-cloth like Yamaguchi himself. They tiptoed up to the huts and shone a torch. The big man was Captain Inagaki, the commander of a river-crossing party, and a company commander of 51 Independent Heavy Transport Battalion. Tsuchiya remembered him well from the days in the Arakan fighting when he had been in charge of the country boats for a river-crossing unit on the Bay of Bengal. Inagaki had managed to find a couple of battered old boats for the headquarters to cross in. Yamaguchi ran back and led the headquarters to the huts. A crossing unit was quickly formed of the General himself, his Chief of Staff and other staff officers, with the secret documents and the comfort girls and mess waitresses who had come even as far as this with the Army. The girls' femininity was not very much to the fore—they had all cut their hair short, and were wearing baggy army uniforms, soaking and mudstained after the endless tramping through the paddy. Sakurai himself used a country boat, taking Iwakuro across with him at two o'clock on the morning of the 28th. There was little rain at the time, but it began again with increased force during the following day, so that the sky could hardly be seen at all. This did not, in fact, prevent the RAF planes coming out on patrol, and Sakurai and his party heard them overhead. Until the end of the day, the party stayed concealed in high reeds, waiting patiently for nightfall before beginning to move again. To the western foothills of the Shan Hills, from the Sittang, there were still 13 miles to go.

Through the night, Tsuchiya could see Very lights going up into the sky, like a firework display. The enemy, he knew, had set up a network of agents in every little village between the road and the Sittang, and wherever Japanese were on the move, or hiding in large groups, these agents were reporting on their moves and using signal pistols to notify British aircraft and artillery. So far, Tsuchiya thought, headquarters itself had been quite lucky: their movements always seemed to be just that one step ahead of the reports of them, so that the village where they happened to have concentrated would be drenched with a storm of steel after they had moved on. Until the 28th, that is. After that day, the guns began to range along the line of march of the headquarters column, moving up to the river—it was lethal to stay in one spot. On the other hand, it was essential for Sakurai to do something more than merely see to the safety of his immediate headquarters: the column moved to Kyaungbya on 30 July, and on the 31st to Migyaunggaung, where Sakurai decided he must call a halt for two days at any rate in order to make some kind of contact with the other formations in the break-out. The news filtered through—*Shini Butai* was across the Sittang, *Baba Butai, Sei Butai,* 54 Division, and Kani Force (the Rangoon Defence Force) had completed their crossing. And at last there was news of Kanjō Force—6 miles south of Migyaunggaung was the village of Welabyin, and information came in that Kanjō was harbouring there.

Figures were still hard to come by, of course, but if headquarters column was any indication, Sakurai knew that losses would not be insignificant. He did not know how much more heavily some of the formations had suffered, but it was noticeable that the tension which had supported the men as they broke out of the Yomas and made for the Sittang began to relax once they were across the river and, in the 13 miles of marshland that stretched to the Shan Hills, numbers began to go sick, refused to march on any further, and had to be left behind in the villages. It became obvious from exploring other villages what happened when they were left behind—the exhausted eyes that closed in sickness or in sleep never opened again, the sleep became the sleep of death. Tsuchiya noticed this time and time again—it was like a spinning-top, he thought; while it's moving, it's like life itself, and then when the movement stops. . . . The units which followed the track of the headquarters column told him as they came in that they had had to avoid certain villages, because the smell from decaying corpses in the tropical rain had rapidly become unbearable.

So the southward trek began. Passing through the small towns of Kyaukkyi and Shwegyin, 28 Army and its subordinate formations moved under the umbrella provided by 53 Division. The journey, a march of over 50 miles, took two weeks. It was not possible during the march to make contact with Burma Area Army, because the batteries belonging to the signals units were ruined by the monsoon rains. But there were compensations. A rumour flitted through the southward-marching troops that at 53 Division's first supply point they would find *shiruko*, sweet dumplings made with sugar and red beans, a great Japanese delicacy. Plain rice would have been enough to spur on Sakurai's starving troops, but the melting thought of *shiruko* was a gastronomic fantasy beyond their wildest hopes. But this was no fantasy—somehow, even in its own state of deprivation, 53 Division had managed to set up a *shiruko* stall at its reception point near Kunzeik. Lieutenant-Colonel Tanaka, the staff officer of 33 Army who had been sent up north by Honda to contact Sakurai, noticed this with amusement as he passed by on his way to the crossing point at the Shwegyin Chaung. Other envoys had gone out too—the indefatigable Captain Mikuria and Warrant Officer Fujimoto had both taken patrols up into the Toungoo area to shepherd Sakurai's scattered rear formations south to Shwegyin and Mokpalin. Noguchi, another 33 Army staff officer, set to preparing stocks of food and medical supplies at points along 28 Army's line of march. This was not as easy as it sounds. Burma Area Army had stocks further south in Tenasserim but the roads had by now been churned into swamps, when they were not actual streams of running water, and the use of wheeled transport was completely ruled out. Rations had to be brought up and manhandled on stretchers. In normal times, it would not have been necessary to bring food to this particular area of Burma at all. On either side of the Sittang there was exceedingly rich farm land, a positive treasure-house of rice, vegetables, fruit, and chickens. But three Japanese divisions had already passed through it long before Sakurai's men were on the move, and they had plucked it clean. Tanaka noticed that the village stocks were totally depleted, and that it was pointless trying to press any more rice out of the Burmese, who were without supplies themselves. They had hidden stocks, of course. Like any occupied people, they tried to conceal whatever kept them alive from the marauding Japanese troops. Occasionally, when the Japanese tried to barter, some rice would be produced in exchange for towels and soap. The Burmese in this area had had no soap for months, and this was very distressing to them. They are a clean people, who bathe frequently, but water by itself had not prevented many of the villagers across the Sittang from being covered in scabies for lack of a thorough wash in soap. Japanese who carried soap in their packs found that a tablet was at times the currency of life.

Coming back along the Shwegyin track, Tanaka realized how hard the march was going to be for Sakurai—not only were the tracks turned into rivers and streams, but even when the Japanese sat down to rest the leeches were at them in an instant, penetrating ragged clothing, sucking away what debilitated blood was left. Like Tsuchiya, who was marching southward at the same time, Tanaka noticed how the number of rotting corpses increased the further south he came —hideously bloated by the monsoon rain, lying in rotting

heaps by the roadside, or making the air noisome and fetid
in the broken-down huts of the villages which the Burmese
had abandoned.

Tanaka was already waiting at the Shwegyin Chaung on
20.July, and was appalled by what he saw. He had passed an
18 Division engineer unit putting together light river-crossing
materials, and noticed the engineer company commander was
carrying a collapsible dinghy. They would need more than
this, he thought, as he looked at the raging *chaung*. 33 Army
had come this way a few weeks before, but it hardly seemed
the same river. It was near this point that it joined the Sittang,
and the Shwegyin Chaung itself had taken on something of
the nature of its destination: no longer a tranquil country
stream wallowing lazily between green banks, it was a strong
and ruthless river like the Sittang. There were going to be
difficulties here, Tanaka realized, as he set to and built himself
a *basha* in which to await the arrival of the first marchers
down the track from Kyaukkyi. They could not walk as fast
as the river current carried the first harbingers of the crossing
—as Tanaka waited, he saw the corpses of 28 Army men being
rolled downstream, an untold multitude of them being borne
seawards. Then, from the beginning of August onwards,
Sakurai's troops began to show themselves in little, forlorn,
tattered groups, on the opposite bank of the *chaung*. The
dramatic figure of Major Yamaguchi appeared, exactly as he
was on the night he and Tsuchiya had looked for a country
boat for the Army commander—*samurai* sword swinging from
his naked hips, clothed in nothing but his *fundoshi* (loincloth).
Yamaguchi waved at Tanaka, plunged straight into the
Shwegyin Chaung and swam across. Tsuchiya had thought of
a mediaeval warrior as he watched him run along the Sittang
bank—to Tanaka a similar image presented itself, as Yamaguchi
rose, dripping, from the waters of the *chaung*: a real man,
Tanaka thought, a soldier of the kind Japan knew so well in
the *sengoku jidai* (civil wars). You could tell that this was a
real *samurai*.

Then he glimpsed Sakurai on the other bank, with Tsuchiya and Fukudome—Sakurai could still smile, he noticed, and seemed in good spirits, but the lines on the face seemed more heavily and deeply etched with suffering than Tanaka remembered. The rest of the main body of Sakurai's columns continued to pass through Tanaka's check point, but what he had suspected from the sight of the rolling corpses in the *chaung* proved to be right: less than half of the numbers of 28 Army which had concentrated in the Yomas was passing down the track to Tenasserim. There had been a very great killing.

The men who came past were in a dreadful state: sunken eyes, listless, dragging along painfully lacerated feet—this was the image of defeat all right, thought Tanaka, who had already seen the extremes of suffering in what was left of 53 Division. And yet—many of them were still carrying their rifles and had ammunition slung from their belts. It gripped his heart to see that these tatterdemalions with their rotting feet, their eyes burning with raging fever, their thighs dripping with the excrement of dysentery, their whole bodies on the brink of total collapse—these men still had the enduring courage that brought them this far. Like Saito and Tsuchiya in the Pegu Yomas, Tanaka had become accustomed to the distant explosions of hand-grenades in the jungles north of Shwegyin. It was usually at night when they occurred, in the depths of the dark forests, when some solitary soldier had come as far as his strength or that of his comrades would let him. There was no question of surrender, and no question of going further—the only answer left was to blow oneself open.

The signal went out from 53 Division headquarters that contact had been made with Yamaguchi, and that Lieutenant-General Sakurai was on his way with a party of thirty-seven men, having reached the Shwegyin crossing point on 9 August. The forces crossing the Sittang numbered 25,000, reported 53 Division to 33 Army. This figure does not refer to those who survived, but is an estimate of those who set out. Only one battalion of Shimbu Force had been met and a search was going on for the others. 54 Division was coming up behind 28 Army. Those who were sick at the start had almost all died on the way. Those who had become sick in the course of the march or the crossing from malaria, beri-beri, or foot-rot numbered 5,000.

54 Division had originally planned to move south to the east of the main body of 28 Army, passing through the Karen territory and its main town Papun. By the time the division —or what was left of it—was over the Sittang, the physical condition of his troops, combined with the extra distance that the detour through Papun would mean, caused Miyazaki to alter his plans, and instead to come straight down the east bank of the Sittang in the direction of Shwegyin. Miyazaki's men were now in the area which was under the protection of Phoenix—56 Division—and Lieutenant-General Matsuyama sent officers to guide them through the Shan Hills. But there was little point in this since Miyazaki did not intend to send his exhausted men through the tiny jungle-covered mountain tracks.

From its distant positions on the Irrawaddy, months before, the Army had done its best to reconnoitre those hills. Even now, officers from the *Hayate Tai* patrol which had been sent into the Shan Hills on an intelligence mission earlier in the year came in to meet the column as it moved southward. It was no fault of theirs that the information they had was now out of date, rendered useless by the thrusting mail-fist of Slim's armoured divisions which had so rudely punched the Japanese armies into the south-eastern corner of Burma. They were amazed to see that Sakurai, the general they had remembered riding his horse, was now being borne along comfortably but much more slowly on the back of an ox. The horse had been ridden into the Sittang, but after a short struggle had been overcome by the current and drowned.

On the fateful day of 15 August, when the Emperor of Japan

was telling his people that they were going to have to 'endure the unendurable' fact of surrender in the face of the overwhelming might of the Allied air assault on Japan, Lieutenant-General Sakurai came into the headquarters of 53 Division at Shanywa. There to greet him were the 53 Divisional commander, Lieutenant-General Hayashi, the Deputy Chief of Staff of Burma Area Army, Major-General Ishida, and the Chief of Staff of 33 Army, Major-General Sawamoto. It was ten o'clock in the morning, and he walked under a wooden archway which some soldiers from 53 Division had inscribed with the characters *'Saku kangei'* ('Welcome to 28 Army'). They were painted on to an old wooden board, but they brought home to Sakurai's staff the reality of 53 Division's protection, and brought tears to their eyes. There were telegrams from Field-Marshal Terauchi in Saigon, and from General Kimura in Moulmein, speaking of the success of his break-out operation. Sakurai glanced briefly through their fulsome congratulations, and folded them away. It was just as well. In the afternoon of that day came the news of the Imperial Rescript bringing the war to a close. It did not come to an end for Sakurai. He knew his Army was still creeping southward—it could barely be called marching any more—and men were dropping out of the columns to die, dying as they moved slowly on, or taking their own lives. That road along the east bank of the Sittang to Shwegyin was rightly called by Lieutenant-Colonel Tsuchiya 'The Road of Corpses'. 'Even "corpses" is wrong,' he remembers. 'White bones were all that was left in many cases, and flies and bluebottles by the thousands swarmed over them: and in the middle of the paddy fields, clouds of vultures gathered....' And Sakurai had to move on from Shanywa. Surrender or no surrender, he had an order to fulfil, his Army had to be brought into some semblance of unity again and quartered in villages which did not, as these villages by the Sittang did, resemble cemeteries. Those who were fit enough had begun by burying the dead they found lying by the side of tracks, but soon the numbers grew so great that the task became impossible. In every village along the length of the great river, hut after hut contained the reeking bodies of the dead, filling the air with a noisomeness that no one dared to penetrate. After all, even the living were little different; men marched along with holes in their buttocks into which you could fit a man's fist, with maggots breeding in them as they walked.

It is understandable that the stragglers and deserters in this condition were easily picked up by British, Indian, Gurkha, or Burmese patrols. As they came into the British hospital at Penwegon, their skeletal frames racked with fever, their eyes burning with the final glow, the interrogators who had to bend over them to hear the faint whispered replies to questions could hardly endure the stench. Sometimes it was more than that, even—a pain-racked body would suddenly arch up, the tortured innards would squirt out a yellow fluid between the bony thighs on to the stretcher, and the whispered answers were gone for ever. These were too far gone to worry much about the eternal shame branded on the Japanese soldier who allows himself to be taken prisoner. But there were others who found themselves bound hand and foot by Burmese villagers as they tried to snatch a moment's sleep in a bamboo hut on the river banks, and, sick as they were, begged and pleaded with their interrogators to be allowed to kill themselves. One young lieutenant from Shimbu Force, who refused to believe that any Japanese officer had ever been taken prisoner before,[7] spent the entire afternoon of his capture weeping his heart out. He should have died on the field of battle, he repeated to his captors, he could never see Japan again, all he wanted was to commit suicide, life was finished anyway.

The corpses did not, as Tsuchiya soon found out, come to an end in Shwegyin. In the stretch of land between the Shwegyin and Madama Chaungs, which British maps mark as 'dense mixed forest', their numbers increased astronomically. Some had been wrapped in Rising Sun flags, as a final tribute from comrades who had decided to struggle on a little further; but the number of the corpses made it intolerable now even to go into the edge of the forest to rest or eat. Unless, of course, they had boots. Since many of the men had nothing on their broken feet at all, there was no question about being squeamish over removing boots from the dead. More difficult to bear were the quiet resigned voices of the dying, at the edge of the track, calling out to the soldiers passing by to take the boots off them if they wanted to.

Officers did what they could to stop the men resting before rest was ordered: it became evident that rest of this kind soon slipped into death. Some of them had to resort to drastic measures to prevent men slipping into the jungle when the march became unendurable. Major-General Koba's men had perhaps the roughest time of all. They were an independent force of 54 Division, and he had taken them up into the Shan Hills, where they lost their way. Koba picked for himself a switch of green bamboo, and whenever he noticed a man trying to drop out of the column would move up to him and thrash him with the switch, bellowing *'Aruke! Aruke!'* ('Keep moving! Keep moving!') It was not long before his switch began to look like the end of a Japanese tea-whisk, splintered into fragments as tiny as the hairs on a shaving-brush—but there was plenty of bamboo, and he kept taking a fresh supply from the jungle. The men did not react violently: they were brought back into line, and walked on, but just as if they were moving in a dream, as the blows from the switch lashed about their shoulders and buttocks.

Many of these men, hundreds and thousands of them, who missed the collecting points, but still doggedly pressed south, simply did not hear the news of the war's end and could hardly believe it when they did. To have come through such agony as they had and then find that the effort had been in vain, that hundreds of men who had been their friends had been left behind in the hills or the boggy fields of Lower Burma, while their country had capitulated thousands of miles away, was almost unthinkable. Their minds could not grasp the enormity of what had happened. Sakurai knew that it would be a difficult task to convey the news to scattered groups of men like this but somehow it had to be done, otherwise even those who had survived the final rigours of the march might find themselves engaged in futile combat with British troops or Burmese guerrillas and meet a pointless death at the very moment when dying in battle should be coming to an end.

33 Army sent out a signal on 23 August: 'According to a broadcast from the B.B.C. in London on 22 August, 200 Japanese troops, who have not heard of the surrender of the Japanese Army in Burma, are in conflict with British forces as they move south through Shwegyin down the east bank of the Sittang.' It was astonishing for a hostile army in the field to find out what was happening on its own doorstep from a B.B.C. broadcast but this was typical of the broken Japanese armies in Burma in August 1945. When the surrender came, their enemies knew better than they did themselves where their own units were. Still, as 33 Army's signal went on, protocol had to be observed: it was the responsibility of 28 Army to ensure that the order to cease hostilities reached all its subordinate units, on whichever side of the Sittang they happened to be, and aircraft and officer patrols would be used for liaison purposes. If 28 Army wished to set up a tactical headquarters in 33 Army's area for this purpose, 33 Army had no objection, and assured Sakurai of their co-operation.

There would be no rest, then, at least not for a while. Sakurai knew this in the hut where 53 Division welcomed him, and it was with this knowledge that he pressed on south to Moulmein though every fibre of his body cried out for him to halt. The rainy season was gradually beginning to draw to a close, the downpour was much less insistent and the sound of the guns had stopped. All over the battlefield the silence of peace descended. The Burmese began to show themselves in the villages as the Japanese came through, but Sakurai's officers were dulled by the shock of the news. A hollow feeling possessed them as if they had been emptied of all emotion.

On 18 August, Sakurai crossed over from Martaban and landed on the quay-side at Moulmein. In the dark night on the jetty, a little group was waiting for him. Tsuchiya, who accompanied the Army commander, saw that it was Kimura himself, the Burma Area Army commander, with his senior staff officer, Ashikawa. He watched Sakurai's face as the old man walked straight up to Kimura, without ceremony, and offered a firm hand-clasp. Kimura put his arm round Sakurai's shoulders and said, so mildly and quietly his voice became a murmur, *'Nagai aida, kurō wo kakete sumanakatta'* ('It's been a long time. It's been very tough for you. I'm sorry.') As the two generals looked at each other in the darkness, Tsuchiya saw the gleam in Sakurai's eyes.

CHAPTER FIVE

TSUWAMONO: 54 DIVISION AND THE ENDLESS RETREAT

In addition to the units directly attached to his headquarters, Sakurai's command included 54 Division, Shimbu Force, and 105 Independent Mixed Brigade, together with a number of smaller units moving more or less independently. The largest of these subordinate forces was 54 Division, which was over 9,000 strong. Miyazaki had brought 54 Division out of the Arakan in two groups, a northern group through the An Pass, and a southern group *(Baba Butai)* from Taungup. Koba Force (two infantry battalions and two companies with 100 mm guns) had moved south from Mount Popa to join the main body of the division, crossing to the west bank of the Irrawaddy to do so. The taking of Allanmyo on 28 April by 20 Indian Division meant that Miyazaki's 54 Division was cut off and could not cross the Irrawaddy from Thayetmyo, where it had been concentrated. His vanguard (two infantry battalions under the regimental commander of 154 Infantry Regiment) had reached the southern outskirts of Thayetmyo, and was so taken by surprise by the rapid advance of 20 Division that it just managed to transfer its headquarters and one battalion over to the east bank of the Irrawaddy, leaving the rest cut off on the west bank. The division therefore moved south to Kama and crossed the river south of the town, using seven country boats which had been collected in the area between 26 and 31 May. On the morning of 1 June the division crossed the Prome-Allanmyo road and moved into the western foothills of the Pegu Yomas north of Paukkaung the same night, using 153 Infantry Regiment and III/121 Infantry Regiment as a vanguard. Between 2 and 16

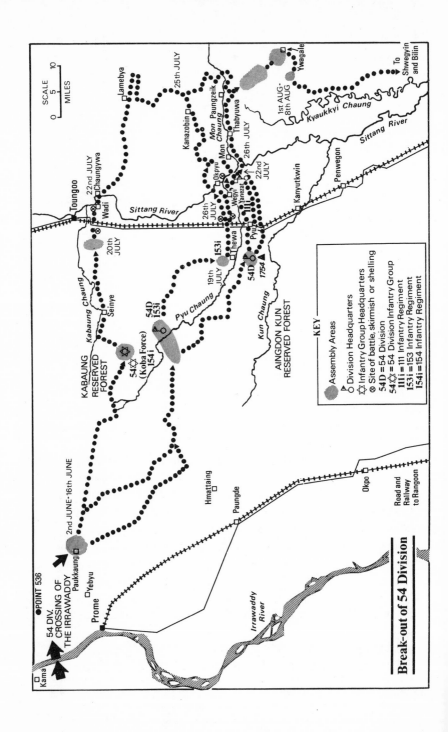

Break-out of 54 Division

KEY

▲ Assembly Areas
○ Division Headquarters
⬡ Infantry Group Headquarters
⊗ Site of battle, skirmish or shelling
54D = 54 Division
54⬡ = 54 Division Infantry Group
111i = 111 Infantry Regiment
153i = 153 Infantry Regiment
154i = 154 Infantry Regiment

SCALE
0   5   10
MILES

54 DIV.
CROSSING OF
THE IRRAWADDY

● POINT 536

Kama

Prome

□ Yebyu
Paukkaung

2nd JUNE-16th JUNE

Hmattaing

Paungde

Okpo

Road and
Railway
to Rangoon

Irrawaddy River

KABAUNG
RESERVED
FOREST

Kabaung Chaung

Seinye

Toungoo

Wadi
□ Chaungywa
22nd JULY

20th JULY

Sittang River

19th
JULY

54⬡
(Koba Force)
154i

**54D
153i**

Pyu Chaung

153i

Thewa

54D

1754

Kun Chaung

AINGDON KUN
RESERVED
FOREST

Kanyutkwin

Penwegon

Sittang River

Lamebya

25th JULY

Kanazobin

Mon Paungzeik

Mon Chaung

Okpu

Wegyi

Yanezu

Thabyuwa

26th JULY

26th
JULY

22nd
JULY

Pyu

Ywagale

1st AUG-
8th AUG

Kyaukkyi Chaung

To
Shwegyin
and Bilin

June, 54 Division made Paukkaung into a stronghold, with a defence zone divided into three sectors, each controlled by an infantry regiment. Here the division began to forage. Those who were not foraging or collecting materials for river-crossing took a rest to recuperate the strength they would need to cross the Yomas and the Sittang. The British made attempts to infiltrate into the Paukkaung positions and mounted small-scale attacks upon it, but there was never anything on a scale large enough to warrant a riposte by the main body of the division.

On 16 June, the division began to move out of the Paukkaung area in three columns, through the jungle-clad hills west of the Pyu Chaung. This part of the Yomas is largely teak forest interspersed with bamboo jungle, and has virtually no paths or tracks or human habitation. The division was forced to camp in these trackless hills. The monsoon had begun over a month before and the indescribable conditions made the movement of heavy guns impossible. Every gun over 75-mm had to be abandoned. In addition, the division was largely moving blind. The RAF attack on the divisional signal unit at Thayetmyo on 29 April had destroyed most of its wireless equipment, so there was no contact between the division and 28 Army headquarters.

Miyazaki was much exercised about the proposed date of the Sittang break-out. The original plan had been for 28 Army to move at the end of June, before the monsoon season reached its height. But he was given to understand that two reasons compelled a change of date: one was the slow concentration of his own division. Another was a hoped-for relaxation of vigilance by the British IV Corps at the height of the rains, and 20 July was therefore considered to be more appropriate. Miyazaki knew that it would be 10 July before his forces would be completely concentrated in the Yomas, since the progress of 111 Infantry Regiment had been delayed. There had already been a gross lack of contact over the business of supplies. At the time of the move to

Paukkaung and the skirmishes with the British forces trying
to probe the Japanese positions, Miyazaki, obsessed by his
experience during the Imphal campaign and wanting to
ensure that his troops carried at least a month's rations with
them in the Pegu Yomas, was relieved to learn that the Army
had arranged for dumps of munitions and food to be available
at Paukkaung. His relief turned to dismay when the dumps
could not be found. They were not in Paukkaung at all, but
at the village of Hmattaing, about 19 miles further south,
close to Paungde on the Rangoon Road. So he had to use up
the energy of his forces, already tired with the retreat from
the Arakan and the Irrawaddy crossings, in collecting rations
in the Paukkaung area. This, though, he fully intended to
do. He was not going to prejudice the men's condition by
trying to meet the Army's jumping-off date if it meant
forgoing supplies, and he thought it preferable to linger at
Paukkaung and hold off the enemy when necessary rather
than to withdraw further into the Yomas where, he rightly
anticipated, food would be scarce. So he drew up plans to
defend the Paukkaung area from the British attack which he
knew would follow him up from Prome.

The attack duly came. On 5 June, about 1,000 to 1,500
men of 7 Indian Division, with ten guns, broke into the
central area of the Paukkaung defences. On Miyazaki's flank
another British unit, about 1,000 strong with ten to fifteen
guns and a number of mortars, was attempting to break
through to the rear of his forward emplacements. On the left,
no large enemy forces had been observed, but they seemed to
be on the increase on the road from Prome. Using *Katsu Butai*
(I/153 Infantry Regiment) and 3 Battalion 54 Field Artillery
Regiment as reinforcements, Miyazaki put in a strong
counter-attack on his right flank. The attack began at dusk on
9 June, Miyazaki having moved his tactical headquarters on
that day to Pagyine, closer to the right flank. As it happened,
it was an awkward time for one of the infantry units in the
hills overlooking Paukkaung to the north: Colonel Murayama,

the regimental commander of 154 Infantry Regiment, suddenly began to show unmistakable symptoms of cholera and after several hours his condition grew steadily worse, so the commander of III Battalion, Major Hatake, took over temporary command of the regiment. The plan was to send in 154 Regiment (less one battalion) and II Battalion of 121 Infantry Regiment, to hit the British probing advance hard on its left flank, and this succeeded.

At the same time, by the 6th, increasing pressure was being exerted by reinforced British units on the centre and left flanks of the Paukkaung position, in particular on the crucial Hill 643 from which the plain could easily be dominated. The units in the central area (111 and 153 Infantry Regiments) put up a stiff resistance, but were gradually overcome, and the British attackers were soon masters of the hill positions. In fact some of them managed to move in even further and penetrated into the plain round Paukkaung itself. Miyazaki then withdrew I Battalion of 111 Infantry Regiment from his right flank force to reinforce his left.

While this was happening, the Mountain Gun Battalion, equipped with three mountain guns, discovered a British artillery unit with five guns at Yebyu, a village halfway between Prome and Paukkaung, on 6 June. They attacked at once, over a range of 6,600 yards, and with their first round hit a bull's-eye right in the middle of the British unit's ammunition dump. There was an enormous explosion and a huge fire blazed for two days.

Miyazaki withdrew his tactical headquarters on 12 June and placed his Chief of Staff, Kurazawa, in charge of operations on the right flank. He returned to divisional headquarters the same day. Here conditions were deteriorating: the rivers and *chaungs* were overflowing, the rain having fallen endlessly for days and days, and troop movements had become almost impossible. Inevitably the foraging had come to an end and communications were almost non-existent. It became impossible to shift those rations which had been collected into dumps. And worse was on the way. What had happened to Colonel Murayama had been a foretaste of what was to come for many men of 54 Division. Virulent cholera broke out among the men of the main body, claiming hundreds of victims among officers and men, from the end of June onwards. Murayama himself, as if by a miracle, continued to be optimistic about his own fate and in fact survived, but the officer commanding *Katsu Butai,* Colonel Takeda, fell a victim to the dread disease—it was a matter of days since he had been promoted colonel. Miyazaki took his loss hard. Takeda had done well since he had taken over and Miyazaki had come to rely on his unit for work in tight corners. The divisional commander thought of Takeda as one of the bravest and toughest and most genuine of his subordinate commanders. His death could not have come at a more inopportune moment, when commanding power, courage, and initiative were going to be needed in 54 Division more than ever before.

Then plague broke out. It was imperative, Miyazaki began to realize, to leave this area of the western foothills of the Yomas and move further into the mountains. The place was becoming a morass of mud and disease and he still had the mountain crossing to complete before the rest of the operation could be concluded. The order to move was issued at four o'clock in the afternoon of 13 June. The monsoon had reached heights of fury and the *chaungs* had become instruments of death—this, too, had repercussions on the division's movements, because the signal units' batteries were soaked and their remaining sets useless. Communication between headquarters and subordinate units had to be by runner, and many of these were carried away to their death in the raging waters. On 14 and 15 June, all units of the division began secretly to leave their positions in and around Paukkaung. The division moved off on the 16th, expecting to complete its fresh concentration further into the Pegu Yomas in the latter half of June. The men carried a month's rations, as Miyazaki had sworn they would; but the cholera and the plague were a problem. It was solved, if that is the word, by a casualty-collecting unit which assembled all infectious troops together as far to the rear of the main body as possible in order not to spread the infection.

An advance guard moved east on 15 June, then the main body of the front-line troops left their positions at eleven at night on the 16th, making as little noise as possible. Small bodies of men were left behind here and there to cover the withdrawal, and these began to come out at five in the morning of 17 June, with almost no reaction from the enemy at all. An order of march had been laid down by divisional headquarters, but the tracks were little more than threads through mud and water and it was not long before the troops, labouring under their heavy equipment, began to suffer terribly, as the days went by under the endless monotony of the rain. 54 Division had been unlucky: although every single unit of 28 Army received a pounding from the enemy and the climate and the river in its frenetic rush to the shelter of Tenasserim, few of them were intercepted on their first move into the Yomas. But 54 Division had to fight most of the way, first to emerge from the Arakan, then to find a crossing point on the Irrawaddy, then during the crossing itself; and lastly in the Paukkaung Plain, where it had hoped briefly to rest and forage, it found itself harried by a relentless enemy.

So Miyazaki gradually led his men further and further into the unfriendly Yomas, along the road that the men learned to call by the name 'Yasukuni Road' from the name of the shrine in Tokyo where the ashes of dead soldiers are reserved and honoured; or, more harshly, 'White Bone Road'. For underfed troops, harassed by the fatigue and the endless rain-sodden march, and pursued by cholera and plague, death was never very far away. And there was little food to fend it off. One warrant officer of 121 Infantry Regiment, Kagehi, remembers the desperate recourse made to yams once the little ration of rice had dwindled to nothing, then the picking-off of fragments of meat from the bones of dead cows crawling alive with maggots. The alternative was the perennial bamboo shoot, which, like the rest of 28 Army, they made palatable in a myriad ways.

As with the other units, it was the few women who came along with them who had the worst time of all. Kagehi recalls being summoned for a patrol into the Sittang Valley to find out for the Division what the suitable crossing points would be. He was to go with a sergeant and five men, dressed in *longyis* like the Burmese, but wearing their Japanese loin-cloths underneath as a pouch for carrying two hand-grenades. Two days later they stopped for a while at a hut which bore the grandiose title of 'Kempei Garrison Unit'. There were seven women there, and when the soldiers came up they joined their hands together and begged and beseeched them to give them food. 'Rice, please, please give us some rice!' 'I suppose they were comfort girls [army prostitutes] or something like that,' Kagehi says, 'but neither they nor we could strike up a single spark of desire between us. We had about twelve pints of rice, and gave them a cupful each in both hands, and it would have made you weep to see how happy it made them.'

The first thing in Kagehi's mind when they drew near to a village near Pyu, from which the plain could be seen quite clearly, was to ask for rice. The villagers were armed with bows and spears, but they seemed good-hearted enough, and offered the men rice to eat. As they were eating, there was a sudden burst of machine-gun fire and five of Kagehi's comrades spun round and fell. The silence was terrifying after the burst of firing, and Kagehi felt how alone he was in the darkness of the night, with the sound of pouring rain, and beside him the dead bodies of friends who had been thankfully swallowing rice a few seconds before. He knew the village was surrounded by the enemy, but he had no intention of being taken prisoner. He lay flat, and moved inch by inch away from the pile of bodies in the darkness, reaching down into his loin-cloth as he did so, to commit suicide if anyone attempted to take him alive. Two or three yards from the roadside where he had been were clumps of tall grass, and he slid slowly along towards one of them until his body was completely hidden. He slipped the hand-grenades out of his loin-cloth. Then, whether from an empty stomach, or excessive tension, he began to doze off fitfully.

A grunting sound woke him up and he was surprised to see the eastern sky filling with light. Then he looked along his body, and the grunting sound was explained—his body was covered with mosquitoes, and a pig was making a meal of them. He slipped free, made for the *chaung* which was close by, and slipped his head into it; then rose and turned into the thickening forest and back again into the Yomas. In spite of the danger through which he had passed, he still had only one thought in his mind, 'I'd like to eat rice again, just once, before I die.' He thought he would retrace his steps back to the company position by the simple expedient of following a track made by elephant prints in the mud. He walked until sunset, and tried to shelter his head from the incessant rain by covering it with leaves of dwarf-bamboo. Since all he had to eat, apart from the fistful of rice he had managed to swallow before the machine-gun fire, was edible grass and bamboo shoot, he began to have diarrhoea, and nothing he could do would make it stop. He went on in this way for several days. Along the side of the narrow tracks white bones were scattered here and there. He attempted to tell where he was by the sun, and by the moon on the nights when there was a moon, and finally, by some miracle, arrived back at the spot where his company had harboured. But by this time he was in such a fever that his body seemed strangely remote from him, and as he walked he kept wondering whose body it was that was making its way through the jungle. When, at the end of his tether, he found his company ready to move off east, he decided he could not walk another step.

'I can't move, I simply can't move an inch,' he told the company commander. 'I'll catch up with the company later.' But the company commander knew better. 'If you get left behind here, it'll be the end as far as you're concerned. At any rate, try and walk as far as you can.' He made a brief attempt to do so, but found he was right: he could not move. It was decided to leave him behind with another soldier, Hosota. They threw their rifles away, not having the strength to use them, and retained only their hand-grenades. This did not mean, in their case, that they'd given up hope. Each encouraged the other to have a go at walking, and they made themselves bamboo canes with which to support themselves as they tried to hobble along, inch by inch.

Soon they were not alone. They emerged from the hollow where they had been left on to a small track, and found other men of 54 Division in the same condition as themselves, almost asleep as they dragged themselves along, the only thing alive in them being the eyeballs staring ahead and glowing with fever. They muttered to themselves in low, heavy voices: 'What's the use, what's the use, we're done for.' But nonetheless, like Kagehi and Hosota, they kept heaving themselves slowly along. Finally there came a moment, still in the mountains, when the Sittang Plain glimmered in the distance, and they could see Japanese troops moving to left and right of them, making for it. They came out on the plain at night, and as they passed by a clump of trees the sound of small-arms fire came at them, 'patsu! patsu!' They were sure they were being fired at, but nothing hit them.

Gradually the fever abated and they noticed they had become a group of ten men—then it was five men, then three, the groups began to form and split up as they came to a point a few hundred yards short of the Sittang, and the men wandered about aimlessly here and there, wondering how to cross. Kagehi went into a nearby hut and found twenty or thirty Japanese in it, from Shikoku, they said. (This makes it almost certain they were 55 Division men.) 'We're going across tonight,' they told him. Fortunately the rain had ceased for the time being, and there was a moon, even though it was covered with cloud.

Suddenly the hut was filled with the noise of rifle fire, and screams of pain. Men hurled themselves out of it and fell to the ground, and inside the hut the spurting blood seemed like a shower of rain. Luckily Kagehi managed to crawl out without being hit, but he knew that to linger nearby would certainly be fatal, and so without even taking his bearings he made for the river bank and slipped into the waters of the Sittang. Seven or eight men were clinging to a raft made from lengths of bamboo formed into a triangle. Oddly enough, he recognized one of them, a soldier from Kobe called Nishikawa, but before he had time to say anything the current had swept Nishikawa away. There was a terrified scream in the darkness and then nothing but the sound of the river, broken by a single rifle shot. He and the rest tried to swim the raft across. The opposite bank was several score yards distant, and as they drew near they heard voices in Japanese calling out to them, 'Swim as hard as you can, there's enemy further downstream!' But the current was far too strong for exhausted men, and they were swept downstream. It was not long before a group of five or six men came out of a clump of grass and fired at them as they went by. One of the men near Kagehi was hit, and he used the corpse to shield himself from the firing which went on until they were out of range. Then, quite unpredictably, the river gave a great swirl, and hurled the raft against the bank. Kagehi dragged himself off it, went along the bank a little way, and found a hut. It stood a little apart from the rest of the village, and for Kagehi a Burmese hut still meant rice. There was a woman sleeping in the hut, and Kagehi shook her, calling out in Burmese, '*Main-ma, Main-ma!*' ('Woman, Woman!') As the woman awoke in fear Kagehi saw an enemy soldier carrying a rifle coming close to the hut. He had no energy left with which to flee, but somehow or other he was out of the hut and into the swampy ground round the village in no time. If they came after him, he never knew, but finally dozed off.

When he awoke, he heard the sound of aircraft overhead.

It was daylight. There were several planes, and they were flying low over thickets and clumps of elephant grass looking for groups of Japanese. He lay still until nightfall, then painfully climbed into the branches of a tree and fell asleep again. The branches were thickly leaved, and proved to be a safe shelter. When it was dark, he came down and made out at the edge of another village close by a group of five or six men standing naked in front of a hut. They had a fire going and were eating something—what it was, he could not make out. Nor could he tell whether they were Japanese or not. He was past caring anyway. Brandishing a grenade in his right hand, he hurled himself in front of the man who was nearest the fire. The men scattered at the apparition, thinking a maniac had descended on them. One of them, not so nimble as the rest, only got as far as the doorpost of the hut, and stood clutching it, shaking with fear. Kagehi still could not see very well, and could not make out whether the men were Japanese or Burmese. Then the man at the hut door called out to him, '*O mae, Nihonjin de wa nai ka?*' ('Hey, you, aren't you Japanese?') in a trembling voice. When Kagehi said he was, the men drew near again—'When we saw the grenade in your hand, we really had the wind up,' they told him, and he could see their relief at finding out he was Japanese turning into anger at having been put to flight and startled out of their wits by one man. They turned out to be part of a unit 200 strong, from Gumma Prefecture, under the command of a Captain Fujiwara. Kagehi sought out the captain, explained that he had not been able to find his own unit and asked to be taken along with them. The captain agreed, and Kagehi finally reached the safety of the Shan Hills.

What happened to Kagehi could be duplicated many scores of times over in the chequered history of 54 Division's crossing of the Yomas and the Sittang and Miyazaki knew exactly what was lying in store for himself and his men. He had experienced it all before, a year ago, during the bloody retreat from Kohima. In command of 31 Division's rearguard, he had been left to cover the withdrawal of the main body of the division. Its commander, Lieutenant-General Sato, had openly refused an order from the 15 Army commander, Lieutenant-General Mutaguchi, to take his division into battle again. 'I'm not going to have my men act as fodder for Mutaguchi's imperial dreams,' Sato stormed to the visiting army chief of staff. 'He's sent me no rations, no ammunition, nothing except orders to advance. What am I supposed to advance with? This time he's overdone it, I'm going back to the Chindwin.' And go back he did, knowing full well that the threat of court-martial for cowardice in the face of the enemy hung over him. In effect, he was never court-martialled, because his evidence on the lack of preparations for the Imphal campaign might have caused too many other heads to roll. His decision is still a controversial one. The survivors of his division say they owe their lives to him. On the other hand, officers of 15 Army staff declare that if Sato had not ratted they might have finally won through to Imphal after all and changed the course of the war in the Far East. It is a clash of personalities as much as of strategic ideas and as both major protagonists are now dead the controversy is not likely to find a solution. But as far as Miyazaki was concerned, Sato's decision was of great consequence. He was the infantry group commander of 31 Division and would have fought to the death if ordered to do so. He was told to hold off the British as they followed Sato's men to the Chindwin, and by a series of courageous delaying actions Miyazaki did manage to save hundreds of Japanese lives—at any rate for a time. He combined toughness with real solicitude for his men and it was with the object of saving as many of them as possible that he dictated his orders for the crossing of the Mandalay Road and the Sittang, once 28 Army had refused his plea to cross north of Toungoo.

All preparations for the crossing were to be completed by 19 July, by which time the division was expected to be 28 Army's northernmost unit lining the eastern edge of the

Yomas. After sunset on the 20th the division was to move off from the starting line in unison. There would be a northern element which would cross the Road just south of Toungoo; and the main body, which would make the crossing on either side, north and south, of the town of Pyu, between Toungoo and Penwegon. After the river had been crossed, the division would concentrate at Ywagale and make for Bilin through Papun, the chief town of the Karen State. The units would attempt to break out in the gaps between the enemy's positions, but if this was not possible then every unit would simply have to fight its way through.

The northern element would be constituted by the Koba Column, under the division's infantry group commander, Major-General Koba, who had already led the column in the fighting around Mount Popa. Koba would leave on 20 July, and cross south of Toungoo, concentrating his forces later at Lamebya (east–south–east of Toungoo) before moving on to Papun. At Lamebya he was to make contact with 56 Division, which was assisting the break-out by carrying out diversionary guerrilla activities in the Toungoo area against 19 Indian Division.

The main body was to assemble by 18 July at the latest at Point 1754, behind a line running through the village of Thewa, and complete its break-out preparations by the following day. The main body would split into two columns, the northernmost or left column consisting of *Katsu Butai* (153 Infantry Regiment) while the southernmost would split again into three. River-crossing units would start out first and be responsible for the collection of rafts and country boats at the crossing points. The right column's echelons would start off at intervals of a day between them. If the division started to move at nine in the evening, Miyazaki and his staff estimated they should be crossing the Mandalay Road by eleven that same night, and should be on or near the banks of the Sittang by dawn on the 21st. The break-out columns would ensure that the first units to reach the road would form a protective shield on it against any enemy attack. They should also cut the telephone wires between Toungoo and Penwegon. As soon as the Sittang was reached, every column was to send a liaison officer to divisional headquarters—ten in the morning of the 21st was the pre-arranged hour. Once the river was crossed, the columns were to concentrate their men in units of roughly battalion strength and then march off to the divisional concentration area, the right column to concentrate at Paungzeik, a village on the Mon Chaung east of Pyu, the left column at Kanazobin, a few miles to the north of Paungzeik. Ywagale was the divisional concentration point, from which it was expected to move on 27 July.

There would be three crossing points on the Sittang: a right crossing point near the confluence of the river with the Mon Chaung, a central crossing point near Yaneza, and a left point near the confluence with the Pyu Chaung. Miyazaki's order then distributed the units among the various columns. He assembled all unit commanders at divisional headquarters on 7 July, and explained his plan of operations to them. Each unit was to use part of its force, he told them, to ensure proper foraging was carried out. This in itself was the cause of some delay, as in many cases half the foraging parties failed to turn up on time in the concentration areas and it seemed likely that most of them would be a day or two late in starting. Each echelon set out from the assembly point under pouring rain from 11 July onwards, cutting a path through the jungle where necessary with an elephant in the lead. There were in fact wild elephants in the Yomas, but the Japanese were using forestry elephants which had once belonged to British timber firms. The wild elephants were given a wide berth, since some of 28 Army headquarters troops had been severely injured by a herd of them in the Aingdon Kun Forest, south of the Kun Chaung, as they made their way towards the Mandalay Road. By the evening of 17 July, all the columns were concentrated in the eastern foothills of the Yomas, but there was no news from the river-crossing units which had secretly despatched a

company of engineers earlier to the Sittang to reconnoitre and collect boats.

Miyazaki decided to have a last conference with the
break-out column commanders and the commander of the
river-crossing unit at divisional headquarters. From information
which had been brought in by *Kempei* and other scouts, he
gave them an outline of what he believed to be the enemy
situation across the path of advance of their break-out:

1. In Pyu he reckoned there were between 500 and 600
British-Indian troops. At every sizeable village along the tracks
leading from the Yomas to the Sittang Plain, there appeared
to be units of weak Burmese troops, mixed with one or two
regulars in each case.

2. North of Pyu, there was no information forthcoming.

3. On the Sittang itself, the situation was far from clear.
The river was about 220 yards wide, and the surface of the
plain leading up to it was waterlogged paddy. The ground was
thoroughly soaked with the monsoon rain, particularly east
of the main road, where there was a belt of ground with water
reaching sometimes to chest height. There was no shelter or
concealment of any kind other than in the villages. On the
River Sittang itself, there were no boats and no rafts at all.

It was futile to pretend that this was other than grim news,
but it was not unexpected. Major-General Koba, who had been
fighting continuously since leaving the Arakan, was under no
illusions and was fully aware that this looked like being the
hardest fight of all. On 5 July he had left Seinye, a little village
south of the Kabaung Chaung, in the Kabaung Reserved
Forest, a few miles west of Toungoo, in order to reach
divisional headquarters in time for the conference. On the
way, coming along the jungle tracks, he met officers and men
of the division, trying to catch up with their units—men
sunken-eyed and hollow-cheeked, walking skeletons some of
them. When he asked them why they had not had enough to
eat, they told him they had not been able to endure the weight

of the rations on their backs and had only brought very little with them. So they filed past him, leaning on bamboo canes for support, a line of men threading their way through the forest with a sadness that defied description. What worried Koba was whether their condition was the result of the decision they had all agreed to, to move into the Yomas in the first place. Could it be that they had been mistaken, and that this was not to be the escape route Sakurai had told them it would be? There had been cows and horses accompanying the units, of course, as Koba knew, and the men told him that most of these had been eaten already. The men who had first go at them tore off the flesh, those who came afterwards pulled out the innards, and the last-comers had to be satisfied with gnawing at the skin and bones and the flesh sticking to them. Koba thought of the deep water lying ahead when these men came to the Sittang Valley. Most of them were stragglers because they were sick, and the conditions of the march were intolerable, the muddy tracks and wet bamboo forest taking their toll. Liaison was constantly interrupted, no one could be sure of getting a message through, and this was why the advance guard units, after reaching the break-out starting line, had to wait four hours for the units to come up behind them. On Koba's front only 2,000 were lined up on time, as dawn broke on 20 July.

Miyazaki was to be out of luck again. 19 Indian Division was waiting for him at the crossing points on the road. To start with, 150 men were killed and wounded between the assembly point and the road on Koba's front, which was shelled constantly throughout the day. Three days later, on 22 July, he was bombed from the air and shelled, and British tanks put in an attack on him, as a result of which he lost another thirty men. Contact between his engineer company (54 Engineer Regiment) and part of his field artillery battalion, which was the rear group, and his forward echelon (154 Infantry Regiment under Colonel Murayama) was lost completely about the time they broke across the Mandalay

Road. Attacked before it reached the road, the rear group retreated west again towards the Yomas, losing many officers and men in the process. Koba himself, with II Battalion, 154 Infantry Regiment, and a section of engineers, put in an attack on the bridge across the Kabaung Chaung just south of Toungoo and destroyed it.

At dawn on the 21st, the infantry group headquarters, with 154 Infantry Regiment's advance guard, reached the village of Wadi, south-east of Toungoo, but got bogged down in the swampy ground, which delayed its move to the concentration area. Koba tried to carry out the river crossing even though it was dawn and the skies were clearing, and sent III Battalion, 154 Regiment ahead to start the crossing. Captain Abe, the acting battalion commander, went on in front, with the companies following him through the swamp as best they could. By some miracle, Abe found a raft and made it to the opposite bank. The river at this point was 220 yards wide. Koba was keen to make the rest of the units cross after Abe, but was dissuaded from ordering them to do so. It was fully daylight by now, and the risk from enemy artillery and particularly from enemy aircraft was very great. The crossing of the main body of Koba Column was therefore put off until the night of the 22nd. The artillery unit attached to it was delayed, too, and if the crossing had been carried out immediately it would have been left behind to cross alone. But Koba was in a fever of impatience to get his men across the Sittang and out of range of the enemy's guns as fast as possible. The artillery battalion had in fact become separated from the main body of the column, and broke across the Mandalay Road on its own, away from the tracks used by the rest. Dawn came on them as they continued their march eastwards, so the battalion decided to harbour in the nearby jungle throughout the hours of daylight. Naturally enough, Koba had no means of knowing this. The main body of the column waited near Wadi during the daylight of 21 July, putting guards round all sides, and was attacked by a British armoured force coming from Toungoo. The enemy began to shell Koba as soon as they came within range. They had three M3 tanks and one light tank and a strong force of infantry in about twenty vehicles. Murayama's 154 Regiment engaged them, and there was a brisk exchange of fire; but by evening it was possible to disengage.

Halfway through the night of the 23rd (about one in the morning, in fact), Colonel Murayama attempted the river crossing, carrying his regimental flag with him on a raft. A single small country boat had been discovered, and Koba followed him in this. It served to ferry the other units across as they came up to the river banks.

There were places where the water temperature was extremely low, particularly where a *chaung* ran into the Sittang, and if the men were in the water too long at a place like this they began to lose all sensation in their arms and legs, and the swirling waters of the Sittang carried them away. Others died of heart failure in the water. There were other dangers, too: Burmese under British command, firing from the opposite bank, or hidden in the leafy branches of trees, kept picking off individual soldiers on rafts as they neared the shore. Bodies slipped off the bamboo, and were lost in the cold, swift stream. Some rafts had been made of rotten wood, and those who rode on them or clung to them soon sank into the Sittang. It was not far, perhaps 220 yards, but it was a nightmare crossing for many, and many others never came to the opposite bank at all. Those who survived made their way to the column concentration point at Chaungywa.

The main body of the division, further south, set out from the starting line on 20 July. At midnight, the left and centre break-out columns of the right column broke across the Mandalay Road. They were attacked at once and Colonel Yagi, the commander of the left break-out column, met his death on the road near Pyu. The centre break-out column lost touch with its subordinate units in the pitch blackness, and soon the night was a milling mass of confused Japanese troops.

Fortunately order was restored, of a kind, and by dawn on the 21st the column was on its way to Kinwain.

The right break-out column was attacked by rebel Burmese in the foothills of the Yomas and retreated back into the hills, coming out again at dawn on the 22nd to break across the road. By 21 July, the river-crossing units of each column had occupied the area of the crossing points more or less without a hitch and the columns followed them, dodging as best they could the vigilant eyes of British aircraft. The men got to know the intervals of the reconnaissance planes and managed to use the time in between their departure and arrival to move in a little further ahead, from one swampy thicket to the next. The first and third battalions of the left break-out column were doubtless in the greatest difficulty. After Colonel Yagi had been killed, the column was in a state of great confusion, and the men crossed the road individually, without reference to the new column commander, Major Yamamoto, passing through Mon and then making their own way to the concentration point at Ywagale. Until they were actually concentrated in that area, divisional headquarters had no knowledge of their whereabouts, and the worst was feared.

The main body of the left break-out column was made up of 111 Infantry Regiment, and the second battalion of 54 Field Artillery Regiment. These pushed on and occupied Wegyi, a village on the Pyu Chaung about 8 miles east of the Road. It seemed a restful place for a little repose after the exertions of the crossing; but they had been spotted, and the village itself had been ranged on by British artillery. About 2½ miles to the east of Wegyi, in Okpyu on the west bank of the Sittang, there were about 500 troops under British command with two guns, and they at once began to bring the fire of these two guns to bear on Wegyi. As soon as they did so, the British in Pyu began to fire also and the shelling poured in from two sides at once. Under the curtain of this fierce artillery bombardment, the British put in an attack on the column. It was a ferocious, bloody battle, and nearly every single officer and man of the regimental headquarters was either killed or wounded, including the new commander, Major Yamamoto. Nonetheless, the Japanese managed to hold on to the village of Wegyi until the 25th. The Japanese themselves tried to take Okpyu with another force, III Battalion, 121 Infantry Regiment under Captain Yamane. The battalion was making for its west bank crossing point and arrived before Okpyu on the evening of the 22nd. They found it full of enemy and attacked at once, but the village resisted stubbornly and they could not take it. On the night of the 23rd, Yamane decided to break off the confrontation, moved his battalion half a mile further south and tried to cross the river there; but the volume of water had increased so much that only one company could cross.

This kind of move was not untypical, and was bound to happen. If a unit bumped a British or Burmese position and found it could neither pierce through it nor circle round it, then it was necessary to look for a crossing point other than the prescribed one. The right column was relatively lucky in finding boats, because after Miyazaki's warning it had expected none. As it happened, there were enough small boats and rafts available for it to cross from the night of the 23rd onwards. The first and second battalions of 111 Infantry Regiment were in a very bad state, after their column had been attacked, and together with the main body of 54 Engineer Regiment, which was supposed to move along with the centre column, they completely lost track of the route they were supposed to follow and ended up by coming out at a point on the river in the zone of the right break-out column.

Miyazaki and divisional headquarters were attacked by a negligible force of Burmese on the river bank—evidently lying in ambush waiting for groups of Japanese to prepare their rafts—and beat them back. They then crossed the river in two days, 24 and 25 July.

The headquarters and III Battalion, 111 Infantry Regiment, which had suffered heavy losses at Wegyi, crossed the Sittang on the night of the 26th. Their regimental flag was taken over on the morning of the 27th by a flag party consisting of a sergeant and six men who then made for the concentration area of divisional headquarters.

The left column consisting chiefly of 153 Infantry Regiment *(Katsu Butai)*, broke out across the road well north of Pyu by 20 July, and was harried by the enemy as soon as it had crossed. It was under continuous attack for two days until it crossed the Sittang on 22 July. On the river bank the headquarters of 153 Infantry Regiment came under heavy fire from an enemy unit, 300 strong, using a trench mortar. It could have become a very nasty situation, since the Japanese were on their crossing point and to look for another one would have risked dispersal and fragmentation of command. So the acting regimental commander, Lieutenant-Colonel Noda (the commander—Colonel Takeda—had died of sickness in the Yomas) seized the regimental flag and put in a charge, knowing his men would not see their flag captured. The enemy were forced to withdraw, though a mortar bomb put paid to Noda's bravery. Only then did the men begin to cross the Sittang.

This business of the flag preoccupied another unit of 54 Division on this dreadful journey. 111 Infantry Regiment (left break-out column) made its way across the flooded Sittang Plain using a compass, and successfully crossed the railway· line and then the Road, hearing the sound of rifle-fire coming from a distant village. At night, however, the condition of the ground was such that the rear half of regimental headquarters could not advance as far as the first rest-point, and the headquarters was reduced to a few score men under Colonel Yagi, who pushed on without waiting for the rear portion to catch up. They then ran into wetter and muddier ground, so bad that the fatigue of the men made it impossible to go on. They had something to eat at their first objective, a village along their prescribed route, at seven o'clock in the morning. As the advance guard left the village to continue eastwards, it came under small-arms fire from a spot in the jungle 330 yards from the village on their left. When this was reported to Yagi, he ordered an immediate attack on the jungle ambush and was killed in action himself as he led it.

The death of the regimental commander and his successor made the officers think the flag was clearly in danger, and that it should be taken to safety. Headquarters carried the flag and, while advancing through waterlogged paddy on the 27th, four men were killed by an enemy ambush. The headquarters switched its line of advance, but to no avail, since fifty more of the enemy were bumped and the Japanese were forced to retreat after a brisk exchange lasting thirty minutes. On the 28th, they were near their crossing point, and decided to have a meal during the hours of darkness. At three o'clock in the morning, as the cooking was going forward, the enemy artillery started up, and ground troops followed. Captain Uruno, who was in charge of the flag party, showed the men where the crossing point through the paddy fields was and split them up. The flag-bearer rolled the flag round his belly and they all began to creep forward across the paddy. For a few yards all went well, then the rifle-fire began. The flag-bearer was hit in the leg and could not move, so he passed the flag to a sergeant near him, Sugita, who made for the crossing point along the track on the embankment which divided the paddy fields. As Sugita went forward, the rifle-fire increased in volume and the shelling began, churning the paddy into an inferno of mud and shrapnel. Officers and men began to fall on all sides, but Sugita went on. The few survivors reached the crossing point with him and waited for evening before crossing, totally exhausted. 'The monotonous tale of ambushes, killings, pursuits, drownings, etc., was repeated in this area (between the Pyu Chaung and the Kun Chaung)' writes the historian of the Indian Army,[1] 'till the break-out attempt had exhausted itself. On /sic/ certain places the Japanese were too exhausted physically and were killed without offering any resistance.' The area in question, across

which the three-fold centre column and the right column of
54 Division broke out, was controlled by 'Flewforce' of
which the nucleus was 64 Brigade of 19 Indian Division,
under Brigadier J. G. Flewett. Flewett's section of the road
ran from Milestone 129½ (the Kun Chaung Bridge) to
Milestone 143 (the Pyu Chaung Bridge). He had three
battalions to start with—the number was later increased to
four—with a detachment of tanks and medium guns, and two
artillery batteries. Immediately to the north of Flewforce was
98 Indian Infantry Brigade (Brigadier C. I. Jerrard). Through
these two heavily reinforced British-Indian formations came
the main body of 54 Division and a good part of 28 Army.
Even the mistakes made by the British sometimes resulted in
Japanese casualties. During the fighting for Wegyi, for instance,
which the Japanese held so strongly against 1/6 Gurkha Rifles,
the official Indian history speaks of 'a cab-rank of Spitfires'
being in attendance on the attacking infantry. The Gurkhas
called on them to strafe a village called Aukkon, and the
Spitfires promptly zoomed down on another village by the
name of Leeinzu—no doubt there had been a mistaken map
reference somewhere—but it was of no consequence that
someone had blundered, for Leeinzu, like all the villages in the
Pyu Chaung area, was a shelter for Japanese, and scores of
them sprinted for shelter—uselessly—as the Spitfire cannon
tore into the bamboo huts.

Nor is it likely that the slaughter could have been avoided,
even if the Japanese had not broken column, as so many of
them did. The war diary. of 111 Infantry Regiment refers
sharply to the regimental commander (Yagi) failing to show
clearly to each and every one of his battalion commanders
the objective of the advance. He relied too much, the
implication is, on his own presence, and when he was killed
in action the battalions naturally lost contact and began to
move independently (and erroneously). The diary gives,
incidentally, a fuller version of Yagi's death. Apparently he
went into the hut of a village headman to eat and rest,

intending to stop exactly one hour. The village headman was so pressing that Yagi lingered not for one hour but three, at the end of which time, as he was preparing to leave, the hut was attacked and he was killed. The village headman, the war diary states, seems to have led the enemy up to the hut, no doubt realizing that Yagi was a person of more consequence than the rest of the troops who were taking a break at the same time.

From north to south, then, from Toungoo down to Kanyutkwin, 54 Division came out of the Yomas, crossed the Mandalay Road, and made for what one of its regimental histories calls 'the swirling maelstrom of the Sittang'. What it suffered on the way can be gauged by a very brief glance at the casualty figures. At the beginning of May, when he moved into the Pegu Yomas, Miyazaki had under his command over 9,000 men—9,300 is the figure given in the *Japanese Account of the Operations in Burma* published by the British XII Army in 1945. At the end of the break-out, when the division was concentrated in Tenasserim and then moved into camp at Payagyi, its strength was just under 4,000. The British always assumed the Japanese figures were inflated, but even so, it is likely that the proportion of losses is roughly accurate—nearly 60 per cent of the division died of disease, enemy assault, or the hazards of the Sittang waters.

CHAPTER SIX

COLONEL SAITO AND THE FATE OF SHIMBU FORCE IN THE PEGU YOMAS AND OVER THE SITTANG

From talks with Lieutenant-Colonel Saito Hiroo in Saigon in the spring and summer of 1946, it was immediately evident that he was a much more cultivated man than many Japanese regular officers had the time or inclination to be. Behind the dark saturnine face was a smiling courtesy which helped me out when the complexities of his statements were suddenly beyond the range of my still rudimentary knowledge of his language. He was, at the time, being extremely useful to us. When the war ended, his own 55 Division, less Shimbu Force, had managed to transfer itself to French Indo-China and he was later, when the rest of his friends had returned to Japan, detached to the Japanese Rear Party headquarters to help the British and French round up those deserters who had gone over to the Viet Minh. There were not very many of them —about 650—in an army several thousand strong, and it is not difficult to see why: the temptation of escaping forced labour from the British in order to live laborious days (and nights) with a Communist guerrilla force can hardly have weighed very strongly against the possibility of returning home. Sooner or later the deserters came into Saigon and gave themselves up to the OC Rear Party, Colonel Kōdō Teiji. Because of its shrinking numbers, the Rear Party itself gradually became a rather pathetic institution: soldiers, sailors, and civilians had at one time wandered freely about the Cochin-Chinese capital and naturally found their circumscribed present a strong contrast with their imperial past. Saito was diplomatic in the extreme in his relations with the British, but inside the outer surface was the core of a passionate patriot and a soldier who despised weaklings and cowards. For this reason Saito was prepared—as many were not—to take the side of Lieutenant-General Hanaya, and insist that his mode of approach to his officers had to be understood in the context of Japanese training.

Certainly neither officers nor men were strangers to beating and physical brutality, which was almost a normal component of military education. And Hanaya's gruff dismissal of the pretensions of young staff officers found an answering echo in Saito, who had a great contempt for the staff of Burma Area Army. 'They had no battle experience at all,' he said, 'they made plans and drew up maps and operation orders without any inkling of what conditions in the front were like Womanizers.' The Japanese Army was not exactly puritanical in its approach to women, so this last comment is rather strange; and it would have been appropriate to other figures of the Burma campaign too. Mutaguchi is said to have had the reputation among the men of 15 Army of having two passions, *main-ma* and journalists, though no doubt his motives differed in each case. *Main-ma* is the Burmese for 'woman', and it may be doubted that Mutaguchi's sexual proclivities did him anything like the damage caused by his fondness for newspaper publicity. But Saito had, in this matter, perhaps a different standpoint.

He was born in Paris and brought up in a French mission school in Japan, and entered the Army in 1932, spending four years at the Military Academy in Tokyo before being gazetted to 26 Cavalry Regiment. After a period as instructor at the Academy, he became a squadron commander of 15 Cavalry Regiment. In 1936 he was in Manchuria—it is strange how these Burma campaign officers have this period in their backgrounds, as so many of the victorious divisional and corps generals on the British side seem to have blooded themselves in North and East Africa. In 1941 he was on the staff of the Kwantung Army for two years and came to

Akyab in August 1943 to join the staff of 55 Division as a lieutenant-colonel.

Hanaya impressed him at once. 'Another bloody greenhorn who thinks he knows all the answers,' was the gist of how Hanaya greeted him. 'Well, you don't, and you have a hell of a lot to learn, and I'm going to see you learn it.' Later on, when Colonel Nagazawa Kanichi moved from 54 Division where he had been regimental commander of the 121 Infantry Regiment and took over command of 55 Division Infantry Group, of which Saito was Chief of Staff, he noticed at once Nagazawa's softer, milder manner and felt ill at ease with it. It seemed unexpected and inappropriate in the kind of man of decision an infantry group commander should be.

On the staff side, he was fortunate in having Iwakuro to advise him. Under his aegis, 28 Army had developed the intelligence networks which had been set up by 55 Division in the Arakan to work into India and among the Arakanese population. These had been created long before Saito arrived and one of the things that impressed him most about his new job was the interest in intelligence activities all the way up the divisional and army organization. In a sense, the work of these organizations made possible whatever measure of success the break-out operation across the Sittang had in 1945.

When a conference was held in Rangoon for the study of the next phase of campaigning, once it became clear that Central Burma could not be held, staff officers from divisions fighting at the front against the British spoke up very frankly. They said that the staff of Burma Area Army G.H.Q. had shown a total lack of knowledge of the true condition of front-line units—especially of the fact that officers and men were in a state of utter exhaustion and short of almost every material of war. They also accused them of being unaware of the strengths put into the field by the British and of miscalculating the enemy's speed of advance. Saito was quite clear in his own mind where the fault lay: it was the young staff majors, Kono and Kaetsu, full of self-confidence but lacking in campaign experience, working out mere paper plans without any knowledge of what it was like to command a unit of fighting soldiers.

Those in command were no better. General Kimura himself, the Commander-in-Chief, was basically an administrator of talent, rather than a man to command fighting troops. Paradoxically, his Chief of Staff, Lieutenant-General Tanaka, was essentially a combative individual, lacking in the diplomacy which smooth working of the staff requires, and much more fitted to command a unit in the field; and Colonel Aoki, a senior staff officer who would have been more appropriately placed in some form of civil administration—his interests lay in the field of military education. Nor could they agree among themselves. There was no harmony in the headquarters of Burma Area Army, quite the opposite, in fact, and the often violent and wordy disagreements between Kimura and Tanaka were soon public knowledge. Saito also had the same attitude of mind to the easy life which he imagined was being led by these young staff officers as British front-line troops may on occasions have entertained about the fleshpots of Delhi, Calcutta, and Kashmir enjoyed by those who had had the sense to carve out staff jobs for themselves. 'Night after night drinking and womanizing,' thought Saito, 'no wonder there is hatred and ill-feeling for Burma Area Army.' In his own mind he compared them with the headquarters staff of the Japanese Army at the time of the Russo-Japanese War, and found total difference, like that between snow and ink. He felt this more deeply because he wore the sword of his adoptive grandfather who had been a lieutenant-general in the heroic days of 1905, and had died in the attack on Port Arthur. The calibre was different.

When, therefore, he heard that Kimura had expressed the conviction that he could crush the British assault on Central Burma on the banks of the Irrawaddy, and later that the British would be defeated at Meiktila, and later still that they could be held north of Toungoo until the autumn of 1945, he smiled derisively—it was no longer possible to give any sort of credence to what the Commander-in-Chief said.

In a sense, Kimura suffered by comparison with Sakurai, as far as devoted officers like Saito were concerned. Sakurai was, after all, the man who had been instrumental in driving the British out of Burma, it was he who had taken the city of Rangoon in the first place—and he saw that his staff were kept up to the mark and frequently visited front-line units. There was no hiatus between the staff and front-line units of 28 Army but this feeling of mutual confidence had disappeared from other formations. No doubt Saito was making the best of a bad job in summing up the situation in this way. Not every staff officer of 28 Army would agree with him, and at least one thought the Army's morale—at any rate by the time it had been a few weeks in the Yomas—was pretty low, and that although it was not short of weapons and had plenty of ammunition, the men lacked fighting spirit. Half of them, if not more, were starving or malaria-ridden. The morale of Shimbu Force was adversely affected by the move of its commanding officer, Hanaya, with the main body of divisional infantry to the battle along the Rangoon-Mandalay Road, where he tried desperately, but unsuccessfully, to hold Pyawbwe against the advance of IV Corps.

In conversation among themselves, it was soon evident that many of the officers, though outwardly loyal and optimistic, took a very dismal view of the future of their country after the fall of Okinawa in June. There was something so final and direct in this threat upon the homeland in a way that had not been implied by any of the other Allied victories in the Pacific. This did not mean that the notion of surrender was anywhere in their minds—for nearly all of them, that solution was so far out of the question that the only alternatives presented were victory or suicide. At the very top there were rumours that must have been hard to take: after 28 Army had been a month in the Yomas, Lieutenant-General Sakurai heard a short-wave broadcast describing the surrender of Germany.

All-India Radio, from Delhi, kept hammering away at this, and transmitting information from Japan that industrial circles there had asked for peace from the Americans, through the offices of Soviet diplomatic officials, but that since unconditional surrender was not mentioned, their approach had not been accepted. This was at the beginning of June 1945. Later in the month came a Tokyo broadcast denying that Japan had asked the Soviets to mediate, and attempting to give the lie to this rumour which, it said, was circulating throughout Japan. Sakurai was no fool—some of his staff might think him a feeble old man who had to be helped on to his horse, but he was shrewd enough. The purpose of the broadcast was to tell the Japanese people that they must struggle on to the bitter end towards achieving the object for which the war had been started; but it was also an indication of conditions inside Japan that the emphasis was required. He had brought his men out of the Arakan, across the Irrawaddy and into the Pegu Yomas, and was soon to hurl them in scattered formations across the Sittang Valley. Many hundreds of them—thousands—would die. Were they to die as part of a final holocaust which would be shared by their families in Japan? Or were there those at home—impossible thought—who were getting ready to treat with the enemy and sue for peace?

Sakurai kept these inner doubts to himself, but they must have been a grievous burden to bear. He was in supreme command of an army surrounded on all sides by powerful and victorious enemy forces, who had put a ring of steel around him and were going to smoke him out of his hill-tops sooner or later. Nonetheless the broadcast did not affect his determination to conduct the break-out to a successful finish. He held in his hand the life or death of tens of thousands of men on the brink of starvation and exhaustion, and with a single throw of the dice he could try and bring them out of the trap. This was the confidence he needed to show, and it was this that Saito saw when he visited 28 Army headquarters.

He and Nagazawa called there on 15 April 1945, and were told by Sakurai and Iwakuro about the difficult situation that had developed around Toungoo and what 28 Army planned to do to hold the British advance where it could. It was clearly becoming urgent by this time to concentrate Shimbu Force in readiness to move before it was cut off by a British advance down into the Irrawaddy Delta. As soon as Saito returned to Henzada, which was the site of Shimbu Force headquarters, he sent instructions to Colonel Inoue, the commander of the mountain artillery regiment, to concentrate an infantry battalion, a mountain artillery battalion, and a platoon of pioneers in the Letpadan area, astraddle the road and rail communications to Rangoon. The rest of the Force was to concentrate in the areas of Henzada and Bassein, with small parties left behind at Gwa, Kyause and Pagoda Point. Then news came through on 25 April that Burma Area Army had abandoned Rangoon and established itself at Moulmein, at a safer distance from the advancing British forces. Saito was not surprised. The standing of Burma Area Army could not have been lower, and when he heard that men from 18 Division, a crack Kyushu division which had given a splendid account of itself in North Burma against the Chinese and then taken the brunt of the fighting in Central Burma, had hurled abuse at the retreating headquarters as it passed the east bank of the Sittang at Martaban, and even used their fists on the troops who were coming away from Rangoon, he could not feel anything other than sympathy for them. Had he been there, he would have felt like doing the same. In the meantime, it was necessary to know what developments this would bring, so Saito drove south down the Rangoon road to Taikkyi, in a captured armoured car. It was brilliant moonlight, and British planes were strafing the road, but he reached 28 Army headquarters safely on 27 April, at dawn. Armed with fresh instructions, he left for Letpadan and Colonel Inoue's force at sunset that same day, and told Inoue to get himself and his men ready for an anti-tank battle north of Letpadan. Then back to Henzada.

On the main road he kept meeting parties of dejected-looking Japanese troops moving south in the direction of Rangoon. They were officers and men of the Southern Fuel Depot, attached to the Rangoon Defence Force, with some men of the Indian National Army. They had not the slightest inkling that the Japanese had already abandoned the Burmese capital, and Saito felt another upsurge of anger at Kimura and his staff: so much for the *samurai* tradition.

Shimbu Force was split into three groups, or columns, commanded by Colonel Inoue, Colonel Kimura, and Colonel Murayama, reading from north to south in terms of position. Kimura Column and the Force headquarters were to concentrate in the area east of Okkan and Letpadan in the foothills of the Pegu Yomas. Murayama Column was to concentrate east of Taikkyi, further south. In theory, Kimura and H.Q. could have concentrated fairly quickly, since they were to use rail and road communications, but raids by British aircraft on trains and night-bombing of the tracks made movement slow. Murayama Column, which was to move by river, found that the rebel Burmese National Army was sitting on the banks to harass Japanese movement and to isolate and kill any small groups of Japanese who happened to be separated from the rest. Headquarters was to leave Henzada on 5 May. Then, at four in the morning of 3 May, urgent news came from 28 Army headquarters that the Palaw line had been broken. Headquarters decided to move at once and left Henzada that same night. The following day they were in their concentration area.

What the Force now had to ensure was that the main body of its troops could move out of the Arakan, across the Irrawaddy and into the Yomas before the British caught them in a pincer movement between forces moving up from Rangoon and others advancing south from Prome. Inoue Column was to hold the area Minhla-Letpadan until at any rate 12 May, by which time it was expected that the whole

Force would be well out of the Delta and across into the Yoma foothills. Inoue had an infantry battalion supported by four 25-pounders and six mountain guns to defend the Minhla position, and Nagazawa, the Force commander, was furious when the Inoue Column moved into the Yomas early, leaving the forces crossing the road and railway to Rangoon at the mercy of the British troops who inflicted far heavier casualties than the Force had anticipated.

There was to be no let-up. Concentration was complete on 12 May, and on the same day orders were issued to all columns to move off into their concentration areas on the eastern flanks of the Yomas. The columns moved at a rate of 4 to 8 miles a day through the hills in which the Pegu River rises, up steep slopes which, as one Japanese said, 'even pack-horses and bullocks would have found difficult', through thick bamboo jungle, where the villages were few and far between, and then ceased altogether. Between 23 and 25 May the whole Force except for the Inoue Column was spread out along a line connecting Myogyaung and Letpadan.

At this point, there arose the question of information. The paths and roads by which the Force expected to cross the Mandalay Road and railway and make for the Sittang had to be reconnoitred, so while the main body rested and waited for its stragglers along a line north-south of the village of Mayan, some of the men who had been trained by Hachisuka's *Hayate Tai* now found the opportunity they had been waiting for. About thirty-five of them were grouped together under a *Kempei,* Lieutenant Ota, and, with the title 'Divine Wind' Unit, set off from the village of Myogyaung. Besides the men there were two Karen women and a Burmese priest and soon they were moving carefully into the villages held by the British Army on the Mandalay Road—at some risk, as will be apparent later.

Saito had already rid the Force of one major responsibility, which had been gnawing at him ever since he heard that Kimura and his headquarters had left behind in Rangoon the army prostitutes (*ianfu*—'comfort girls') who had been, as he put it, 'the means by which they fulfilled their beastly desires'. These comfort girls, Koreans mostly, were a characteristic feature of the Japanese Army throughout East Asia, and may have found Saito's thought for them somewhat improbable. But then Saito was a man of some sensitivity. All comfort girls attached to the Force were to be properly escorted through the mountains, according to the instructions of 28 Army headquarters, but Saito made a counter-proposal. Boats were available in the Delta, and there was at any rate one officer who could be trusted to run the gauntlet of British sea patrols with the maximum courage and flair—Captain Asanaga, a veteran of Bias Bay and Java, who had spent the spring and summer of 1943 fighting British gun-boats on the Mayu River. With crews taken from 4 Shipping Engineer Regiment, Asanaga loaded forty motor-boats with one of the oddest passenger lists ever seen in Burma. Eighty comfort girls and hundreds of casualties who would never have survived the move into the Yomas, let alone the crossing of the Sittang, escorted by a single armoured vessel, started out across the Gulf of Martaban, ten days after Rangoon had been taken by the British. They moved far south of the usual shipping routes and were told to keep wireless silence for forty-eight hours. At Force headquarters the wireless operators kept a constant watch, working in shifts until, over two days later, a message came through reporting that all the boats save four had reached the village of Ye, about 180 miles south of Moulmein. Some days later a further signal told Saito that all the boats had reached safety. Saito's forethought for these most unconsidered of women saved at any rate eighty of them. Others, with different 28 Army formations, were not so lucky; nor were the Japanese nurses, who stuck with the Army to the end.

On 3 June, Saito decided to pay a visit to 28 Army headquarters high on a hill to the east of Okpo. They had begun to find that the old British maps which (like most other Japanese units) they still used as the basis of their movements and plans failed to correspond with reality: villages had moved and although they went by the same name their positions did not correspond to those on the map. Still, they were not for the moment in too great difficulties—there was arable land here and there, and there were other things to worry about. The original plan had been to cross the Sittang Valley at the end of June, but there had been no contact as yet with 54 Division, and neither Kanjō nor Kantetsu Force had been able to make their positions known. Until liaison was renewed, no overall plan could be made. Iwakuro had handed over the plan of operations to the Chief of Staff of 54 Division at Prome on 29 April, but no wireless communication had taken place between the main body of 54 Division and 28 Army headquarters and there was no way of finding out whether the plans had succeeded.

There were odd pieces of information available about the other units. Kanjō Force, under the command of Colonel Furuya, had moved south in its retreat from Mount Popa and had encountered units of Kantetsu Force under Colonel Ohara. Ohara had told them that 28 Army was on the move with the intention of reaching Chiengmai in Siam. A liaison officer had come in from *Shini Butai*. They had been asked by 54 Division Chief of Staff to protect Division's crossing of the Irrawaddy until 15 May. But the crossing was postponed so *Shini Butai* moved off into the Yomas east of Okpo. Lieutenant-Colonel Tsuchiya was with it, on attachment from 28 Army headquarters, so this information was regarded as trustworthy. Apart from 54 Division, the other units under command of 28 Army seemed to have completed their concentration east of the Irrawaddy and into the Yomas, so it was decided to send Captain Tsukamoto to a point in the hills where 54 Division units were likely to pass, to make contact. With this information, Saito returned to his own headquarters. There was a lot to do.

'Army want us to act against the area Letpadan—Tharrawaddy—Hmawbi with minor guerrilla actions,' he told Nagazawa, 'and since it doesn't seem to be known yet whether the initial break-out will be in the early part of July or the middle, we will have to do something about our rations. Somehow or other we will have to lay in stocks of food for a month. And all the other preparations for the break-out will have to be detailed at once.'

Saito aimed at maintaining a week's supply of rations on the Japanese army C scale (about 400 grammes of rice) in addition to a month's supply on the B scale (about 200 grammes). The Force Intendance unit was given the task of foraging with the column in the Letpadan area and 13 Naval Guard Unit, which later joined in the break-out under the command of 105 Independent Mixed Brigade in the eastern foothills. The foraging was not a success. It was undisciplined: the troops who were gathering food took more than they needed, by force if necessary—a sure sign of an army that does not think that it will be coming back—and fed themselves well in areas where it was possible to do so. Nagazawa acted promptly when he heard of the pillaging and reprimanded Colonel Kimura as the column commander responsible. To start with, at any rate, Shimbu Force had a fair proportion of necessary foods—unhulled rice *(momi)*, vegetables for vitamins and poultry for fats, which meant that vitamin injections could be used sparingly. Saito had already anticipated food tests in the Arakan, and more than ten varieties of *nogusa* (edible grasses) had been logged. Once inside the Yomas more than thirty-eight varieties were discovered and tested. But the real manna of the mountains was the eternal bamboo: bamboo shoots were for the taking, in abundance, and it was necessary to eat ten times the yearly average that the troops would have been accustomed to in Japan. This diet kept down beri-beri, but that was not at the moment the greatest risk: 98 per cent of all ranks in the Force had had malaria since their days in the Arakan and, more seriously, for many of them this was complicated by constant attacks of dysentery.

Two problems were involved in the break-out: crossing the

Mandalay Road through the British positions and crossing the Sittang. The road and rail communications to Rangoon ran parallel to the eastern edges of the Pegu Yomas, and were about 20 miles east of the concentration point of Shimbu Force at Mayan. From the road to the crossing points planned at the river was another 10 miles. Shimbu intended to slip its units through the British positions, if that were possible; if not, then it would fight its way through to the river. Once there, those troops with long battle experience and some knowledge of long-distance swimming would take charge of the *han* or sections into which the columns would divide. The difficulty was to find suitable officers to take charge of the subdivided units. In Saito's view, many officers were inefficient and there was inadequate knowledge of other arms—signals did not know about engineers' problems, and vice versa, and in the case of one column, Inoue's, the column commander himself lacked adequate field experience of battle.

The engineers began to play an important role. All kinds of tests had to be carried out on whatever items had been brought into the Yomas to act as river-crossing materials, and whatever could be supplied on the spot. The Pegu River was used for testing individual rafts, group rafts, rafts using inner tubes as flotation chambers, the construction of bamboo 'baskets' for carrying equipment without letting it sink, 'float-boats' which used a combination of bamboo and tents. Buoyancy tests were carried out on dead bamboo, on individual water-bottles, on the weight of rice likely to be carried, and on the proper length and breadth of bamboo to keep one man buoyant in the water across a river 110 yards wide.

The problem of rafts had already begun to preoccupy the Army headquarters, too, and the Chief Staff Officer, Colonel Okamura Aiichi, had already developed some possibilities even from the almost non-existent sources in the Yomas.[1] Okamura had celebrated the Emperor's birthday (29 April) in Allanmyo with Sugimoto, the officer commanding *Shini Butai,* before returning to 28 Army headquarters. He was in Tanbingon, in the eastern foothills of the Yomas, about 13 miles east of Okpo just before dawn on 2 May. He had been away for two months, and found the Army in the midst of break-out preparations. Sakurai greeted Okamura with the news that Iwakuro and the younger staff officers were fully occupied with working out movement details, and said, 'You can stop being a C.S.O. and become a Colonel of Engineers again! I want you to give special consideration to one thing: the crossing of the Sittang.' Sakurai was deeply disturbed about the prospect of what the Sittang would be like, the longer he had to delay the crossing operation. He was short of engineers, it would be the height of the monsoon and none of his units had any of the materials needed for transporting large bodies of men across river obstacles. Okamura felt that there was a shortage of reliable information on the river itself: he had to gauge the situation on the banks of the Sittang from a map dated 1937, and he knew Burma well enough to realize that there could have been great changes, particularly in floodable areas, since then. The river's course might have changed slightly, villages might be inundated or have moved from where the map put them, and so on. The whole thing needed study, and Okamura formed a temporary river-crossing unit from 28 Army Heavy Transport Unit to do nothing but spend the days and nights in the Yomas going into every detail of the crossing problems: how to get the right materials when there were none, how to choose crossing points on the banks of the Sittang, and so forth. It was an irony of fate that Okamura himself, for three years previous to this, had been an instructor on military river-crossing techniques at the Military Academy in Tokyo—but he had never worked on a situation quite as hedged around with impossibilities as this one.

As we have seen, there was bamboo in abundance. But it was useless having bamboo poles—other than for individuals— without any means of binding them together. For ferrying groups of men across the river, large and small rafts were going to be needed, otherwise it would be impossible to control the crossing. Yamaguchi's acute observation saved the day. Yamaguchi was a handsome moustached staff officer of 28 Army headquarters, an expert in lines of communication, and a great friend of Colonel Tsuchiya. He had heard that Okamura was perplexed by the problems posed by the lack of rope. 'Some of our men have watched the Burmese,' he suggested, 'making rope by stripping the bark from some trees which have a broad leaf and look like mountain maples.' Anything was worth trying and Okamura got his river-crossing unit to work on this bark rope. It certainly worked; the rope that resulted was not as strong as manila, but rather tougher than hemp palm rope, and the tree that it was taken from grew plentifully on the mountain slopes. Okamura had stationed his unit at Thabyu, further into the interior of the Yomas than headquarters at Pinmezali, and on the edge of the North Zamayi Reserved Forest, which became the source of what Okamura termed, not unnaturally, the 'rope of life.' Okamura went to see Sakurai, and asked him to issue an order throughout the army to the effect that every man was to make his own rope from the tree bark, 2 yards long in each case, and carry that rope with him. Okamura calculated that with rope to bind them, three lengths of bamboo about 4 inches in thickness would be adequate as an individual raft to support one man and his equipment of rifle and pack. But this had to be tested first, and two staff officers (Fukumiya and Yamaguchi) built rafts on this model and tried them out successfully in the rivers in the Pegu Yomas.

Among the officers of Shimbu Force, Saito had picked up a windfall of a kind no army could have expected to tumble into its lap in such incredible and yet appropriate circumstances: Lieutenant Kitamura. One of the finest long-distance swimmers in the world, Kitamura had won the 1,500 metres at the 1937 Los Angeles Olympics. In the intense nationalism of international games, he had swum for the glory of Japan as much as for the delight in competing in the exercise of a difficult and exacting sport. But the demands made on his tough muscular body in California were trivial compared with what Saito expected of him now, and what was at stake was no cup or medal, nor any sense of patriotic conquest of East over West, but the very lives of thousands of his friends and comrades in 55 Division.

The youth of 1937 was now, eight years later, a bearded Japanese Army officer, but under the uniform he was still 'the champ' *(ōja)*. This time, though, there were no cheering crowds bawling encouragement from the stands. The work of exploring the *chaungs* of the Pegu Yomas and then of testing the current of the Sittang was done at great risk and in the utmost secrecy. Kitamura's energy was boundless. Back and forth he went from Shimbu headquarters in the hills, slipping through Burmese guerrilla encampments and British positions, sliding into the water under a mask of weeds to note the strength of streams, if and where they were fordable, what could be expected of unfit men swimming them at the height of the rainy season, and so on.

He trained the men too. It was hopeless to expect that in a few weeks, in the physical condition most of them were in, they would be able to cross the Sittang by swimming alone. But there were ways and means of helping them achieve the buoyancy which was needed to give them courage to tackle the crossing. Tests were carried out with single lengths of bamboo to find out just how much was needed to keep a man afloat while he traversed 110 yards of stream. For those who would not risk this, all kinds of rafts were contrived. A few inner tubes were available, and, in combination with bamboo made up into a basket-type of container, individual and group-rafts were made. The illustration opposite page 45 shows Saito's drawings of some of these. The individual rafts could be carried on the back, and a piece of bamboo 20 inches in length could be added to this to increase buoyancy. More complex was the joining together of rafts to give a kind of catamaran effect. Bamboo poles were wrapped round with tents, which made a primitive canoe. Secured together, these provided a small vessel adequate to take four men across a river. The rope problem had already been solved by Major Yamaguchi's observation of Burmese rope-making from tree-bark.

The men hero-worshipped Kitamura, and with good reason. Not only the Japanese, either. There was one young Burmese who had accompanied Shimbu Force from the Arakan and who clung to Kitamura like a son. The boy, Than Tun, was born in Kyaukpyu on Ramree Island, and his spoken Japanese was so good that the men of 55 Division had conferred a Japanese name on him, and called him Araki. Than Tun always stuck close to Kitamura when the latter went on his reconnaissance patrols behind the British lines. Whenever Kitamura reached the *chaung* or river whose conditions he was to test, he stripped off his Japanese uniform before slipping into the water. Than Tun would hide the uniform among the reeds and keep a watchful eye on them until his idol returned. On these occasions he always hung back a little behind Kitamura. When it was a question of checking up on villages, the conditions were reversed, and Than Tun always went on ahead. He would stroll whistling into the village, wearing a cap. If he could be sure the village was empty of guerrillas, he would take the cap off as a hint to Kitamura that he could come forward. If he sensed there were hostile Burmese in hiding in the huts, he would keep his cap on and wander, still at the same strolling speed, out of the village at the other end.

It was a risky procedure, and it was not long before the inevitable happened. Than Tun walked into a village one day to find it packed with Indian troops, who took him prisoner. Kitamura could do nothing to help him, and made his way back to Shimbu. Than Tun was safe enough. The end of the war was not far off, and when Lieutenant-Colonel Tsuchiya of 28 Army came to Pegu as a peace envoy in September 1945, and visited the Japanese POWs in the IV Corps cage there, he was amazed to recognize a face he knew. Tsuchiya had been in overall control of espionage and reconnaissance, and had leaned heavily on Kitamura's information. He knew Than Tun by sight, and was able to tell him that Lieutenant Kitamura had survived the great holocaust.

Gradually the army began to build up an emergency river-crossing technique. There was a certain virtue in this from other points of view too: many of the men were sick and hungry and it was necessary to sustain their confidence and also to keep them on the qui vive. For the officers, pistol-shooting rallies were held, and for the men, competitions in gathering bamboo shoots. There could hardly have been a less sophisticated occupation, but almost anything was preferable to allowing masses of tired men, subject to bouts of sickness, to brood about their condition, because the end product of that was desertion and suicide. Both these things happened in the Yomas. After a month of the life there, and seeing no end to it, many men began to sneak away from their units, in the mistaken belief that they would be welcome in the Burmese villages in the foothills. In fact, so much had Burmese opinion veered once again that few Japanese soldiers were safe for very long in these villages, particularly if they were on their own. Even in small groups they risked being bound while sleeping and handed over to a British patrol. There were others who felt that they could be surer of a welcome: one *Kempei* N.C.O. who was very proficient in Burmese had left a mistress behind in the Delta, and suffered exceedingly from the painful contrast between life as a member of an occupying army in what was—strategically at the time—a backwater as far as military activity was concerned, and the hectic and exacting life of being a *Kempei* in the mountains with a force trying to escape the enemy. The riskiest exercises were for the *Kempei,* and they were supposed to be more inured to hardship and to have undergone a tougher training than the ordinary infantryman. They *were* tough and hard, but one or two cracked, and either deserted or—even more unthinkable in the traditional context of the Japanese Army—allowed themselves to be taken prisoner.

To keep up morale, Saito thought of other things too: the sodden forests of Lower Burma, the almost uninhabited stretches of wild jungle, had somehow to show forth the promise of home, and with exactly the same instinct that led Wingate to christen his Chindit strongholds 'Aberdeen', 'Blackpool' and 'White City', Saito began to devise Japanese names for the collections of *bashas* that were dotted around the hillsides of the Yomas. Sometimes these names were simply nouns that might symbolize light and hope: 'Asahi' ('Rising Sun') Village (17 miles east of Letpadan); 'Hikari' ('Light') Village (a track junction 5 miles south-east of Asahi); 'Akatsuki' ('Dawn') Village (in the western foothills of the Yomas), and 'Tsukimi' ('Moon-viewing') Village. Sometimes they were meant to bind the troops closer with memories of the region from which most of them came. 55 Division was centred on Zentsuji, and its catchment area was the island of Shikoku in the Inland Sea. Towns in the prefectures of Shikoku lent their names to Shimbu's villages: Yoshino, in Tokushima Prefecture, Matsuyama, in Ehime Prefecture, Kōchi, in Kōchi Prefecture, and Kotohira, in Kagawa Prefecture. Since the majority of the troops came from one or other of these prefectures, the psychological effect on the troops, thought Saito, would be like setting out from one's native village.

Then there was nomenclature for luck. Another village was called Misogi, a Japanese religious term signifying 'a purification ceremony', 'ritual ablution'. The word implied to the Japanese soldier the notion of praying to the gods to achieve a state of great beauty and strength in which to break through the enemy, as if their bodies would suddenly be purified and washed free of all evil by plunging into a cascade in the depths of the mountains. In this village, under Saito's direction, the units under command of Force headquarters wrote their wills and messages to comrades.

Shimpei Village was next. The name was composed of the character for 'god', *shin*, and for 'soldier', *hei*, the idea being that after purification *(misogi)* the soldier was nearer to God or the gods, transcending his fate and the issue of life or death, and, in effect, becoming himself a god. Lastly, Point 2256, where the Force concentrated before its final burst out of the Yomas and across the Mandalay Road. This was to be called Kachidoki Village. *Kachidoki* is the Japanese word for a 'shout of victory' or 'battle-cry' and was an appropriate name for the start of the advance because it implied success in battle from the first instant of the advance. Other names were used for purposes of deception. The Mandalay Road was given the name of Japan's celebrated tourist attraction, Hakone Yama. The Sittang was called the Japan Alps, and the track running east from the Sittang after Japan's fabled road, the Tōkaidō, or 'Great Eastern Highroad'.

So much for keeping up morale. To conserve physical strength, the day's march across the Yomas was reduced to 2½ - 4 miles, and all units were made responsible for providing temporary huts for casualties, able to hold twenty men, at an average interval of half a mile. Whenever a unit had to cross a *chaung* on its way through the hills—this was very frequent—the occasion was used to provide exercises in river-crossing techniques by mooring a raft to a tree and using it to ferry across part or whole of the unit.

The Kimura Column was the easiest to concentrate and the fastest in its advance over the hills. Inoue's was the slowest, but there was some excuse for this since it was transporting guns and ammunition through country difficult enough for a man with nothing more than a rifle and pack. The column had four mountain-guns with 100 rounds per gun, and it was almost impossible to concentrate it on the starting line by 19 July. Finally six elephants were used, borrowed from the Force headquarters and another column, to be returned when Misogi Village was reached. This slowed the other column down and created a difficult situation for it when it emerged to attack the British positions at Penwegon.

Murayama's column could only concentrate a total of 300 men at its starting point, so difficult was the going through the slippery hills. He had with him the Regimental Engineer headquarters, some engineers and a section of cavalry; but two infantry companies, a mountain-gun company, and some other troops had been 'mislaid'. When this situation became known at Force headquarters in Misogi Village, Major Fukuyama of headquarters staff was sent off with some elephants from Inoue Column to bring forward the units which had begun to straggle. The Force's casualties were collected together in Akaho Village and came under command of Major Matsuo. It was with the stretcher casualties that morale began to crack.

They set out, one by one, from Akaho Village, passing through Matsuyama Village, and, in Saito's words, 'suicide by hand-grenade broke out like an epidemic.' The Force commander tried to put a stop to it, but the despair of those who were sick or wounded and were being carried in unspeakable conditions through the rain-sodden mountains was too strong for official orders to be effective in preventing it. To some extent, there was the motive of not wishing to be a further burden to comrades who had the job of carrying them when they were barely fit enough to move themselves along; but there was also the fact that many of the suicides occurred in units which had only recently been attached to Shimbu Force for the break-out, men from the Southern Army Supply Depot, and from railway regiments who had been stationed in Rangoon. They believed themselves to be cut off from escape to the east and were consequently without hope. 'This is the time, now,' they told each other. 'We're going to die sooner or later anyway; it might as well be quickly, with a grenade.' The hills began to reverberate with the explosions. Saito was no stranger to death, but the repeated hollow boomings began to tell on his nerves. The Force commander was no help. Nagazawa viewed the war situation, as he always did, pessimistically. Lieutenant-General Hanaya had taken the measure of Nagazawa, Saito thought, when Nagazawa was a regimental commander of 54 Division on Ramree Island and the garrison had been ordered to retreat too late and had been cut to pieces as a result. It made Saito angry to hear him always praising 54 Division and disparaging Shimbu Force. Nagazawa was also doubtful of the success of the reconnaissance carried out on the Mandalay Road and was sure that British tanks would be spread out along the road at intervals of 500 yards to stop the Japanese getting through, which Saito rightly thought was ridiculous. Against Saito's disparagement of Nagazawa must be set the high regard in which he was—and is—undoubtedly held by the regiment of which he was the commanding officer, 121 Infantry Regiment of 54 Division. It was his close attachment to this regiment, which he had commanded from the day it was raised, that made him retire in the district from which its men came (Tottori in Western Japan) and keep in constant touch with their families. By a not unfamiliar assimilation of contraries, Saito may well have admired the ruthless brutality of his own divisional commander's behaviour. But Hanaya and Nagazawa were at opposite poles: Nagazawa had a real affection for his men, and a care for their welfare which derived directly from the regional association of his regiment. Even, therefore, when the command of Shimbu Force promoted him to the rank of Major-General, he was still to a large extent emotionally attached to his old regiment and gave voice to those unfavourable contrasts in his mind which, inevitably, can only have been a constant irritation to 55 Division officers like Saito.

As it happened, Lieutenant Kitamura returned from a reconnaissance (see page 155) the very day the Force set out from Akaho Village, and when it reached Misogi, Lieutenant Oda, in command of the *Kamikaze Tai*, arrived to make his report, so Nagazawa's fears were set at rest. Phase Three of Operation MAI, breaking out from the Yomas to the Sittang

Plain, could get under way.

Shimbu Force began its movement out of the eastern foothills of the Yomas on 20 July, moving from the start line at five o'clock in the evening and reaching the village of Yee west of the Mandalay Road at eight o'clock. An infantry company was put into the village to secure it as the men of Force headquarters stared with anguished longing eastwards. They were still high enough to look right out over the Sittang Plain, now filled with evening mist, and they gazed and gazed, their hearts full. This, too, was a sign that morale was changing. What the Sittang Plain meant to many of them was not a valiant charge through a beleaguering enemy, and a readiness to fight him again. It was an escape eastwards, out of Burma —out of battle if possible—a search for a haven, not for a respite before the next battle. Their reverie was brusquely interrupted.

Inoue again, Saito thought. The left break-out column, consisting of the Divisional Mountain Artillery Regiment (less two battalions) and half an infantry battalion under Colonel Inoue, had begun to pile up immediately behind headquarters, having mistaken its own route. The men poured all over Force headquarters and forged on into the darkness, delaying the advance of the headquarters unit by about two hours. As they began to move forward again, along the motor road which leads from Yee to Penwegon—it is a track for most of its length—they heard the sound of intense heavy and light machine-gun fire from the direction of Penwegon. They knew Penwegon was strongly held and that a British headquarters was there—the reconnaissance had made that clear. There would be no question of securing it, as the Force Operation Order for the breakthrough had decreed. But the British and Indian troops in the village would be held long enough by a diversionary attack to allow the main body to pass north of the village without interference.

An attack was put in under Lieutenant Kurokata whose men hammered away at Penwegon throughout the night of 20/21

July, losing eight dead and seventy-six wounded. Penwegon was a known risk. From information provided by the reconnaissance made by the *Kamikaze Tai* under Lieutenant Oda, Shimbu Force headquarters assumed that the village was held by a force of about 4,000 infantry, with sixty guns, and at least ten tanks. In addition, it was reckoned that several hundred Burmese irregular troops would be in the area. From the middle of June, Saito had sent out parties to forage from the village of Myogyaung, on the edge of the Yomas, and to bring back information about the roads between Myogyaung and Penwegon. The parties were of the *Hayate Tai* pattern, dressed in Burmese garb, and carrying the little shoulder-bag which the Burmese wear, but containing two hand-grenades.

One at least of the parties managed to infiltrate its members into the village of Penwegon in their Burmese disguise. Since Penwegon was the headquarters of 17 Indian Division, it was strongly held and contained a great variety of units, including a military police unit which was responsible for the 'cage' holding Japanese prisoners-of-war who had been brought in in increasing numbers over the past few weeks. The infiltrator, who moved around the village in the dark, found the cage and had some hurried whispered conversations with the prisoners before he opted for prudence and took the road west into the Yomas through Dodan, Zibyugin, Gyobinyo, and Yee. He was lucky, too, since a Burmese who chatted with him in the village of Penwegon penetrated his disguise without much difficulty, but evidently said nothing to betray him to the British. Others were not so lucky. If the headman of a village thought the risk worth taking, and the Japanese let his guard drop even for a brief space of time, he could be caught while sleeping and handed over to a British patrol. One *Kempei* sergeant got away just in time in the village of Kanyutkwin, just a few miles to the north of Penwegon. He and a private of 28 Army headquarters had been sent to reconnoitre a number of crossing points on the main road. They were dressed in *longyis*, carried a bag with a pistol and grenades in it, and were told to report back to Lieutenant-Colonel Tsuchiya on 17 July. Another five similar parties had been sent out by Tsuchiya to check other points in the area for the crossing of Army headquarters. The sergeant reached Kanyutkwin in the early hours of 16 July, having taken far longer than he anticipated to cross the swollen Kun Chaung and reach the road through waterlogged paddy and elephant grass. He and the *Kempei* private moved across the Mandalay Road and railway and walked another two miles to another village, eastwards in the direction of the Sittang. They then decided to return via Kanyutkwin and, as they were passing separately through the village, the private was stopped and questioned by an Indian patrol, who were singularly unimpressed by his explanation and took him prisoner. The sergeant made himself scarce.

Fragments of information from units of this kind gradually permitted the Japanese to build up a picture of the forces likely to be opposing them, though they were never absolutely sure of identification or strengths.

Saito began to come across other difficulties. The *Kamikaze Tai* reconnaissance had been only moderately successful. Men had been lost, the information brought back was often fragmentary, and there was one drawback which had not been foreseen: the huge increase in rainfall in the ten days which had elapsed since the last reconnaissance report had radically altered the topography of the paths they had explored. He had not been able to keep in touch with Murayama Column, even though an officer patrol had been sent to make contact. The Inoue Column which had been ordered to hold and secure the bridge across the Kun Chaung and to attack the artillery emplacement near Tawgywe-in, had (as he expected) failed in its tasks. Lastly the leading company reported back that a stationary British patrol consisting of a number of men under one officer was sitting across the Force's path of advance about 1,650 yards from the Mandalay Road. The officer was keeping a watch with binoculars in the direction of the Force. Saito's Arakan experience then came into play. If the British kept to their habits, he thought, that patrol would be withdrawn at sunset. He decided to use the waiting time imposed by this obstacle in forming up the Force break-out column into echelons of forty men each, and made up a column with the Force commander in the centre and an infantry company to act as screen, with a machine-gun section and an infantry-gun section (with one gun) disposed ahead of it, to await the turn of events.

 As he had anticipated, the British patrol withdrew at nightfall. Saito sent forward a patrol of his own to reconnoitre the movement of men and vehicles along the Mandalay Road and at ten o'clock started the column moving forward. In two hours, at midnight, they were on the line of the Road. The men began to pour across, whispering to each other excitedly how strange it felt to be walking on a paved road after all the time in the Yomas on mud and grass. They were not fired on as they crossed and soon the Force reached the railway. Units had been stationed across the Road to counter-attack any British units which might attempt to hinder the crossing. These were withdrawn and the Force as a whole was concentrated along the line of the railway. As agreed with each column beforehand, a red signal shot was fired into the sky —it had been captured from the British in the Arakan. As the red signal curved higher and higher in the heavens, and then arched down, Saito's eyes blurred with tears. The tension of the past few hours had been difficult to bear, and suddenly his mind was full of the images of thousands of men and animals streaming out of the Yomas on lines parallel to his own, and he prayed for them, with an intensity born of relief at having brought the Force at least this far. Now for the river.

 In theory, and looking at the distance on the map, this should not have taken long. The point on the railway where Saito stood was about 3 or 4 miles to a crossing point on the Kun Chaung, which ran into the Sittang a few miles further east. From the point where the road from Penwegon met the

Kun Chaung to the confluence of the *chaung* and the Sittang was about 4 miles. But it was the nature of these miles that began to set the time-table awry and delayed the crossing dates for every single column. The right column crossed on 30 July, ten days after the break-out had begun, the centre column on 4 August, the left column from 30 July to 5 August, and the Force headquarters unit as late as 13 August. The Force commander, Major-General Nagazawa, describes the conditions:

During eight days' continual slogging march through water, the height of the water often reached to our waist, our neck, our chin, until our whole body was submerged. For three days and nights of that period we had nothing to eat, were under constant attack from enemy aircraft and so had to stand still in the water throughout the hours of daylight, sometimes in the tops of trees, and had to wait until nightfall before we could move on again. The reeds sometimes reached a height of 9 or 10 feet and made the way impassable, and we scrambled and slipped and fell through them. Our speed of advance was cut down to a crawl, and in the pitch blackness of the night the only means we had of guiding those behind us was the occasional flash of lightning—by this time we were completely without maps, watches, or pocket torches. Bit by bit the units began to lose their way, the formations broke up into complete disorder.

I kept swimming my horse round, moving him here, there and everywhere in an attempt to maintain some kind of control over the formations. I thought I would never manage without my horse, but when he was drowned later on I found unexpected reserves of strength which kept me going.

The most difficult point was about 330 yards from the village of Thinganbin. Here the water was so deep that our heads went under, and to add to our discomfiture units of the rebel Burmese National Army were taking pot shots at us from the village. It became completely exhausting to swim through water filled with dense clumps of reeds, so long that they constantly hampered our swimming movements, and many of the men by this time simply died in the water. We finally reached the village, and heaved ourselves up on to the land, but the men continued to die, from sheer exhaustion. The medical officer, Lieutenant Fujii, died here. His assistant, a medical corps cadet called

Asakura, kept going as best he could without drugs or medicines—and we had endless cases of diarrhoea and dysentery.

Lieutenant Inoue, the adjutant, lost our code-books in the water and was overcome with what he had done. His sense of responsibility drove him back into the water, and after fishing around for a while he retrieved the codes. By the time I saw him again, it was clear he simply could not stand, so I decided that headquarters should recoup its flagging spirits by resting for a week in the Thinganbin area. I passed on the order 'Start again a week from now', but Lieutenant Inoue, whose legs were in a terrible state, started to do physical jerks to get himself in condition again—almost frantically—and he was in fact able to set out with us later. We also managed to assemble numbers of stragglers at this point, and got the men to pound unhulled rice so that everyone could have a full stomach before struggling on any further. The instant we reached the bank of the Sittang, light machine-gun fire ripped at us from the opposite bank. Judging from the sound of the firing, it was the Burma National Army again. I had an attack put in by the leading platoon, and heard later that the lance-corporal in charge met his death while clearing the position, shouting *'Tennō Heika Banzai!'* ('Long Live the Emperor!') As soon as the opposite bank had been secured by our vanguard, we discovered one small boat which had remained undestroyed by enemy aircraft and local guerrillas. Using this boat, repeating the crossing scores of times throughout the night, we managed to get the whole of the Force headquarters across. By the dawn of 13 August our crossing was complete.

While the Force headquarters unit was moving in the direction of the Sittang, Murayama lost contact completely with the central break-out column. The headquarters moved forward on a separate route and, as Nagazawa says, lost a great number of men in the water in the Thinganbin area. But this was merely the same pattern as that of the other columns. Exhausted men in every stage of starvation and disease endured the most horrible sufferings in order to reach the bank of the river which represented salvation for them, only to find that it was merely another obstacle, perhaps even the hardest of all. The official British history of the campaign describes the monsoon of that summer of 1945 in terms which make it easy to realize the agonies undergone by Sakurai's men. General Kirby writes:[2]

On various occasions the opposing forces engaged in the fighting in Burma had gone through periods of extreme hardship, but probably the monsoon of 1945 was the worst of all, particularly for the Japanese with their hopes of survival rapidly disappearing. During June, conditions got steadily worse as the monsoon strengthened and pouring rain alternated with sweltering oppressive heat whenever a break in the cloud resulted in a few hours of sunshine. In the plains the flood level rose steadily, even tracks above flood level often becoming nearly knee-deep in mud and the seriously wounded drowned unless quickly picked up. In the hills, paths turned into mudslides and streams into raging torrents, while everywhere vehicles slithered off the so-called all-weather roads into ditches or down mountain sides. Added to these difficulties were myriads of biting insects, prickly heat and jungle sores which made life about as pleasant as the mediaeval concept of purgatory ....Fighting...was nearly always bitter since the Japanese fought desperately for survival against opponents determined to ensure that few if any of them would live to fight another day.

Saito had planned to reach the village of Natlaung but learned that the Engineers' river-crossing unit had taken that route. He decided to change direction towards Ma-ubin. Soon the soaked ground became a sea of mud, the water went up to their thighs, and in two places they found they had to cross *chaungs* in spate. It was after sunrise by the time they reached the bank opposite the village. There were two Burmese agents in Ma-ubin—half-castes, Saito thought— who had turned the villagers against the Japanese. It was not difficult. 'Look at these Japanese soldiers,' went the whispering campaign, 'they aren't up to much now, are they? No boots, no uniform, they're a miserable-looking lot.' The fact that these men moved freely and confidently about the village made Saito think he was near a British guerrilla encampment. However that might be, the Kun Chaung had to be crossed if they were to make any movement towards the Sittang. The *chaung*'s width was about 55 yards at this point, and it was running fast. Saito got hold of the officer commanding the scout company and ordered him to get across the Kun Chaung by any method he could use and occupy Ma-ubin. He expected they would soon be shelled once the Burmese agents in the village reported their presence to the British and the crossing operation began at once, during daylight.

As the men began to straggle out into the stream, they were horrified to see corpses bobbing down towards them. From their appearance Saito judged they had been in the water at least two days. It was a sight Shimbu Force was to grow used to in the next few weeks, and in fact on this particular crossing Saito saw two of his own men swept away in whirlpools, beyond the reach of their comrades. Fortunately there was a moon, and although it became plain that most of the officers and men would have preferred to spend another night in that village—it was a pleasant change to find a spot where there was plenty of rice, for one thing—Saito could not allow them to let up, and urged them forward on to the crossing.

The route which Saito had intended to follow led from Natlaung to Pyinmabin, but he anticipated that the British artillery position at Kungyaungwa would turn its attention on the Force and so concentrated his main strength at Nga-to-kin. For the sake of security, Saito assembled the villagers and told them it was strictly forbidden for them to leave the village for the space of one day while the Japanese troops used their huts to rest in. Exception was made for the cowherds, and fortunately these were not spotted by the British planes which flew low over the village on reconnaissance.

The first echelon should have sent back to the second the information about the village of Natlaung, but—in this matter as in so many others—failure of communications was complete, and the second echelon moved into Natlaung and was promptly shelled by the British, who were using time shells. As it happens, the second echelon sustained no casualties from the firing, and moved on to a village south of Nga-to-kin to rest.

At dawn on the 25th, Saito looked around at the village in the pouring rain and the sea of mud in which it was set, and reflected bitterly that it was the day on which, if the speed of the moves had gone according to plan, Shimbu Force would already have been in Kyaukkyi in comparative safety. At sundown, they moved off towards Pyinmabin and reached a point just west of it at ten o'clock in the evening. Saito sent out scouts, who were fired upon and returned with the news that there were about 200 or 300 British-Indian troops in Pyinmabin. Not only that, it looked as if they were being reinforced, and there was a constant to and fro of vehicles on the opposite bank. There were also sounds as of engineering work in progress. There was jungle to the north and north-west of Pyinmabin, too, the scouts said, in which the water went up to your thighs. Saito weighed up the impact of these messages, taking into account the distance still to be travelled to the Sittang, the time available, and what was visibly happening to the sodden landscape around him. He determined on a change of direction, obtained Nagazawa's agreement, and after about a mile's advance to the north began a compass march towards the river bank opposite Wettu. An advance guard cut a path through dense reeds taller than a man and the march went on at the rate of 500 yards an hour. Saito remained on horseback, riding back and forth endlessly, checking the state of the ground and looking for landmarks and areas where the water became shallow.

They came close to Nga-to-kin at dawn on the 26th and Saito at once sent out an officer patrol under the command of Second Lieutenant Yamaguchi, the Machine-Gun Section commander of the attached infantry company, towards Wettu. The unit rested their swollen feet and legs a long time in the swampy ground. About four o'clock in the afternoon, Yamaguchi returned and made his report. The ox-cart track leading to Wettu was submerged up to chest height, and it would be necessary to swim or float part of the way. The rest of the way the depth of the water was below knee height, and if the first part could be avoided by a detour, it would be possible to reach the village.

On the 27th, after marching by compass through the night, Saito reached a point on the track where the water was at knee height. Suddenly Yamaguchi came up to him and pointed to a big tree—they had expected to spot this tree 500 yards earlier. 'I recognize this tree,' he said. 'The track goes south about 500 yards from here, and there is an ox-cart road, which I've been along before. Wettu is about a mile further on, and the water goes up to knee-height.' Saito was cheered by this and the advance guard was sent off at five o'clock in the afternoon. They had gone no further than 200 yards when the water came right up to their chests. The water had risen this high in the two days since Yamaguchi had been along the track. The episode underlined the impossibility of relying fully even on recent reconnaissance of the waterlogged country up to the Sittang, and Saito ordered his men back to the position they had been in at noon, not wishing to risk a further advance along the track and losing them in the water. The water rose again, the men ate what little food they had left and drank the rain-water. There was no rest for Saito. Picking four officers and the scout section he moved east, looking for ground where the water was shallow, but with increasingly little hope of finding it.

By 28 July the Force commander was at the end of his tether. Nagazawa was in the advance guard in the early hours, and raged wildly at Saito. He had no confidence in him at all, he shouted, his control of the operation was worse than useless. Nagazawa was reflecting, uncannily, the mood of the men. Many of them were beginning to behave very oddly, many were shedding the heavier bits of equipment, and one or two would burst into wild song and break away from the main body to go back along the path by which they had come.

Saito began to wonder about his own sanity. He was under the illusion that the point he had reached at dawn on the 28th was one he had already reached before. He had the eerie sensation of watching himself on the brink of going mad, had the good sense to realize what was happening and tried to relax his extreme tension by resting for three hours in the branches of a tree. But when he awoke he was still angry and resentful at the dressing-down he had had from the Force commander, the more so since it had been done in the presence of some of his fellow officers.

The following day, Yamaguchi went out again in search of the village he had reconnoitred some time previously, and on this occasion was lucky. He heard rifle-fire, and then the cackling of hens, and came across three Burmese fishermen in a little shack only half a mile away, so the Force moved on towards it. On the way, Saito, still on horseback, was fired on from a clump of trees and shouted to his men, 'They look like Burma National Army, they couldn't even hit me when I'm on horseback. Bring them down from those trees and take them prisoner!' The rifle-fire ceased abruptly, and the headquarters unit reached a *chaung* less than 110 yards wide. One of the men shinned up a tree and reported that, judging by the number of roofs, there was a fairly large village to the north. A raft was made from four oil-drums which had been brought this far at the cost of a good deal of pain and labour, and soon everyone began to cross. Some of the men by this time were incapable even of crossing with the aid of the oil-drums and Saito was appalled to see them stay in the water, with that look of madness in their eyes, a heart-rending look that betrayed the despair that was in them and that held them in the water when Saito yelled, 'Don't give up, don't give up now! The village is just over there!' But even those who managed to cross had lost any desire to hold on to their guns and many of them were lost in the water.

The story could be repeated endlessly for this unit as for many others. 'We were close on 600 men when we came out

Above, left: Tsutsumi Shinzō, whose account appears in the last chapter, as a naval sub-lieutenant in 1940; *right,* a family snapshot taken from the body of one of the sailors in the jungle

Right: A Chinese 'comfort girl' is questioned by a British Intelligence officer

After the Bomb, the tragic moment of surrender: Major Wakō Hisanori
hands his sword to the British officer commanding the 1/10 Gurkhas

of the Yomas,' Saito remembers, 'and now we were down to 134.' The official British history, speaking of Shimbu Force's break-out, quotes an anonymous account of this period between the road and the Sittang:

During the day the men lay concealed on small floating islands of bushes that dotted the swamp and at night floundered on through the morass, often up to the neck in water, feeling for a footing in the inky blackness. During this nightmare march losses were heavy. There was no food and exhausted men lost consciousness and sank into the bog, their comrades unable to help them. Many went mad from the horrors of the swamp, others made their way back to the west. Only those in the best physical condition and with the highest morale survived to complete the march.

Those who did not complete it were, in most cases, inevitably abandoned by the men who pressed on. Before the final trial of the river crossing came, Saito agreed with the Force commander that prayers should be offered for those who had died, in the last village before the Sittang. Those who were too sick to continue, or were too severely wounded, were left with some medicine and one grenade per man.

On the evening of 7 August, Saito was in the village of Yele, heavy in heart at the casualties who had been left behind with one certain fate in store for them; but he was tense and buoyed up, too, by the immensity of the effort which lay ahead. The infantry company attached to Force headquarters was to cross the Sittang at Yele and secure the opposite bank, seize any small boats that happened to be available, and help the rest of the headquarters unit across. They came under attack from Burmese units at noon on 8 August, and there was a brisk exchange of machine-gun fire. Saito waited for sundown, and then asked for volunteers for a 'forlorn hope' party to cross to the opposite bank. The soldiers who came forward were lucky enough to find a sampan capable of holding about a dozen men, and up to dawn on 9 August about fifty men crossed the Sittang, forced the Burmese Army unit to retreat from the village on the opposite bank, and occupied its northern edge. But the Burmese had been well trained in combat tactics by the Japanese—at least this unit had—and they courageously put in a seventy-man attack on the village on the afternoon of the 9th, and finally broke through. The 'forlorn hope' party was still in being, and put up a stout resistance, which resulted in the death of the youngest of the party, a twenty-two-year-old second lieutenant called Mononobe, who fell bravely while attacking a Burmese machine-gun position. He did not die at once, and Saito heard his last whispered words, and a faint *'Tennō-Heika Banzai!'*('Long Live the Emperor!'), but felt no sadness at all. The young subaltern's death had been too courageous, too much in the pattern of the soldiers Saito admired, for him to feel any regrets.

The river crossing began again in earnest as soon as darkness came down on 9 August, but not unattended: as soon as the crossing began, artillery began to range on the village on the river bank. Saito judged that it came from the direction of Penwegon. Fortunately for Shimbu Force, it seemed to be fire-shells that were being used, and almost no damage was done. The crossing was a slow business with one sampan, and by dawn on the 10th 300 men of the first echelon had crossed, the journey taking about half an hour. Saito had begun to know when the artillery attacks would be put in and spent a lot of time judging the direction and timing of the shelling. At 0810 hours it began again, but the Force suffered no casualties from it that day and in the evening began to put across the second echelon. It was clearly dangerous to linger anywhere near the river banks or the villages alongside them and Saito began to profit from the arduous experience of the previous two weeks on the right bank of the Sittang. If small boats could be used, the rigours of marching through waterlogged paddy and swamp would be reduced, and Saito managed to commandeer some small boats and pressed some Chinese who were in the village into service as guides. In this way, the Force headquarters unit moved in the direction of Thinganbin. Dawn came as they were still *en route,* and for safety's sake they began to disperse into the thickets of jungle on either side of the track, where it was decided to rest until late afternoon. The rest was not entirely without incident. About three in the afternoon, a Burmese scout stumbled upon a party of Japanese, panicked at seeing more men than he had anticipated, fired and fled. Two hours later, movement began again, and at dawn on the 11th the Force headquarters was in Thinganbin.

Here, at last, news began to come in of the other units. A *Kempei* who had been sent from Kyaukkyi on reconnaissance, and who spoke Burmese, came into Thinganbin with a youth from a nearby village. From him Nagazawa and Saito learned that the infantry battalion attached to the Inoue Column was on the river bank opposite Kyaukkyi. Contact was made with them, and the Force headquarters managed to secure command of the second echelon. Inoue, the column commander, was told to reach Kyaukkyi as soon as possible. The Force headquarters was there itself on the evening of 13 August and made contact with Inoue Column and Murayama Column. To the north of Kyaukkyi, they learned, was *Baba Butai* from 54 Division, and to the south of a village called Dagala Karenzu—a few miles south of Kyaukkyi along the Kyaukkyi Chaung—was the main body of 112 Infantry Regiment, of Kanjō Force. Between them and Kanjō was the Kimura Column of Shimbu Force and the Matsuo and Fukuyama units. Liaison officers were despatched immediately to contact all these units. On 15 August, Force headquarters joined up with the Murayama Column and was preparing to set off from Kyaukkyi when an advance guard from 54 Division passed through. According to this advance guard, 54 Division, split into six echelons, intended to pass straight through Kyaukkyi on the understanding that Shimbu Force was to act as rearguard and protect 54 Division's withdrawal.

There was worse news than this. British aircraft began

dropping leaflets on the sodden and dispirited soldiers: 'Through the mediation of Soviet Russia,' they read, 'an armistice has been arranged between Japan, Britain, the U.S.A. and China.' In confirmation of this there was a rumour that a British peace envoy had been seen in the neighbourhood of Dagala Karenzu. Nagazawa was not in a sceptical mood about this news, and he did not want to stay where he was if an armistice was to be declared here in Burma. He and his men had had enough of the Lower Sittang Valley and it was agreed that all units should march south as fast as they could go. They should at all events attempt to reach the area south of Shwegyin. Movement began on 17 August with Kanjō Force in the lead, followed by the Kimura and Inoue columns. The last man of the Inoue Column was over the Shwegyin Chaung and on the south bank on 28 August. The path between Kyaukkyi and Shwegyin was strewn with dead and dying, and Saito's heart was filled to bursting with the pathos and grief of defeat and the futility of the sacrifice of these men, dying beside a waterlogged track in the Burmese jungle in the first few days of peace.

So it was over, Saito thought. And not too soon, for some people. Had the campaign continued, some heads were sure to roll. Inoue, for example. In his column, as far as Saito could see, only the Mountain Gun Battery commanded by Major Hamaoka had carried out its duties properly. The column commander himself had not, and was roundly reprimanded by Major-General Iwakuro when 28 Army headquarters passed through Kyaukkyi on 5 August. 'You stay put here in Kyaukkyi', Iwakuro told him, 'until Shimbu Force headquarters passes through, whenever that is. However long they take, you wait here for them.' Saito learned of this when he finally reached Kyaukkyi. Major Hamaoka came up to him, red in the face with suppressed anger—the more surprising since he was normally of a fairly affable nature—and pleaded with Saito to have the regimental commander removed. 'I don't want to serve under a regimental commander

like him!' Hamaoka exclaimed. In contrast Lieutenant-Colonel
Murayama stood out like a pillar of strength. Murayama was
an engineer, and trusted by Hanaya, the divisional commander
—a rare enough achievement in itself, largely because
Murayama was unafraid of Hanaya's bullying tactics. It was
because of the control Murayama exercised, and because he
was known for his courage, that his column was given the task
of putting in the attack on Penwegon, which was anticipated
to be the most difficult part of the operation. Murayama was
wounded in both legs during a skirmish on the banks of the
Sittang.

Major Matsu, formerly a battalion commander of the 143
Infantry Regiment, was an intelligent and charming officer,
and liked by Hanaya; but he did not make a good job of the
business of conveying the force casualties up to and over the
Sittang. Many of them were simply abandoned in the mud
and rain. He seems to have been an ambitious man, eager to
rejoin the larger units, and when he was gazetted to the staff,
paid little heed to the duty he should have carried out, of
reporting the dead and missing from the units under his
command.

But these were complaints on a personal level. In more
general terms, there were misconceptions about the planning
of the break-out, in Saito's view. For one thing, in spite of their
reconnaissance parties, there was inadequate knowledge
of the conditions obtaining in the Lower Sittang Valley. As
Miyazaki of 54 Division had wanted, the operation should
really have been carried out north, not south, of Toungoo.
The entire force of 28 Army could then have followed
roughly the withdrawal route of the main body of 55 Division,
south through Papun and into Tenasserim. In a sense, the
staff should probably have argued more strongly against the
decision about the place of crossing, and about the time.
Saito later thought he should have insisted much more
strongly on starting the break-out on the 23rd, since
preparations would not have been completed by X-Day,

20 July. Had he had the use of those three days, Saito is convinced that the losses not only of Shimbu Force but also of the other forces in the break-out would have been reduced. The thought of the dead began to oppress him. He remembered the 3,000 graves of Japanese troops who had fallen in the Arakan, believing in the inevitable victory of Japan. He remembered the 500 men who had died in those terrible days in the water on the approach to the Sittang, many of them retaining to the end the discipline of politeness imposed by Japanese life, making not a single murmur of complaint, but whispering, 'Thank you for helping me' as the death throes overcame them.

It was this obsession with the dead which made Saito fulfil his responsibility towards his army to the very end, in Indo-China, rounding up deserters, ensuring that the fragments of the Japanese army finally made their way home again—though it was to a homeland broken by defeat in which, he felt sure, nothing would survive of soldierly chivalry, of codes of gentlemanly behaviour, of the *bushidō* which had been his life's ideal and which had upheld him in the nights of desolation and madness in the flooded rice fields of the Sittang.

CHAPTER SEVEN

RAGTAG AND BOBTAIL: *KANI HEIDAN* AND THE RANGOON DEFENCE FORCE

The southernmost formation to take part in the battle of the break-out was 105 Independent Mixed Brigade, or Kani Force, to use the term by which it was most commonly known. This brigade had been formed originally for the defence of Rangoon. 28 Army had been responsible for the defence of the Rangoon area from the autumn of 1944. The direct defence of the city itself, as opposed to that of the surrounding area, was the responsibility of two units, the Rangoon Anti-Aircraft Unit and the Rangoon Lines of Communications Unit. Later still, on 10 March 1945, *Kani Heidan* was formed, with a name that was far more imposing than the reality: the first character of Kani, *kan*, means 'bold' or 'adventurous', while *i* stands for 'power' and 'authority', qualities singularly lacking in the motley fighting force commanded by Major-General Matsui. Kani Force took under its wing all the various units which had been preparing the defence of the city and centralized them: lines of communications units, anti-aircraft units, naval garrison units, railway units, airfield protection units, and so on. It was also responsible for the *Kempei* in its area, military or naval hospital patients, and the troops running the POW cage, the Central Gaol in Rangoon. Ultimately the Force incorporated civilians who were thought to be able to contribute something to the city's defence, shopkeepers, clerks, journalists, businessmen, teachers. After the rebellion of the Burma National Army in March 1945, Kani Force came under the direct command of Burma Area Army, and one of its first functions was to carry out operations against the

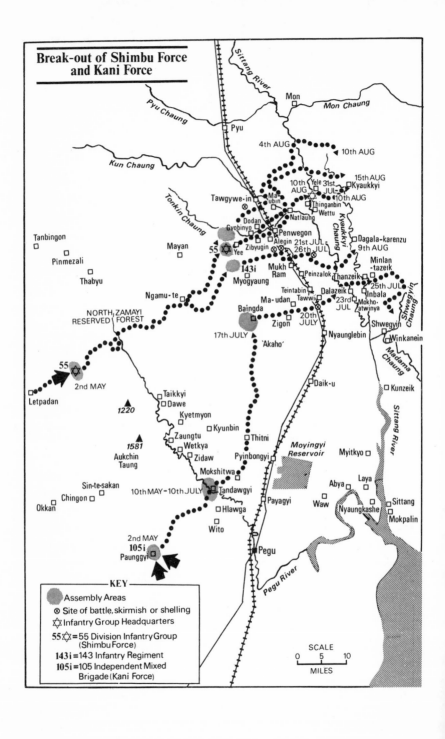

Break-out of Shimbu Force and Kani Force

Sittang River

Pyu Chaung

Mon

Mon Chaung

Pyu

4th AUG   10th AUG

Kun Chaung   15th AUG
                                        Kyaukkyi
Tonkin Chaung   Tawgywe-in   Ma-   10th   Yele 31st   10th AUG
                                   ubin   AUG   JUL
Tanbingon   Dodan   Thinganbin Wettu
          Pinmezali   Mayan Gyobinyo Natlaung
                                        Penwegon   Dagala-karenzu
                                        Alegin 21st JUL 9th AUG
      Thabyu   55   Yee Zibyugin 26th JUL   Minlan
                                                          -tazeik
                        143i Mukh   Peinzalok Thanzeik
            Ngamu-te   Myogyaung Ram   25th JUL
                                        Teintabin   Inbala
NORTH ZAMAYI   Ma-udan Tawwii Dalazeik Mokho-
RESERVED FOREST   Baingda   23rd atwinya
                                        Zigon   20th JUL
          55   17th JULY   JULY   Shwegyin
                                        `Akaho' Nyaunglebin   Winkanein
     2nd MAY   Madama
Letpadan   Taikkyi   Daik-u   Chaung
                                Dawe   Kunzeik
              1220   Kyetmyon
                        Kyunbin
                Zaungtu
              1581   Wetkya Thitni
     Aukchin   Zidaw   Moyingyi
      Taung   Pyinbongyi   Reservoir   Myitkyo
                Mokshitwa   Laya
   Sin-te-sakan 10th MAY-10th JULY Tandawgyi   Abya
 Chingon   Waw   Nyaungkashe Sittang
Okkan   Hlawga   Mokpalin
                        Wito
     2nd MAY
     105i   Pegu
     Paunggyi
                        Pegu River

KEY

- 🔴 Assembly Areas
- ⊗ Site of battle, skirmish or shelling
- ✡ Infantry Group Headquarters
- **55**✡ = 55 Division Infantry Group (Shimbu Force)
- **143i** = 143 Infantry Regiment
- **105i** = 105 Independent Mixed Brigade (Kani Force)

SCALE
0   5   10
MILES

Burmese. But when the British-Indian forces burst through the ineffective screen put up by 33 Army at Toungoo on 22 April, Burma Area Army ordered Kani Force first to defend Rangoon, then to move up to Pegu and Payagyi and prevent the British breaking through either directly on to the Rangoon road, or down the road to Moulmein.

Matsui's men had been engaged in what the Japanese called a *tōbatsu* or punitive expedition to suppress the rebels of the Burma National Army, but the approach of the British divisions was a far more serious threat to Rangoon than that presented by Aung San and his Japanese-trained forces, so Matsui promptly called off the *tōbatsu*, concentrated his forces in the city of Rangoon, then moved out to the Pegu and Payagyi areas after Burma Area Army issued an order to that effect on 27 April, i.e. by the time it had completed its abandonment of the city. In addition, Matsui was instructed to destroy all important installations in Rangoon itself, wharves, electricity generators, munitions, warehouses, and any anti-aircraft guns which could not be moved out. There is no doubt, as the Japanese official history points out, that the issue of this order to Matsui showed a clear intention to abandon Rangoon to the enemy before the end of April.[1] But it cannot have had the same clarity for poor Matsui himself because, three days after the first order was issued, a second one came through (30 April) in very different terms: 'The brigade will return at once to Rangoon and defend it to the last round and the last man.' Perhaps Southern Army's insistence had compelled Kimura to go through the motions of ordering Kani Force to perform what had now become an impossible task, or perhaps the conflict of orders reflected the conflict in Burma Area Army headquarters between Kimura and his Chief of Staff, Lieutenant-General Tanaka. Tanaka was a passionate last-ditcher and was prepared to fight the British in Rangoon until the city was reduced to a heap of rubble.

At any rate Matsui was too involved in the fighting round

Pegu to do much about the second order. North of Payagyi he was to attempt a holding action to prevent IV Corps pushing its armour down the road to Rangoon. About 1,700 men of Kani Force were dispersed in covering positions at Pyinbongyi and Payagyi and lost 350 of their number in a desperate and futile attempt to fling the British back. The rest of the force, which was described, in its temporary role, as the 'Payagyi Garrison Force', retreated eastwards along the road to Waw, where there was a battalion of 24 Independent Mixed Brigade holding the line of the retreat open to the Lower Sittang.

17 Indian Division's orders for taking Pegu were issued on 30 April. The town had played a crucial role in many other campaigns in Burma, including the British disasters of 1942. It lies on both banks of the Pegu River, and through it run both the railway and the road to Rangoon, from Mandalay and the north, and (via Waw and Sittang) from Moulmein and the south. The road makes a bridge over the river and there are two railway bridges, one 3 miles to the north of the town, another only half a mile from the north side of the town where the railway comes in from Moulmein, joining the railway from Toungoo and Mandalay on the right bank. Matsui left Rangoon on the night of 28 April, made his way to Pegu, and reached it halfway through the night. He at once concentrated his forces there, intending to reinforce the Payagyi Garrison Unit with them, but the time was already past when this could have served any purpose, as the British armour had already broken through that shield.

The Japanese were subjected to fierce aerial and artillery bombardment on 29 April, but the fighting came to an end with the approach of night, and they observed the British tanks being put into three harbour sites while the crews rested, east of the main road. The Japanese estimated that the British had about 170 medium and light tanks, of a total number of around 2,000 vehicles. The British returned to the attack early on the morning of the 30th, and a fierce

anti-tank battle developed, with Matsui using the 12 and 13
Naval Guard Units as his fighting force. The sailors fought
well, but sustained heavy losses, including Commander
Kōno, their commanding officer. It was at this juncture that Matsui received Kimura's order of 30 April,
telling him to return to Rangoon and defend it to the death.
The same order instructed 28 Army to advance to the area
north-west of the city and prepare for future attacks there.
Matsui was in despair. The sheer impossibility of carrying out
the order should have been obvious to the fools at Burma
Area Army who had sent it. But he was a soldier, and
attempted promptly to extricate his forces from their
involvement with the troops of 17 Indian Division who were
now pressing in on Pegu, inexorably, from all sides. What was
worse, Matsui had tasted the immense attacking energy of IV
Corps' mechanized forces and knew perfectly well that if
they caught Kani Force on the way south to Rangoon his
formation would be cut to ribbons. He decided to concentrate the Force at Paunggyi, on the southern edge of the
Pegu Yomas, and after completing the concentration of his
tired and battered men, to move on Rangoon from there. The
Force's front line would be moved west of the Pegu River on
the night of 30 April, Matsui hoping to gain time for his
withdrawal by using the river as an obstacle.

As it happened, the monsoon had begun to turn to the
advantage of the Japanese. It arrived a fortnight earlier than
expected and put paid to the race of IV Corps for Rangoon.
Early in the morning of 2 May, work had started on a Bailey
bridge across the Pegu River as soon as the town was
moderately free of Japanese and the booby-traps they had
left behind. An armoured vanguard of 48 Brigade was soon
across, but the rain began to fall ceaselessly in great torrents
during that night, and although the bridge remained firm, the
roads leading to it were soon hopelessly submerged. For the
moment, Matsui could breathe freely. His units began to
move off, taking a footbridge over the Pegu River and

travelling westwards from the river in the direction of Paunggyi. The guns which could not be manhandled across country were destroyed, and an engineer section blew the bridges used by the formations once the concentrated Force had passed over them.

When Matsui learned that the British had retaken Rangoon he should promptly have forgotten about Kimura's absurd order. In fact, he did not. Kani Force left Paunggyi on 5 May and moved south out of the Yomas towards Taukkyan. While reconnaissance of the Rangoon area was being carried out from there an order came from Burma Area Army to the effect that Kani Force, from its position in the area north of Rangoon, was to begin guerrilla attacks on the British, to prevent them mounting further operations, and to put an end to their plans for an offensive in the direction of the Sittang. This order effectively released Matsui from the moral burden of having to commit his forces against Rangoon and attempting the folly of retaking it from the British.

British-Indian units accompanied by armoured vehicles put in attacks on Paunggyi during this period between 30 and 31 May, but the Japanese held firm in their positions. In early June Matsui could feel British strength building up all round him. Reports came in that there was at least one British-Indian division in the Rangoon area, another in the area between Pegu and Waw, and the Pegu area itself was reputedly occupied by a powerful armoured unit. Both Pegu and Payagyi airfields were being used by a great number of aircraft. By an order from Burma Area Army the naval units which had so far been under Matsui's command now came under the direct command of 28 Army and were told to make for a point north of Taikkyi where 28 Army was said to be. The story of these naval units, under the command of Commander Fukami, is perhaps the most tragic of all those connected with the battle of the Sittang, and will be told in the next chapter.

The break-out plan for crossing the Mandalay Road and

then the Sittang was shown to the Kani Force commander on 28 June. Matsui based his own break-out plan on it, working his movements out in two phases. In Phase One, drawn up at Tandawgyi, the Force's movements were timed to start on 10 July. They were to move north along the line of the eastern foothills of the Pegu Yomas and were expected to concentrate at Baingda, a village about 13 miles west of Nyaunglebin, by 18 July. Break-out preparations were to be carried out in great secret at this spot, and then on the night of 20 July the Force was to break out across the Mandalay Road north of Nyaunglebin. It was then to make as quickly as possible for the crossing point on the Sittang north-east of Nyaunglebin.

Phase Two was drawn up at Baingda. The Force was to follow the pattern of all the other units under 28 Army command and split itself into three columns. It would leave Baingda on the night of 19 July, concentrate until the morning of the 20th in the area north-west of Nyaunglebin and then cross the Mandalay Road on the night of 20 July between the villages of Tawwi (about 2½ miles north of Nyaunglebin) and Peinzalok (about 2½ miles north of Tawwi) and get as close to the Sittang as possible by the morning of the 21st. The Sittang would be crossed at Mokho and in the area north of that village. After the crossing, the Force was to concentrate between Inbala and Thanzeik and then move into the hills east of Minlan-Tazeik. Contact would be made there with Japanese forces of 33 Army and under their protection the Force would move south through Shwegyin and make for Bilin. The Fukami Naval Unit would bring up the rear of the Force.

Like all the other plans of the units under 28 Army's command, the plan was circumstantial and convincing on paper. The execution of it was the difficulty, as those few miles from the road to the Sittang were to prove. The first phase went off fairly reasonably, the force leaving its positions at Tandawgyi on 10 July for Baingda. During the move, Matsui had under his command roughly 3,400 men.

Every unit moved north carefully, using jungle tracks on the eastern edge of the Yomas to avoid being spotted by British planes, and the concentration was completed at Baingda on 18 July. Matsui waited for the arrival of the naval units, but since they did not present themselves at the agreed concentration point, he had no choice but to move on without them.

The British attacks began in earnest once the road crossing started. The right column was attacked near Zigon in the early hours before dawn on 20 July and artillery shelling and infantry attacks prevented the column carrying out the planned crossing on the night of the 20th. In fact only the headquarters of 2 Mobile Unit was successful in crossing the road. The column gradually began to break up under the constant harassment of enemy fire and it was 26 July before the Sittang was reached, and then only at the price of very heavy losses, including the death in action of Lieutenant-Colonel Tokura, the officer commanding 451 Independent Infantry Battalion, who was killed in a skirmish just after crossing the Mandalay Road.

The centre column was a little luckier. It broke across the road halfway through the night of 20 July, without being spotted by the British or the Burmese. Between the night of 22 and 24 July, the column crossed the Sittang at Mokho using rafts and country boats and came under fire from British planes who flew low, strafing the river. The column sustained a few casualties from this machine-gun fire, but otherwise crossed safely.

The right column made a mistake in its route on the night of the 20th, and, because of the difficult terrain, was unable to cross the road as planned. The British spotted the column on the 21st and it began to lose men fast. By the time the columns reached the Sittang, there was no question of the units concentrating. Every one of them made the crossing as soon as possible without waiting for further orders. As a result, the Force found it impossible to assemble in the area Inbala-Thanzeik as the original plan had anticipated, and left Thanzeik on 26 July, dodging enemy air strafing as they made for the hills east of Minlan-Tazeik. It was the end of the month before the remnants of the other two columns finally came under command again.

In view of the confused nature of the orders he was given originally and the motley miscellany of units and non-units he commanded, there is no doubt that Matsui did a very creditable job indeed. A former commander of 113 Infantry Regiment of 56 Division, he had seen some very tough fighting in North Burma before being transferred as a major-general to the command of this ragtag and bobtail brigade. Admittedly, there were trained soldiers and sailors as its nucleus – the independent infantry battalions, the naval garrison units, the airfield and ack-ack units. But there were also the various 'Rangoon units' or *Ran Butai* made up in many cases of men long past the age of conscription, who had been living a comfortable life on the fringes of the army of occupation, had been engaged in business or teaching in Rangoon, or were hospital staff. And there was the inevitable contingent of about forty comfort girls. Oddly enough, at least until they neared the Sittang, the soldiers of Kani Force do not seem to have suffered from lack of rations. Although many of those taken prisoner were in an appalling physical state, their condition was attributable to foot-rot and general debility caused by the unparalleled exertions of the past two months, not to lack of nourishment. Food was plentiful; they had rice, salt, and meat in the shape of bullocks which drew the ration-carts and then were slaughtered and eaten when the bulk of rice to be transported did not justify the use of carts any longer. But the confused situation in which the force had left Rangoon meant that its medical supplies were almost non-existent and there was no soap. The men were told to wash their feet and dry them thoroughly before a fire, but in monsoon conditions this was a counsel of perfection. And since so many had recently

been civilians, the discipline was inevitably harsh. Those
who found they could not keep up with the column were
not initially allowed to fall out, but were first threatened and
then beaten and made to walk on ahead to prevent them
becoming stragglers.

They were all warned that the really dangerous area of the
operation would be the period when they were crossing the
Mandalay Road. After that, there was almost no information,
and the appalling circumstances they encountered once they
were over the road and therefore, as many of them supposed,
at their journey's end or near it, caused a tremendous drop in
morale. It would have been hard enough for fit troops to
bear. For untrained men fresh from civilian occupations and
mostly above the usual age limit for a soldier's life, the shock
was in many cases fatal, and they simply succumbed. When
they reached the Sittang the worst was yet to come. There
were some country boats, but not many, and those who used
rafts often had no strength left to manipulate them. Once on
the rafts they presented perfect targets for the units of
Patriotic Burmese Forces in their guerrilla formations on the
river bank. One medical officer remembered being swept
away down the Sittang on a raft with six others, falling asleep
and awakening to find his companions dead, shot from the
river bank as the raft swept by. Others were caught in the
villages as they rested, like one officer from an ack-ack unit
who was separated from his men two days after the Mandalay
Road was crossed and went into a village until nightfall to
avoid capture. The villagers treated him well and gave him
food, and he was inclined to trust them, but nonetheless kept
his pistol in his hand and his sword by his side; and he made
it evident to the villagers that he was carrying hand-grenades
too. But like so many Japanese soldiers cut off singly from
their unit, he had to sleep some time, and dozed off. When he
awoke, he found his pistol and hand-grenades had disappeared. The villagers flung themselves on him, bound him
with ropes and took him in to the British.

When he came before the interrogator, his horror knew no bounds. He had committed the unforgivable sin of being taken prisoner, and sobbed that he should have died in battle. Life was over for him now; if after the war he was compelled to return to Japan, he would commit suicide.

By the summer of 1945 this was not necessarily a universal reaction. There were men – and officers too – in the Japanese Army who had gone as far as they could with the militaristic adventure of the thirties and forties and knew now that they and their entire people were treading a path that led inevitably to defeat and mass slaughter. This was evident in some of the regular army formations and more so in the case of a scratch unit like Kani Force, which included a high proportion of recently conscripted civilians. Those one-time shopkeepers and teachers could – and did – fight like veterans. But when the tide of battle washed over them and they were left as individuals, abandoned to their wounds, possibly, in some deserted village, then the futility and misery of the war was brought home to them and they began to question the rigidity of the code which had brought them to these straits.

One such was an academic, a university lecturer whose training in economics had told him that in the long run Japan stood no chance against the industrial might of the Western Powers and that the sooner the war ended the better. Although he was aware that the Allies considered the Japanese soldiers to have behaved with roughness and cruelty to their prisoners-of-war, there was no question in his mind of betraying his friends by revealing the dates and places for the crossing-points. In fact, when it became clear from his interrogator's questions that the British knew all the Sittang and Mandalay Road crossing points and had watched the various Japanese reconnaissance patrols checking them, he tried to suggest that these were feints and that the break-out would take place further north, where the risks were less. But there was no point in refusing to reveal his own mood of despair about his country and its present situation. From conversations with officers and N.C.O.s for whom the sufferings of the past few months had been too extreme and for whom the future was unrelievedly dark, it had become clear to him how low morale was in those formations locked up in the Pegu Yomas. Many of them had overheard staff officers describing the forces for whom they were planning, in highly unflattering terms: Shimbu's morale was low, according to one, half its men were sick and they had rations for one month only; according to another dyspeptic view, *Tsuwamono* (54 Division) had a bad reputation and always avoided battle areas, but were likely to be in better shape than some other formations under 28 Army command since they had been living in villages and obtaining food. 28 Army itself was reasonably well furnished with light weapons, he had heard – 1,000 rifles, 100 L.M.G.s, and 50 heavy M.G.s up in the hills; but little of its fighting spirit was left, and half its troops were sick with malaria and lack of food.

Unlike this intellectual, who thought the British would treat him properly, very many Japanese were amazed not to be shot out of hand. They were even more astonished when they were not only well fed but given expert medical attention – sometimes from Japanese nurses, incidentally, since several of these were captured during the campaign, and put to work among their own men. As many of Kani Force knew, since they had sometimes been involved in administering occupied territories, this underlined the contrast with Japanese treatment of beaten enemies and subjugated peoples. 'Everywhere we occupy', admitted one of them, 'is soon wrecked or falls into disrepair. Perhaps there *is* an underlying streak of barbarity in us.'

CHAPTER EIGHT

ZENMETSU: THE SAILORS IN THE JUNGLE

High above the City of London, Brackenbury House rises with a slightly clinical air, storey after undistinguished storey reaching up into the same sky that reflects St Paul's and Nicholas Hawksmoor's St Mary Woolnoth. It looks, and no doubt is, expensive to rent, for the multitude of companies whose office names fill its signboards. One of them, at any rate, is not likely to be too much concerned with cost, since it must be one of the richest and most diverse commercial enterprises in the whole world: the Japanese firm of Mitsui. No upstart in the world of business, the Mitsui sign can be seen on Japanese woodblock prints early in the eighteenth century, and its origins go even further back. It deals in everything, shipping, banking, general trading, and has branches in every major country on the planet. Its London office is on the tenth floor of Brackenbury House and in one of its rooms, sparsely but richly furnished, sits the assistant general manager, Tsutsumi Shinzō. He is a handsome man, tall in Japanese terms, with an indefinable aristocratic air, and a pleasant smile hovering over his lips as he looks out over the capital city of the country whose armies, a quarter of a century ago, harried him mercilessly through the jungle-clad hills of Burma, and tore his unit to shreds until there was almost nothing left. The amazing thing is, Tsutsumi was an officer in the Japanese Navy. How he and his men became caught up in Sakurai's break-out is perhaps the most fascinating story of the entire campaign. Because it is, I would like to treat it with more detail than perhaps the size of the unit may be thought to deserve. After all, it was only 600 men strong, whereas huge formations like *Tsuwamono* had close on 10,000 and Shimbu Force over 6,000. But the events through which Tsutsumi passed, and his reactions to them, mirror in small the sufferings and courage of the other formations, as well as reflecting a certain desire to move independently of the Army. They therefore have an interest which transcends the purely numerical.

Their saga is referred to briefly by Sir William Slim who writes:[1]

The last Japanese to attempt the break-out were 12 and 13 Naval Guard Forces formed from the Port and Shore Establishments of the Imperial Navy in Burma. They amounted to about twelve hundred men in all and, strangely enough, chose to make their attempt last and alone on the 31st July. As they struggled across the road, losing heavily in the process, all our forces within reach were turned upon them. Rapidly growing fewer, as our troops and artillery took toll, they approached the Sittang, only to find their way blocked by one of our battalions and to be caught between it and another pursuing one. The country was flooded and numerous *chaungs* near the river were in spate. It took nearly a week for an Indian and a Gurkha battalion to close in on the sailors, but of the four hundred to which they were now reduced, as the Japanese themselves afterwards told us, only three escaped.

It is no wonder that on Japanese maps illustrating the Battle of the Break-out, where 54 Division, Shimbu Force, 28 Army headquarters and Kani Force all show blue lines leading from the Yomas across the Sittang Valley and then arching southward into Tenasserim, one line moves up from the south of the Yomas, crosses the road, and then comes to a full stop between the road and the Sittang, with two characters beside it, reading *zenmetsu* — 'wiped out', 'annihilated'.

13 Naval Base Unit, under Rear-Admiral[2] Tanaka Raizō, was placed under the command of Burma Area Army on 18 February 1945, by order of Southern Area Army (Field-Marshal Terauchi was the overall commander of the forces in the Southern Regions). The Base Unit consisted of a headquarters in Rangoon, with just over 100 men, three

keibitai ('guard units'), 12, 13 and 17, the first two over 800 strong, the third over 1,000 strong; and a signals unit of over 200 men also in Rangoon. 13 Guard Unit was stationed at Myaungmya in the Arakan and 17 Guard Unit at Mergui, far to the south, on the strip of land that leads from Burma right down into the Malayan Peninsula. By and large, their duties were those of coastal defence, with occasional transport chores thrown in. Only the headquarters of the Base Unit was lucky enough to be evacuated with Burma Area Army when Rangoon was abandoned in April 1945. 12 and 13 Guard Units stayed to fight alongside the Japanese army. Rear-Admiral Tanaka left Rangoon by car with his adjutant early in the morning of 25 April and made for Kyaikto, after passing his men who were making for the Sittang on foot. Once in Kyaikto, he attempted – unsuccessfully – to contact his Guard Units by wireless. He decided to shift his headquarters to Moulmein, where he was established by 1 May. Before this move of the Base Unit headquarters from Rangoon, two minesweepers and two motor torpedo boats which had been moored in Rangoon harbour set off for Moulmein across the Gulf of Martaban, in the evening of 23 April. Some civilians attached to the Navy were on board, and those members of 12 Naval Guard Unit who had not been formed into the Special Land Combat Unit–about 300 in all–reformed under Captain Kōno, the officer commanding 12 Naval Guard Unit.

This Special Land Combat Unit, a kind of Marine force, was placed under the command of Major-General Matsui and his Kani Force and left Rangoon on 28 April for Pegu, to consolidate its defence against the British IV Corps, which was expected to attack Pegu on its way to Rangoon. The main body of 13 Naval Guard Unit was in Myaungmya in the Irrawaddy Delta, consisting of about 600 men under Captain Fukami and placed under the command of Lieutenant-General Sakurai and 28 Army. They left Myaungmya on 8 May, sailed along a tributary of the Irrawaddy called the

Bawle River and landed at Yandoon on the 15th, afterwards moving into the Pegu Yomas. The unit's torpedo boats and landing-craft, with about 220 men, separated from the main body which was to make a land crossing to Tenasserim, and left for Moulmein by sea. The Special Land Combat Unit, in the meantime, had become involved in a fierce fight with the British spearhead division in Pegu, and on the evening of 30 April they sustained very heavy casualties, Captain Kōno himself being killed in battle. His command was taken over by 1 Company Commander, Lieutenant Nonaka. The unit was gradually withdrawn by Matsui from the Pegu fighting, halfway through the evening of 30 April, and moved into the Yomas with what was left of Kani Force, arriving at Paunggyi on 4 May. The following day they set out for Hmawbi airfield, to the north of Rangoon, and had got as far as Wachangon when the news reached them that Rangoon was definitely in British hands. They moved into the southern end of the Yomas and came to a halt momentarily at the village of Yanthaya on the western slopes.

Here they stayed until 10 June, making small guerrilla raids with Hlawga and Wito villages as their bases. On that day, the Land Combat Unit left Kani Force, merged with 13 Naval Guard Unit, and moved north on 18 June to the villages of Zaungtu and Zidaw. From the time they arrived in these villages, which were in the very depths of the Yomas, malaria and dysentery cases multiplied. They sustained a great number of casualties from bombing raids by British planes, who did not take long to find out where the sailors were hiding. The rest of the month of June was taken up with foraging and looking after the sick.

After meeting Lieutenant-Commander Tsutsumi of 13 Naval Guard Unit in the village of Zidaw where he had gone in charge of a foraging party – this was the first contact the units had had since the theoretical 'merger'–they moved off together in a north-easterly direction, carrying the sick as best they could. Tsutsumi moved to Kyunbin, taking

Lieutenant Nonaka and his men with him and the two guard units finally joined up at this village on 8 July. They were then reformed and made up into two companies, one from 1 Company and the Land Combat Unit headquarters and the second from 13 Naval Guard Unit. The new set-up came under the overall command of Captain Fukami, the officer commanding 13 Naval Guard Unit. The total number of men in the combined units at this time was around 650 – so even before the break-out operation began the sailors had lost about 200 men of their original strength (about 850). *Fukami Butai*, as it was known for short, was placed under the command of Shimbu Force for the break-out operation.

We can see this operation more vividly through the eyes of Lieutenant-Commander Tsutsumi whose account of the battle, *Tenshin* (*Retreat*), is livelier than the few pages of his colleague's formal diary which appear in the Japanese official history.[3] Tsutsumi's experience was wide. In his six years' service he had been stationed at the extreme limits of Japan's overseas empire, from Harbin in Manchuria to Singapore at the very tip of Malaya, and then to almost the farthest west of her new possessions, the port of Akyab in the Arakan. Of all the places he knew, Burma remains most deeply imprinted on his mind, particularly those last days during the withdrawal into the Yomas and the desperate fight to break out of them in which so many of his men met their deaths.

For about eighteen months, from October 1943, Tsutsumi's 13 Naval Guard Unit had a fairly pleasant time, at least when compared with the life of those Japanese who were fighting in the hills before Manipur or in the far north against the Chinese. Certainly their base and vessels were bombed, and their patrolling and mine-laying duties may have been hazardous enough under skies completely under the air supremacy of the RAF. But they were not only able to build air-raid shelters and barracks, they could cultivate vegetable

plots and irrigate fields in an attempt to make themselves
self-supporting. Tsutsumi liked the Arakan, with its jungle-
covered slopes – though the hills rarely exceeded 6,600 feet
in height–which cut the region off from the Irrawaddy Valley
and stretched from the Indian border in the north to the
shores of the Bay of Bengal in the south. His unit's
responsibilities – the coastal defence of South-West Burma
from Akyab round to the mouths of the Irrawaddy –
paralleled those of 28 Army on a much smaller scale. For
the city-dweller that Tsutsumi had been until he joined the
navy, they left time to taste what life could be like in the
exotic surroundings of the tropics, with screaming monkeys
flying from branch to branch, the glimpse of birds with
resplendent plumage, and – just occasionally – a tiger
stalking through the jungle. He knew the thrills of shooting
game in the big hills and listened almost with awe to the
sound of his shots echoing and reverberating until they were
swallowed up by the thickly cushioned forest slopes. There
was danger of another kind in this shooting, of course. It
could betray you to aircraft flying overhead, because RAF
fighters flew in and out of the valleys several times a
day, looking for signs of Japanese troops on the move, and
descending on them like 'mountain-storms', as the men called
them – *yama-arashi.*

When the order came to leave the Arakan, in mid-January
1945, Tsutsumi received it with regret. So that the men
should not witness his emotion, he climbed up the hillside
and gazed westward in the evening, watching the setting sun
disappear into the Bay of Bengal. Behind him, the endless
waves of mountains marched across Burma, to India, to
China, and gradually enfolded themselves in the purple velvet
of the tropical night sky. The darkening sea and tranquil hills
made up a landscape of eternal magnificence – he wondered
if he would ever again see anything so splendid; and into his
memory there came echoes, not of gunfire, but of Dvořák's
New World Symphony. He gazed his fill, and came reluctantly

down the slope again to the reality of war.

His unit was to move into the inland Delta area, but by a different route from the way the army marched. A road had been built along the 110 miles that separated Taungup on the Bay of Bengal from Prome on the Irrawaddy. You could look down the cliffs along which it ran and see the shattered frames of trucks whose drivers' mistaken judgement of where the road edge lay had proved lethal. Elsewhere on the road were other burnt-out lorries whose movement had been spotted by Allied aircraft – with equally fatal results. There was no need for the naval guard unit to use road transport, anyway, and in the Delta it was neither so convenient nor so pleasant: they had their own small craft, and in these made their way to the new base at Myaungmya. This was a very different spot from Taungup. There was no need to start plantations to supplement food supplies – this was fantastically rich rice-growing country, where other foodstuffs were comparatively plentiful, too. It seemed pretty secure from landward attack by the enemy, since the whole area was criss-crossed by the *chaungs* and creeks linking the various mouths of the Delta like the meshes of a net. But the jungle had been a screen for Taungup. Here there was no jungle, just an endless, flat watery plain, offering no shelter whatever from enemy artillery, if it should come.

Surely it must come, Tsutsumi thought. There was going to be a decisive battle for the possession of Lower Burma, and this rich area was not likely to be left out of it. The unit was full of rumours: the British had landed from the air, from the sea, and so on. By the end of April the rumours became fact. Rangoon, which was 94 miles east of Myaungmya, fell to the British, the headquarters of Burma Area Army fled the city, and 13 Naval Base headquarters went with them. Cut off from all contact with its parent unit, 12 Naval Guard Unit started to move north of Rangoon to Pegu. Burma Area Army was supposed to be making for Bangkok, in Siam, Tsutsumi heard – surely that could not be true? He was not the only one to hear rumours. The people of Myaungmya looked at the Japanese very differently from the way they had a few months before when 13 Naval Guard Unit first moved in. You could see from their eyes how much the war had started to go against Japan.

Rumours or reality, a decision lay ahead for the commander, Captain Fukami Sakao. The long monsoon season was approaching, and it would be necessary to know if the unit was to break through the enemy cordon which had cut it off from the Japanese forces east of the Irrawaddy, or if it was simply to stay in Myaungmya and defend it to the death. Short, fat, an expert in gunnery, Fukami was prepared for either contingency. He would fight it out if so ordered. But no orders came. He discussed the future with his officers, and a decision was reached to break through the enemy and make for Moulmein. But were they to go by land or sea, and when? Motor torpedo boats were useless for carrying large numbers of men; they could not carry many more than their crew. But they might, with some temporary discomfort, be made to transport casualties, so 21 Torpedo Unit was ordered to start off for Moulmein immediately, carrying sick and wounded. One gunboat, three M.T.B's, and eleven landing-craft were to stay at the base. As a gunnery officer, Fukami had another distasteful choice. If the bulk of the men were to go by sea, it would be impossible to use the boats for weapons and ammunition, and the unit had 25-mm M.G.s and 13-mm M.G.s which would have to be destroyed. This really went against the grain as far as Fukami was concerned and it was decided to split the men up. Some would go by sea, others by land, the main body using the land route. From Myaungmya, making for the Salween and then cutting south, Fukami reckoned the distance to Moulmein would be around 310 miles.

When should they leave? Tsutsumi, backed by the medical officer, Lieutenant-Commander Horiguchi, urged Fukami to leave as soon as possible before the rainy season and before the enemy dispositions were consolidated – say mid-April, or at any rate before 29 April, a convenient deadline for Japanese, since it was *Tenchō-setsu,* the Emperor's birthday. What considerations weighed on the other side for Fukami are not clear, but he opted for a later day, 8 May.[4]

Leaving Myaungmya was itself a busy task. Army scrip had to be destroyed. It was too bulky to carry and, they suspected, would only have a very limited future use. So permission was obtained to incinerate it and masses of occupation *rupee* notes went up in flames to the value of 1,500,000 *yen.*

On 8 May, the whole unit paraded in barracks in field service marching order. As was customary, Fukami read aloud the *Gunjin Chokuyu,* the list of qualities which are expected from members of Japan's armed forces, and the Imperial Rescript declaring war, to remind the men that the imperial purpose was still behind them. They drank some of the local rice wine, and prayed for the success of the journey which lay ahead. In every face, Tsutsumi noticed, was a tension he had not seen in previous engagements, and he had seen many. The heightened colour of the men betrayed the feeling of finality, a sense that if they did not beat their way through the enemy, he had them in a trap from which they would not escape. 'It won't be long, see you in Moulmein!' Sublieutenant Fujimoto called out, and was gone with three M.T.B.s, their white wake visible for a long time in the nocturnal waters of the *chaung* as they moved seawards.

They were off the mouths of the Irrawaddy the following morning and lay at anchor during the hours of daylight. When night fell they started off again and made for the open sea, straight across the Gulf of Martaban for Moulmein. They were running great risks: the eyes of the British fleet were watching the approaches to Rangoon.

The remaining gunboat and eleven landing-craft accompanied the overland unit some way through the channels of the Delta, then they too turned seawards. Tsutsumi's unit then moved north along the Bawle, a tributary of the Irrawaddy, and turned in the direction of the landing point, the village of Hlaing. The sun had already slipped below the horizon.

Movement was bound to be at night. Enemy fighters roamed the line of the *chaungs*, and often came in very low to watch for Japanese concentrations. After passing Bawle on 9 May, the three leading small craft went on ahead of the other nine in order to find a suitable spot near Hlaing at which to land. Tsutsumi was riding in the second craft. By the morning of the 13th, he began to be worried – there was no sign of the first craft anywhere. *Could* it have made so much better time? It was was too risky to press on during daylight, so he decided to postpone pursuing it until nightfall. His and the third landing-craft were pulled into the rushes by the *chaung* banks and remained concealed until evening. When night came they started off northwards once more, but still no sign. Tsutsumi's unease was almost a certainty now. Early the next day, before it was light, he saw a red glow some distance up-river. It was coming in their direction. Hastily, the two craft pulled into the left bank and waited. The red object grew larger and larger and seemed to be coming nearer all the time but they still could not make out its exact shape. The river meandered a good deal, and occasionally a bend obscured their view completely. Then, at a spot about 200 yards upstream from where they lay in wait, flames burst forth. As they strained their eyes into the darkness, they saw the first landing-craft drifting down towards them, on fire.

The *chaung* was about 75 to 85 yards wide at this point. The craft floated past them, half-capsized, looking as if it were about to sink at any moment. The fire was already beginning to smoulder. Nobody seemed to be alive on board. Was this what people meant when they talked about ghost ships? What had happened to the crew?

Tsutsumi and the two craft stayed where they were as it grew lighter. Towards noon, the river began to carry other

objects from upstream − white objects this time, bobbing on
the waters. Corpses. Half-naked, or stripped completely.
They were the crew of the first landing-craft. As if
hypnotized by the sight, the crews of the other two started
up their engines and moved out into midstream to pick the
drifting bodies of their comrades out of the water. The
bodies were covered with bruises, and looked as if they had
been hacked at by a blunt-edged weapon. Tsutsumi guessed
what had happened. They had probably landed and split into
groups of two or three, and been caught asleep by Burmese
who had used *dahs* on them − the *dah* is used for hacking
away at trees or undergrowth and is a murderous weapon.
The sudden and violent death of their friends put the sailors
in an angry mood. They did not want to wait for nightfall
before moving now; they wanted to find the place where this
had happened. Tsutsumi took advantage of a rain-cloud
which came low and darkened the sky and the boats moved
off.

At about four in the afternoon they caught sight of a
cluster of huts close to the left bank. They pretended to sail
on, and then halted a little further upstream. Leaving a sentry
on the boats, they approached the huts − the so-called *'nipa
huts'* roofed with coconut tree leaves, the walls being pillars
of bamboo; the floor is raised to about 6 feet above the
ground, so that even in the monsoon floods the inhabitants
are not disturbed. Tsutsumi went straight to the houses to
search them, while the men of the third craft beat the
surrounding jungle. Not a soul was to be seen, nor was there
any sign of anything untoward having occurred. No signs of
any struggle. It was all very odd.

There seemed no point in lingering any further, and as it
was almost dark they began to return to the boats. Then, by
the side of a little track, they spotted a water-bottle. There
was no doubt it had belonged to one of the crew of the first
landing-craft. So they *had* been here. Something fearful must
have happened in or near these quiet, innocent-looking huts.

Tsutsumi's boats had to make contact with those coming up behind, so it was out of the question to seek out the villagers somewhere else. They made a U-turn in the river and went back downstream.

Just before first light on 15 May, the second and third craft landed at Hlaing. They unloaded the dead men, and awaited the arrival of headquarters. About eight o'clock, a full-throated roar of gunfire was heard, far upstream to the north. 'Enemy armoured columns moving south,' Tsutsumi thought — 'someone is using artillery against our units re-treating into the Yomas.' The men listened tensely to the distant boom-boom. Tsutsumi, bearing in mind what had happened to the first boat, now seriously began to worry about headquarters. Why were they so late? Just then he heard the sound of small-arms fire downstream, and the full burst of a Japanese 13-mm machine-gun. After about thirty minutes, the firing to the south came to an end but it had become clear that there was enemy on both sides of them. Desperately anxious, they continued to wait.

About two o'clock in the afternoon, nine vessels including the headquarters gunboat arrived at Hlaing. Tsutsumi breathed freely again. The headquarters boat had apparently tangled with a small enemy unit on the left bank and this had caused the delay. Two N.C.O.s had been killed and an officer wounded in the right arm. It looked pretty painful, thought Tsutsumi, as he examined the bloodsoaked triangular sling. Ten N.C.O.s and men had been wounded, too. The weapons, ammunition, and food were unloaded, then the men paraded and held a funeral service for the first sacrificial victims of the retreat. A lock of hair was cut from each man, to be sent back to Japan; then the bodies were reverently committed to the waters of the *chaung*.

While the ceremony was going on, the sound of gunfire from the north continued without a break, and seemed to be moving southward. If a fair number of tanks were involved, the sailors looked like being caught between two prongs of a

British pincer, so it was decided to move off eastward that night and make for the Prome-Rangoon Road, which they had to cross to reach the Yomas. The boats had to escape, too, and would run into difficulties if they did not move off before dawn. The gunboat and ten patrol boats were loaded with their crews and the wounded, 120 men in all, under the command of Lieutenant Hirose, and slowly disappeared into the night mists. They had promised each other to meet again in Moulmein – the same promise that had been made to the other crews earlier. But Tsutsumi was to discover later that of the 120 men who set out that night, only twenty-nine survivors ever saw Moulmein. Two boats made the crossing successfully, the gunboat carrying the wounded Sub-lieutenant Terabayashi, and one of the patrol boats under the command of Sublieutenant Mai. The rest were caught by the British either at the mouths of the Irrawaddy or making a frantic dash across the Gulf of Martaban, and were gunned into the water.

It was the turn of the overland unit to move. At eight o'clock in the evening of 15 May, a patrol vanguard set out from Hlaing followed an hour later by the main body. They marched eastward at a good pace, but Tsutsumi knew they could not reach the Prome Road that night, and it was too risky to continue by day. So the daylight hours of the 16th were spent concealed in hollows by the roadside. They reached the road at daybreak on 17 May. From Hlaing to the road the way ran over a broad, empty, undulating plain, dotted here and there with clumps of bushes. As they crossed this plain the men could see British signal lights rising in the sky to north and south of them, but they did not think the British were after *them*; it was more probably units of 28 Army who were being traced. Still, there was no point in taking chances. As dawn brought out a light green colour from the grass of the dark plain, they hid themselves among the bushes and slept. From the sound of the guns, Tsutsumi tried to work out just where the British tank unit was — it seemed to be several miles to the north, on the Prome Road, in the village of Palon. When they reached the road, where the flame trees' dark shapes lined the embankment, the sound of tank tracks did not seem very far away. They had been moving in a single column, but to cross the road in this way would take far too long, so they altered formation into a number of short columns. A vanguard under Sublieutenant Serita having crossed without incident, all the columns went over together. 55 yards to the east, and parallel to the road, ran the railway between Prome and Rangoon. They were soon across it, and saw a little track leading up into the foothills of the Yomas on the other side. They moved along it, and soon the jungle grew thick and dense and began to close in on them. At this stage of their journey it was a godsend. They were over the first obstacle.

Then the weather changed. There had been occasional showers so far, but from the afternoon of 17 May, the skies changed to a uniform dull lead, and a heavy downpour began. The men were already pretty fatigued, since the marching by night and resting by day had upset their routine. Fortunately, once in the jungle tracks, it was possible to revert to normal hours, but not to relax vigilance: they had heard the noise of tank tracks again, as if two or three tanks were moving up along the path by which they had come, and there seemed to be only one path at this point. A small group of sailors was instructed to act as a scout screen to protect the main body, and trees were felled and laid across the sharply-angled corners where the track wound in and out. Holes were dug just big enough for a man to hide in — what we should call 'fox-holes', and the Japanese '*takotsubo*' — 'octopus-pots'. The logs would slow down the tanks, and the soldier in the pit would rush out with an anti-tank mine and blow their tracks off — this was the theory. A petty officer, Matsumura, had been left behind in the octopus-pot to wait for the tanks but the noise of tracks and engines could still be heard reverberating among the hills. It was difficult now to

The end of the line for the Japanese

Japanese prisoners, ragged and foot-sore, are searched and interrogated

tell whether the noises were following them or going back down into the plain again, but there was no explosion from the place where they had left Matsumura. Was he safe? Had the tanks stopped and turned back before they reached him?

They passed through a village called Kemli, marked on British maps as 'Chingon,' where, to their astonishment, they found not Burmese but a settlement of Chins, whose home ground is the Chin Hills hundreds of miles away on the Indian border. On 19 May, they were in the village of Sin-Te-Sakan – the usual cluster of bamboo huts and roofs lined with *napi-ori* (banana leaves). They were terribly thirsty by the time they marched into this village and made at once for a clear stream, about a yard wide, which ran through it. Unhesitatingly, they guzzled great draughts of the cool, delicious water, drinking almost without a pause; and then filled their water bottles. With an immense feeling of renewal running right through their bodies, they continued their march.

About 300 yards further on, higher up the track, they saw something which turned their stomachs. A dead horse lay in the stream – it looked as if it had fallen from a cliff above – half of its body submerged in the water. Its belly was distended by the gases of decomposition until it was almost twice the normal size. From its broken neck and burst rump, white maggots were crawling out and filthy black flies swarmed where the flesh had broken open. The water they had drunk with such delight was only a few yards further downstream.

The sailors moved on higher and higher in the Yomas, until on the afternoon of 20 May they reached a 1500-foot high peak (Aukchin Taung) where they came across an army unit led by Major Nishiseko, the tail-end of the formations which had passed this way into the Yomas. Nishiseko told him that Shimbu Force was concentrating in the Yomas and gave him the code-name of its village – Otome Village (after a Japanese girl's name) – but did not linger; they had several days' delay to make up for, and were soon making ready to be off. There was something odd about them, which Tsutsumi could not quite put his finger on. Then it hit him like a flash, when he heard some of them talk – their faces, whiter than normal, their bird-like voices – these were Japanese women! They wore uniform, and had their heads shaved close like soldiers, and he had thought at first they were just new recruits. Each one of them bore a long pole, with a basket suspended from it fore and aft. Most of them contained food, but one of them, in her front basket, was carrying a baby. To shield it from the rain she had covered the basket in banana leaves. Soon they were off again, following Major Nishiseko, up and down, moving slowly along the slippery mountain tracks, until they were out of sight.

Tsutsumi's men moved off next, from Hill 1581 northwards to Hill 1220, then east towards Taikkyi[5] and the upper reaches of the Pegu River, which they crossed. The rains had not swollen it too much yet, it was only about waist-high and 60 yards wide at the crossing point. The example was, however, deceptive. Turning north-east to Dawe, they had to cross the Dawe Chaung, a tributary of the Pegu River, and found that although it was barely 30 yards across, it was both deep and fast-flowing and could not be crossed on foot. Here the sailors showed their ingenuity. They went into the jungle, collected rattan, and made enough rope from it to pass a length across to the opposite bank. They then made a raft from bamboo poles lashed together, with a little wooden wheel in front through which the rattan rope passed. A few men at a time rode the raft across the *chaung*, and another rope pulled it back, for the process to start again. Of course it only carried a few men at a time, and was a slow method, so they started another one further downstream. Even so, it took the whole unit two days to complete the crossing.

As they went further into the hills, the conditions began to take their toll. Men went sick with malaria, dysentery broke out, and the continuous rainfall soaked them to the skin regularly. The rain-clouds freed them from the risk of continual surveillance by British aircraft, but sickness and discomfort weighed down the 'other pan of the balance. At first the sick could be carried on hastily improvised stretchers, but the stretcher-bearers themselves, as with other units who did the same thing, gradually began to fall behind. Tsutsumi then adopted the 'ladder' solution: a ladder construction of bamboo which had two fit men, one at each end, to support it. Those men for whom dysentery, diarrhoea, or high fever made walking difficult, were set in the intervals between them and compelled to keep moving. Staggering along in this way, the sailors moved through the rain for another three days before they reached Akaho Village on 1 June. Akaho Village, as Tsutsumi knew, was only a code-name. It was, in effect, a hollow in the ground, with no human habitation in sight, high up near a mountain peak: but it was not a bad place for a halt — there were plenty of bamboo shoots, sweet potatoes and edible grasses, and running water.

Here Tsutsumi rested for a while and then set off with his Commanding Officer, Fukami, and a few men to make contact with Shimbu Force on 3 June, since 28 Army had put them under Shimbu's command. Otome Village was not very far, according to the information he had had from Major Nishiseko, and indeed, after spending the night of 3 June in the open, they reached Shimbu headquarters about noon on the 4th. Nagazawa and the 55 Division staff greeted them with delight and shared their midday meal with them. Tsutsumi had not had a cigarette for a long time, and drew with gratitude on the one offered him by Lieutenant-Colonel Saito from a packet of *Koa*. So to business. Shimbu Force would spend the next three weeks, they told him, preparing to break out over the Sittang. The date — X-Day — would be 20 July. Taking some rice with them for their men, Fukami, Tsutsumi and their party set off on the return journey.[6]

He was back at Akaho Village on 5 June. The next day

was his second wedding anniversary, he thought ruefully. He had married at the age of twenty-eight after being appointed paymaster to the naval air arm unit at Ōminato, on 6 June 1943. Three months later he was on his way to Burma. Still, it was no use brooding. There was much to do. The men had to carry one month's rations with them, and of the 500-strong unit over half were now sick with malaria or dysentery. After much discussion it was decided that Tsutsumi should take the 220 fit men, or at any rate those judged capable of a few days' march, south to the village of Zaungtu on the Pegu River, as a foraging party. It was a fairly sizeable village and should have some rice. When they reached it, it was almost an island, rising darkly a little way above the flooded rice fields. Not a soul was in sight. There was only a small amount of hulled rice, but plenty of unhulled, some salt and the vegetable the Burmese call *ngape* — every hut had a great store of this in pots. And, of course, there was fish. The fish had been preserved in salt and when Tsutsumi lifted the lid of the pots in which it was kept, he could see the top layer had begun to ferment, and there were maggots on the surface; but when you threw away the top layer, what was underneath tasted delicious. *Ngape* was bitter, but it was not the first time the sailors had tried it and they had acquired a taste for it. The difficulty lay in carrying it, which they solved by cutting yard lengths of bamboo, hollowing them out and packing the *ngape* into the space. There were other things they decided to make a meal of before returning — chicken and coconuts — in fact they ate until their eyes were almost bursting from the sockets. It was a long time since they had eaten their fill, and with such variety. They finished off with ripe mangoes, which hung from the branches like great coloured bells.

Perhaps the unaccustomed food was too much for stomachs which had grown unused to it. At any rate, ten of Tsutsumi's party found themselves unable to walk, whether from malaria or diarrhoea, and certainly incapable of carrying food back to their comrades in Akaho Village. Tsutsumi stayed four days in Zaungtu, employing the men on hulling rice. They were strafed on three occasions by RAF fighters and some were wounded, but not seriously. On the return journey they carried whatever they could on their backs and, though they knew the road by this time, the going was made even harder by the fact that they had to get used once again to having their meagre uniforms soaked by the endless rain, against which the village huts had to some extent sheltered them. Men began to fall out and the history of hand-grenade suicides, familiar to all the other formations, began to repeat itself. After all, they were convinced, if the enemy came upon them separated from their unit they would certainly be killed out of hand. The number of deserters increased rapidly – in fact of the 220 men his foraging party had started with, eighty-eight disappeared by the time he returned. Of the rest, Tsutsumi only counted twenty-eight as fit men. In desperation, he sent three men on ahead to the main body at Akaho Village to come in and fetch them. Two days after the men had been sent out, Sublieutenant Tanaka arrived from the main body with a number of men. Disquiet had grown in their absence over the delay of food supplies and also about the risks of breaking out from the Yomas very much later than the army units. So they were all going to move south. Hearing this, Tsutsumi fixed a spot where it would be possible to join up with the main body, the village of Kyetmyon where they now were. He explained all this to Tanaka, left him with the sick, and took thirty fit men with him back down the track to Zaungtu. There had been so many deserters from the foraging party that the supplies finally brought back by it would be inadequate, and Tsutsumi was impelled to bring up more supplies by a feeling of duty or at any rate by the sense that otherwise he would not properly have accomplished his mission. Once back in Zaungtu, he set his men to pound the rice free of its husks – there was no point in loading themselves with what the men would not eat — when he heard the sound of gunfire, far off down-stream.

He decided he had better go and reconnoitre. He passed through the village of Wetkya and came to Zidaw, about 3 miles downstream from Zaungtu, where, to his amazement, he came upon 12 Naval Guard Unit, or what was left of it, under Lieutenant Nonaka. Nonaka gave him an account of the vicissitudes of the past month, how they had been cut off in Pegu by British forces, and how 12 had lost two-thirds of its strength in the fighting. He was down to 190 men. Tsutsumi told them about the food stocks in Zaungtu, and Nonaka and his men came along to help shift them northwards. By 7 July, the reinforced forage party was back at the rendezvous of Kyetmyon. Thinking to anticipate the commanding officer moving southward, Tsutsumi went a little way up the northward track to meet him. What he saw instead was a group of wild-looking sailors, with luxuriant growths of beard, coming towards him, using their rifles as sticks to help them along. He encouraged them by saying the rice had arrived and was in the village nearby. Then, about four in the afternoon, he went a little further on and saw ahead of him one of his men, Kanetaka, carrying a hefty ammunition box along the slippery mountain track. They caught sight of each other when Kanetaka was about 10 yards away, and Tsutsumi could not help himself, he cried out involuntarily, 'Kanetaka!' But it proved a fatal thing to do. Kanetaka, startled by the voice, slipped in the mud and fell forward with his burden. Tsutsumi ran forward to help him up, put his arms round his shoulders, and was horror-stricken to find that Kanetaka was dead. He learned afterwards that he had been suffering from malaria and dysentery. His body was in a state of extreme fatigue but he had nevertheless opted to carry a heavy load and had almost managed to bring it to the rendezvous. The shock of the fall proved too much for him. Tsutsumi wept as he drew his sword and cut Kanetaka's little finger off his right hand. They buried him at night by the side of the track. The same night, with other members of his unit, Tsutsumi solemnly burned Kanetaka's finger, wrapped the incinerated finger in a small cloth, and placed it in his pocket as a memorial for the dead man's family.

The unit stayed almost a week in Kyetmyon, recruiting its strength again and waiting for stragglers to turn up, and wondering whether the army units to the north of them might not already have broken out across the Mandalay Road, leaving them behind, the only Japanese in the Yomas. They assembled on 15 July, around 600 men in all. Of the 550 who had left Bawle two months before, 150 had died in battle or from sickness. To the 400 survivors were added the 200 men from 12 Guard Unit. To them all, Captain Fukami read again the *Gunjin Chokuyu* and the Imperial Rescript, prefacing it by the brief phrase-'This is the last lap.' No more pauses, no more villages – a straight march east, and a straight drive across the road.

On 22 July, the sailors reached Baingda in a corner of the eastern foothills of the Pegu Yomas. 'Corner' is all it was – no houses, nothing, just jungle. But moving a little further east, they could make out, in the distance, the vast plain of the Sittang. Under the pouring rain, two or three men began to fall sick every day, and when there was a brief interval in the rain the RAF came out to look for them. Medical supplies had already run out. Fukami and his officers decided to think out a policy for the break-out, because clearly not all the unit was even going to reach the Mandalay Road at this rate. 'We are behind the army, as far as I can see' – was the case he put. 'The road and railway lines to Rangoon will be even more strictly guarded as a result, when we cross. It will be like plunging to our death, the success rate will be very low. What I propose is this. Bear in mind that the alternative is: if we stop, we die; if we march on, we die. There *is* a solution for the sick. Those who cannot walk unaided will stay behind in Baingda. They will

follow the unit if they can walk again. One medical officer
will stay behind with them.' Lieutenant Kinoshita, a graduate
of Keiō Medical School, was given this duty, and forty men
were left behind with him, as the relatively fit sailors began
to come out of the mountains on 24 July. They did not carry
much food with them, the idea being that they only needed
enough to last them the time it took to reach the railway. If
they did not die in the attempt, then fresh steps could be
taken to get more food. In the meantime, it was better to
leave the rations with the sick. This was done ungrudgingly.
Kinoshita was in good fettle and accepted his mission
without hesitation. 'You'll make it, you know!' he said to
encourage the rest as they bade him goodbye and told him to
follow on when the sick picked up a little. Then, the farewell
phrase, 'De wa, genki de ' ('Well, look after yourselves'), a firm
handshake, and they were gone. Tsutsumi never forgot Kinoshita's youthful face, and the fleeting smile it wore as they
said goodbye. Behind those clear, fine, limpid eyes lay the
sure knowledge how final it was. Neither Kinoshita nor his
casualties were ever heard of again.

By 31 July, they had reached a village called Ma-udan, just
short of the Road. They waited during the hours of daylight,
then began to march off towards the Road after sunset. The
point which had been fixed for their break-out was a place
called Teintabin about 4½ or 5 miles east of Ma-udan, and
about 2 miles north of Tawwi Station. They did not have
many illusions about crossing unspotted. Just before they
had reached Ma-udan, sixteen RAF planes had strafed them
mercilessly, so they knew the enemy was *au fait* with their
movements. But 'We have got as far as this,' every one of
them thought. 'We either make it now, or get killed in the
attempt.'

At three o'clock in the early hours of the first day of
August 1945, they came out on to the Mandalay Road. No
hail of gunfire met them, not a single shot. It was very odd.
None of them had expected to cross the road unopposed.

They scattered into open formation to traverse the intervening patch of land between the road and the railway, about 1600 yards of wet grassy surface. They were about halfway across, when the night sky was suddenly lit by signal flares, and a green and yellow light tore to shreds the safe blanket of night that had shrouded them. As they threw themselves flat on the ground, heavy machine guns opened up on both flanks. The sailors kept down, and did not reply with answering fire for fear of giving away their position. They began gingerly to inch their way forward. The machine-gun kept up the hail of fire, but most of it went above them.

Very slowly it became light and Tsutsumi could make out the situation. There was a small creek to his left, about 10 yards wide, flowing east towards the railway. Straddling it was a small iron bridge, and heavy enemy fire seemed to be coming from this direction. Another machine gun was positioned to the right of the sailors, who were moving forward over a front several hundred yards wide. As the day lightened, the attack grew fierce, and Tsutsumi, who was in the front of the left flank, decided to move along the side of the creek. The British kept firing signal lights into the sky and as Tsutsumi looked up at them — they were red this time — they seemed to him like a pile of bright copper coins going up and up into the heavens. The sailors were replying to the fire now with their own 13-mm machine guns and light machine guns, and the ambush seemed to be slackening off. There was the railway line, Tsutsumi saw, just in front. An embankment about 6 feet high protected it from the monsoon flooding, and he made his way towards it, inch by inch. To his right, the sailors were moving to the attack and about 30 or 40 yards away he saw his friends begin to fall under the storm of British bullets, Lieutenant Kugimoto first, then Lieutenant Kodo, then Lieutenant Iwanaga, then, much closer to Tsutsumi now, the medical lieutenant, Uchida. But the enemy seemed to be withdrawing from the bridge. Tsutsumi bent double and made a dash forward. Now the Japanese 13-mm was firing from the bridge. The enemy had withdrawn to a little piece of jungle about 400 yards ahead, and slightly to the left, and was again bringing fire to bear from there.

It was broad daylight now, as Tsutsumi reached the railway line and heaved his body up on to the embankment. The rest of the sailors were making a dash for it too, not in any order, but sprinting like rabbits in the intervals of firing. Tsutsumi hurled himself over the opposite embankment and into the deep grass on the other side, flat on his face. The British began to bring other weapons to bear: on both flanks, from a considerable distance away, mortars began to open up on the sailors. He could not make out where the fire was coming from, it was so far off. He lay in the grass, quivering, pressing himself into the earth as if to avoid the shrill rushing scream of the mortar bombs. Then came the last straw — the noise of approaching tanks on the road they had just crossed. The sailors were trapped in a three-sided box.

From all three sides, bullets, shells and mortar-bombs poured into them. The Japanese fought back with what they had, grenade-launchers, light machine guns and rifles, and attempted to escape the hail of fire by crawling along the bank of the *chaung*. But the British 'box of fire' was saturating the entire belt of country through which the Japanese were moving, fragments and splinters of shrapnel screamed through the air, sand and earth flew up in fountains. A shower of earth fell upon Tsutsumi's back and steel helmet and almost buried him. When he looked up again, and around, he saw that the second-in-command, Lieutenant-Commander Wakana, had been wounded in the right eye and was calmly giving himself first-aid. The enemy artillery gradually reached a crescendo of ferocity and Tsutsumi could see the shattered bodies of his sailors flying into the air in broken fragments. And here in this attack, as everywhere in the break-out which had become a retreat, men who were too heavily wounded for help to be of any avail finished the job themselves with a hand-grenade.

Tsutsumi took command of all the men he could control near him, and directed them into the bushes, shrubs and water-covered roots of the little creek. They struggled on downstream, up to their chests in water, for about 300 yards. Then, at a point where the stream ran sluggishly, they swam the twenty yards to the other side. Here too there was flat, level, water-soaked paddy which came over their boots. But most of the time it was too dangerous to walk and they half slid, half crawled for another 300 yards to a small village screened by a grove of trees. This grove was the unit's previously arranged assembly point.

The artillery fire was still too fierce for men to come up out of the *chaung* and many of them kept on going downstream. Perhaps the enemy spotted them – at any rate, shells began to drop along the line of the *chaung*, blowing logs out of the water. But the little village was left alone. Tsutsumi had managed to collect about fifty men and, as if for virtue rewarded, he stumbled across a bottle of raw rice wine in one of the huts, which helped down some of the little rice they found. His watch showed the time to be exactly eleven o'clock.

After a little while, they heard the sound of an enemy observer plane circling round and round overhead. Clearly, it was trying to puzzle out where they had disappeared. They're going to shell this village fairly soon, thought Tsutsumi, and without more ado conducted the men out of it another 2,000 yards further to the east. They found a deep hollow in the ground and decided to halt there without moving, until nightfall. They would move south-east at dark and meet up again with the commanding officer and the rest of the unit. Strangely enough, they did so, but with a sadly depleted force – *Fukami Butai* was now, on the evening of 3 August, no more than 148 men strong. In that battle of 1 August they must have lost over 400 men, including fourteen officers and petty officers.

The survivors finally straggled into the outskirts of the village of Dalazeik on 7 August, fighting little skirmishes as they went. Dalazeik is close to the right bank of the Sittang and the British had set up a guerrilla base there. *Fukami Butai* were, of course, unaware of this as they made their way to the village during the night, and finally ended up a few hundred yards from the British positions. Naturally they were soon discovered and a fierce battle broke out, the Japanese becoming the target for the usual hail-storm of mortar-bombs, grenades and heavy machine-gun fire. They were reduced to four grenade-dischargers themselves, with a few grenades and rifles, but in spite of their inferiority in fire-power they managed to hold off the enemy attack while the main body of the unit slipped round the village in the direction of the river. It was a fatal day for the commanding officer, Captain Fukami: grenade fragments ripped open his stomach as he led the sailors across the fields, and Lieutenant-Commander Horiguchi, the medical officer, was wounded in the side. Sublieutenant Tanaka showed Tsutsumi his steel helmet, which had a bullet-hole right through the centre. Tanaka himself had not even a scratch. But you have to wait until tomorrow before you begin to count a man's luck, Tsutsumi reflected — the next day Tanaka was shot dead. Tsutsumi himself had his own share of luck: in the afternoon of 6 August, he was swimming across one of the small *chaungs* about 3 or 4 yards wide, which criss-cross the entire area near the Sittang, and was about to move into the shelter of thick shrubbery which overhung the opposite bank. It was concealment, at any rate, if not protection, though he thought that where the shrubbery was thickest the fragments might be dispersed. As he approached, he saw that a dozen sailors had already had the same idea, so he swam towards a similar clump 50 yards further on. As he reached it, the mortar fire began again and he saw a bomb fall plumb in the centre of the shrubbery he had first made for. In an instant every man in it met his death. Why he should have escaped it, why those men met their deaths, continued to nag and perplex him – surely someone, somewhere, he thought, is spinning the thread of destiny?

Two days later, on the morning of 8 August, they reached a point where they could see the embankments of the Sittang River in the distance. They were in elephant grass about 6 feet high, about 6 miles to the east of Dalazeik. They had marched throughout the previous night, up to the knees in mud, carrying Captain Fukami on a hastily improvised stretcher. By this time, the sailors were near the end of their tether with fatigue and had eaten nothing for days. They halted for a moment, undecided whether this was the place to take a rest or not, when enemy gunfire started up on three sides, north, south, and west. Whether the British guerrillas from Dalazeik had patiently trailed them throughout the night or had come round some other way, Tsutsumi did not know and was past caring. Whatever the reason, they were beleaguered on almost every side. The enemy closed in and here and there amidst the elephant grass came the sound of shots and screams. The circle of combat widened, and the whole area was a vast *mêlée* of struggling men. The enemy seemed to be Gurkhas under a British officer and they had automatic weapons. The elephant grass hid the enemy from you until the very last instant, Tsutsumi remembers, and when it opened before you, you could never be sure of not firing upon one of your own men. The battle was turning into a handful of close engagements, with pistols, short swords, and bayonets, when the cry went up for the Japanese to break off and retreat to the wood near the embankment. Tsutsumi made off eastward, to the edge of the elephant grass, and saw the sailors emerge in groups of three and four from the grass and go into the wood. With Petty Officer Ueda and a few others, Tsutsumi lay pressed hard down into a hollow of earth as enemy automatic fire came in their direction. Suddenly he saw Lieutenant Okamura hobbling across in the direction of the wood, his helmet gone, and using his sword as a stick.

After the fight on 7 August, near Dalazeik, the 148 survivors of the earlier battle now numbered ninety-eight. But what was infinitely more serious was that almost every officer, including the commanding officer, Fukami, met his death in battle that day. In the evening, the survivors collected at a tiny village called Mokho Atwinya in the lee of the embankment on the west bank of the Sittang. Tsutsumi counted them – seventeen men. But thinking that there might be other survivors who would make for the spot, he decided to wait a little. If the enemy decided to put in another attack, well, here was as good a place to die as any.

In fact, during the night, the enemy attempted nothing. Early in the morning of 9 August Lieutenant Okamura and four men slipped out of the village. Tsutsumi called after them, but to no avail. This left seven men of the original 13 Guard Unit, under Tsutsumi, and six men under Sublieutenant Yoshida of 12 Guard Unit. After some discussion, they decided to remain in the village for three or four days on the offchance of picking up stragglers, and prepared for the crossing of the Sittang. On 12 August, during the hours of darkness, the enemy came at them again. Tsutsumi and Petty Officer Ueda were sleeping in a little hut used for storing rice. They had little ammunition left by this time and swiftly agreed not to fire until the enemy was actually in front of them. Judging from the sound of the firing, the enemy was some way off. As they lay in wait, Tsutsumi heard a soft sound, *pattt*! in the walls of the hut, and after a little while the sound of firing disappeared in the distance. Tsutsumi called out, 'Ueda! It seems all right now!' Ueda was lying full length on Tsutsumi's right. There was no answer. He moved over to Ueda, and shook him by the shoulder. No movement. When Tsutsumi looked down he saw his own chest and water-bottle were covered in blood. Ueda had been hit in the right shoulder, the bullet had gone straight into the heart and he had died instantly, without a murmur. That must have been the sound Tsutsumi heard coming through the hut wall a few minutes before.

He was in despair: Ueda had been close to him, from the very start of the withdrawal, and now, to die like this, just as they were on the brink of making the final crossing that would bring them to safety! It seemed intolerably hard that a chance bullet should put an end to life. At the moment the bullet came through the wall, Ueda's heart and his own could have been separated by no more than twenty inches. If he had momentarily shifted position it might have struck him only in the buttocks or the arm or it might have hit Tsutsumi himself. It was clearly dangerous to linger in this village and Tsutsumi decided to make for the river a day earlier than he had intended. Even with the little information that patrols had brought back, the river was evidently several hundred yards wide at this point, and fast-flowing by all accounts. It would be folly to attempt to cross without a boat. In a small hut further upstream someone had come across a small country boat, and Tsutsumi decided to take this, when it grew dark on the 16th. But it was not so easy. When they drew near to the hut, he saw that it had been drawn up under the first floor, and was protected by wire netting. The hut itself projected ten yards into the water, and there was obviously someone inside. While they were quietly deliberating what course of action to take, someone started taking pot shots at them, and they withdrew cautiously back the way they had come.

But it was out of the question to linger in the village, so on 17 August, not caring now whether it was daylight or not, they decided to cross the embankment and hide in the tall reeds. The morning passed quietly, but at three in the afternoon they heard sounds far away along the embankment which made them think a large enemy force was moving south. Peeping out from the thick clumps of reeds which hid them quite effectively, Tsutsumi and his few surviving sailors watched as four columns of British-Indian troops filed past, along the top of the embankment and through the field beside it. The embankment was about ten yards high at this point, and only about the same distance from Tsutsumi's hiding place. The sailors froze in fear or, as the Japanese put it, 'their liver went cold', and they held their breath. The voices of the marching troops came clearly to them on the faint breeze, but the column seemed to go on and on without a break — it must have been a battalion strong.

What if they were spotted? Should they make a break for it, swim out into the middle of the *chaung* like frogs in a rice field? Or have it out in one final battle, and if that did not end it, kill themselves? This seemed the logical answer, but suicide with a grenade was not now the sure thing it might have been days ago. You could not be sure that water had not penetrated the mechanism, you might make the final earth-shattering decision and pull the pin, only to find that nothing happened. If this did happen to any one of them, they had already agreed that the rest should intervene to finish him off. It was now about five in the afternoon. The last ranks of the enemy battalion vanished southwards along the line of the embankment. They had taken their time!

Now about a dozen Burmese came along, carrying poles across their shoulders from which hung chickens and bananas — an unforeseen *cantinière* arrangement, thought Tsutsumi, who then realized that they were following some distance behind the British unit no doubt hoping to do some business. They too moved along the top of the embankment, then paused for a while, and started over towards the spot where Tsutsumi and his men were hiding. Did one of the sailors move and give them away? He could not be certain, but at any rate the Burmese, as if to make sure, began to throw stones into the reeds. 'They've not seen us!' whispered Tsutsumi to his men. 'Don't move! Don't fire!' Soon the Burmese moved off southwards, in the wake of the British battalion. Whether they had been able to see clearly into the reeds or not, Tsutsumi knew there was no point in taking chances. If they had, the news would be with the British before long, so they moved as far from the embankment as possible and further upstream. It was just as well. About an hour passed, then a dozen British soldiers, accompanied by two or three Burmese, came back along the embankment. The Burmese pointed to the spot where the Japanese had been hiding, and the soldiers took aim and fired into the reeds. They waited a little, and when there was no reaction at all, they shouldered their weapons and marched off again. Perhaps they did not rely very much on native reports, and thought the Burmese had made a mistake.

Assuming that darkness made it safer, the Japanese returned to Mokho Atwinya. It was, of course, a dangerous thing to do – but Tsutsumi wanted that boat, and in the rice sheds and cow sheds there was bamboo for river-crossing materials, enough to make a raft if the boat proved impossible. By the night of 18 August two rafts lay floating in the water. They were hardly in the best of condition – the bamboo was old, and cracked in places, and Tsutsumi wondered whether it had sufficient buoyancy. The raft built by 13 Guard Unit had buoyancy adequate for the men's equipment; the one made by the men of 12 looked as if it would be useless even for that. But they would have to do. At all costs, Tsutsumi and the surviving officer from 12, Yoshida, were intent on coming through, in order to report to their headquarters the fate of their units, now so near to being totally destroyed. Kanetaka's incinerated finger, and other memorials of men who had died in the battles of the last few days, all these had to be brought back, the story had to be told, otherwise this overland unit would disappear totally, like some illusion, into the depths of eternity. This meant they should split up, so that at any rate one of the parties might have a chance to get through. There was no question of combining to ensure a more massive firepower, because even in combination they did not amount to much. After a heated discussion, it was decided that Tsutsumi should cross that night with the rest of 13 Guard Unit. Yoshida would make a fresh start later. In fact, he started off the following day, took a different route, and came through alive.

So Tsutsumi had his men load rifles, pistols, grenades, packs, water-bottles, and boots on the raft, and secured them tightly. The raft was built for six men to fit into the interstices of the bamboo and push the raft as they swam. They were to swim clothed, to protect their bodies from the chill of the river. At eleven o'clock at night, on 18 August 1945, they entrusted their destiny to the waters of the Sittang. The men pushed the raft out into midstream across the dark face of the river, from the shallows, and began to swim. It was easy enough until they reached midstream, when suddenly the current struck them hard, and as they tried to come closer to the opposite bank, it bore them downstream parallel to it. They could see the bank like a darker band of blackness in the thick night, but could make no progress towards it as the river carried them off. On and on they went, hour after hour − it must have been at least five hours, thought Tsutsumi − until slivers of light began to show dawn on the banks.

Then they realized they were not alone in the water. There were other men in it, too, entangled in clumps of floating weed, and seeming to struggle in its grasp. But it was an image of struggling, nothing more. The men were dead, they were soldiers from the 28 Army formation who had tried to cross the Sittang further up and had failed. Rafts were swept along beside them, turned topsy-turvy by the waters which spun them round casually, from time to time, in a powerful vortex, and then shot off once more, spinning downstream with the weeds and the corpses.

As the day grew lighter, Tsutsumi's patience grew less. Was there no way of controlling this raft? Then he saw, far ahead downstream, a blinding flash of white light. The headlights of an enemy patrol boat? That was all it needed.

Tsutsumi began to pray, and as other men in similar situations before him, from the beginning of time, he prayed and begged his mother to look after him, to watch over him, and keep him safe.

His foot felt, just for an instant, the scrape of the riverbed — they must have been brought closer in to the opposite bank than he had realized. 'Put your backs into it, lads!' he shouted to the men. 'We're almost there, one last effort!' The water was still up to their necks, but by a combination of standing and swimming, straining against the powerful thrust of the Sittang, they brought themselves, little by little, closer and closer inshore. Now the water was up to their thighs, and the bank was quite near. A few minutes later, with a sense of unbelief, Tsutsumi was clambering up the river bank with his five sailors.

It was six o'clock in the morning of 19 August 1945. He was not to know it for some time, but the war had already been over for four days. Along the river bank were dotted a few huts and little lights began to appear in them — perhaps it was the morning meal being prepared? But it might be dangerous to enquire, so the sailors made off between the houses, and marched east.

400 yards further on, they came out into water meadows, and as they did so firing began from the periphery of the village. Petty Officer Komemura was shot through the right lung; as he toppled over, he cried '*Tennō Heika Banzai!*' (Long Live the Emperor!) and then began to murmur to himself the Buddhist invocation '*Namu myōhō renge kyō*' ('We pray the Lotus Sutra of the wonderful Law'). He kept repeating this until he died. Tsutsumi is not quite sure where they were by this time — they had, after all, been swimming for seven hours down the Sittang; but he thinks the village was Inbala.[7]

Using only a pocket compass, Tsutsumi and the four who were left kept moving in a south-easterly direction; the map he had carried with him was useless now, soaked through with water. Water had got into the compass, too, and the needle had stuck, so Tsutsumi took off the the glass lid, threw it away, emptied the water out, and took measurements by balancing the needle carefully on the card.

22 August. Morning. They were moving across a field, to a single hut in the middle. Oddly enough — for they had grown used to expecting hostility from the Burmese by now — there was just one middle-aged man in the hut, who welcomed them, and put food before them. Such food, too — they had tasted nothing like it since Zaungtu in the Yomas: chicken, eggs, fluffy white rice — and plenty of it. It was, in the Japanese phrase, 'like finding Buddha in Hell'. The sailors sat down to it with glee, and, after resting, turned to something a little less satisfying: an examination of their feet. They did not knew how much marching lay ahead, and their feet were in a dreadful condition. They had been in the Sittang so long and the water had soaked their feet so frequently that they had turned swollen, puffy and white, except in between the toes, where raw red ulcers could be seen. It was obviously the sensible thing to keep their boots off for a while and stay in the hut while one of them pounded sesame seeds in his steel helmet to make a soothing powder for the raw spots between their toes. After they had started to busy themselves in this way, the Burmese told them he had work to do in the fields, and left.

Three o'clock in the afternoon, and he had still not returned. Without warning, the hut became the target for a hail of gunfire. The sailors were resting, up on the first floor; they grabbed their rifles and flew outside. Under a lean-to shed, there was a pile of bamboo, big round fat logs which had been cut for firewood. Using this pile as a shield, they started to fire back. They could see the enemy, a few heads bobbing up and down, some distance away — there seemed to be between twenty and thirty of them. The backsight-notch of Petty Officer Kiyomizu's rifle was struck by a rifle bullet and bent out of shape, but by some miracle Kiyomizu himself escaped unhurt. In a pause in the firing, Tsutsumi heard something dripping, slowly and insistently, on the curved top of a bamboo section. He looked up, and saw it was blood. He looked round swiftly. Were they all down? No, Petty Officer Harada was not there. 'Harada!' he shouted. 'Harada, are you upstairs?' He could barely hear the groan that was the answer: 'They've done for me, Commander. I'm finished.' He must have been hit by enemy fire coming through the wall before he could follow the others. 'Hang on, I'll be with you in a second!' Tsutsumi yelled, as he kept on firing. 'Keep your head down!'

Whoever they were, the enemy did not seem to want the risk of an open encounter, and were making no move forward. 'Cease fire!' Tsutsumi rapped out. Maybe the enemy thought the sailors had been wiped out by their fire – at any rate, as darkness fell they withdrew. How often he had seen them do this, thought Tsutsumi. They kept one pinned down during the daylight, and suddenly as night fell they would relax and pull back. Perhaps they were afraid of the night raids? There was no doubt at all in his mind why the enemy had come up – they had been warned by the middle-aged Burmese; otherwise he would have shown up sooner or later. Even with the firing at an end, there was no sign of him, so it was obvious what had happened. As soon as he was sure the front was clear of the possibility of an enemy attack, Tsutsumi bounded upstairs. He needed only one look at Harada. He had been hit in the back and had fallen forward. Vivid red blood welled out from his jacket, and great globules jetted out on to the rush matting which covered the floor. Tsutsumi knelt down and removed the jacket – already ants had begun to crawl over it – and was appalled by what he saw. A hole 12 inches across had split the back open like a pomegranate and the raw red flesh looked as if it were trying to force its way out of the skin. The shot seemed to have gone along the middle of the back, and gouged it out. Ants had begun to swarm round the lips of the wound. He brushed them away and told one of the sailors to take Harada's gaiters and wash them in clean water. He made a rough bandage with them, round his body. Harada begged for water, but Tsutsumi knew he had to refuse: if you give water to someone who is losing great gouts of blood, you bring on death more quickly. He had a rice-gruel made in the evening, and fed it to Harada with a spoon. It was no use: Harada vomited it straight back. 'I can't help you, Harada,' thought Tsutsumi, 'I'm sorry, but I can't help you.'

Some upstairs, some down, they settled into an uneasy sleep, taking guard by turns. A bump in the darkness woke them all. Harada was lying by the water container on the bottom floor, his face drained of blood. He was already dead. What must have happened was clear enough: unable to endure being deprived of water, he had crawled down the steps to the bottom floor, put his lips to the container for one last drink, and then simply keeled over. 'Perhaps I should have let him have a drink', Tsutsumi thought to himself, 'if he wanted it so badly. It was too late anyway to do him any more damage.'

They buried Harada and set out again on the 24th. They were down to four men now. They had prepared three days' rations each from the food in the hut — a little cooked rice and some *ngape*, stuffed into hollowed-out bamboo cylinders and then slung over their backs. They noticed aircraft flying over — these were not the RAF fighters they had grown to fear, but transport aircraft, C 47s flying low. They watched as white and yellow parachutes fluttered down in the distance. They kept going south-east, on and on, tormented by a griping pain in the stomach, which they had no means of curing and did their best to ignore — until on 27 August their march came to a full stop. It looked as if the stop would be permanent too. They had come to the shores of a vast lake, which did not exist on the map, but stretched as far as the eye could reach to right and left, unimaginably extensive. Tsutsumi looked closer at the surface, and then realized it was no lake at all. The innumerable little rivers and *chaungs* of the plain, which flow into the Sittang, had burst their banks as a result of the endless monsoon downpour and had obliterated the patches of land between them; but the resulting 'lake' was not excessively deep and here and there you could see the tops of trees projecting above the water, their lower branches being quite submerged. 'We can swim this,' Tsutsumi said to himself, and started the men to work making little rafts for the equipment they had left.

Bananas grew plentifully there, so they put banana stalks together for buoyancy, and placed their weapons on them, pushing the little rafts forward over the water as they swam. They had finished off the food that morning. From the time they started off, before noon on 27 August, to the afternoon of the 31st, when they reached a mountain road on the other side of the 'lake', they swam on and on for five days, without a single bite to eat. They had to do it in bits and pieces, of course: they would swim for 40 or 50 yards, then take a rest on a branch of a tree which happened to be on the same level as the water surface; after a little rest, they would swim on. It was quite different from being in the Sittang, since there was no current, which helped them a good deal. But there were other problems — they did not dare leave their mouths open for the water leeches, and at night, in order to snatch some sleep, they rested in the branches of a tree, but had to strap themselves to it with their gaiters in case they fell into the water. Their soaked clothes were uncomfortable, but even more so were the ants. Their nests would be on the ends of branches, the size of a melon, and they would begin to move along the branches towards the sleeping sailors, light-brown ants half an inch in length, tormenting the sleepers' hands or face. Inadequate sleep, empty bellies, fatigue, leeches, ants — the British attacks seemed to have come to an end, but a whole host of natural enemies had taken over. Surely hell must be something like these nights in the wet trees?

On the afternoon of 31 August, they heaved themselves up

a low cliff which was the opposite shore of the 'lake' and came out on to a mountain path along the plateau which had been their yearned-for objective for so long. It seemed an eternity since their feet had trodden on anything so hard as a real path – they had forgotten what a pleasure the sensation could be, and the sudden influx of joy at the physical contact with a road gave them energy they thought they would never recover. There was still a stiff march ahead, they knew, but the path put them in good spirits and gave them fresh courage. After what had seemed the interminable purgatory of the false lake, the effect on them was as if their lives had been saved after some perilous voyage. They turned south down the mountain road in the evening, and came across a group of soldiers, eighteen in all, under a medical corps sergeant, Fukuda. They were cooking rice by a stream, and although there was not very much, they spared a handful each for the sailors, who spun it out with edible grasses and made a gruel of it, their first real meal since dawn on 27 August. Watching them eat, Tsutsumi realized that his men had reached the limit of the vital force of which human beings are capable. The things they had done, the agonies they had been through, would have been impossible for them in times of peace.

The next ten days were a relatively tranquil time, a slow march, still southward, towards a point 4½ miles east of the town of Shwegyin, where they proposed crossing the Shwegyin Chaung. By the side of the track, rubber plantations spread into the hills. No enemy ambush seemed to await them, but they were continually assaulted by their own inner enemy, the fierce hunger that could not be assuaged. As if to warn them of a fate they thought they had avoided,and which might still lie ahead, the track was strewn with the bodies of soldiers who had fallen sick and died on the spot. They would come across little groups of bodies, huddled round a tree trunk for shelter under the leaves, still leaning against each other – and also other bodies which were mere white bones, picked clean. In the shelter of the rubber forests, they saw the body of a soldier close to the trees — still in uniform — but the face had rotted away under the military cap. Seeing them by daylight was bad enough; but the shock of stumbling across these bodies in the dusk made the sailors feel that the night was full of devils.

It was the same story when they looked for shelter in the occasional huts that lay at the forest edge. They came across one such, rather more splendid than they had anticipated, in among the rubber trees, a real wooden house with two floors. They approached it cautiously — a house of this size could well contain a British or Burmese patrol — but it was empty. They pushed open the door, went in, and climbed the stairs. It was a sight they had never grown used to, though they had now seen it so often: two soldiers lay on the floor upstairs, their whole bodies a seething mass of black flies, as if the corpses were still moving of their own volition. But the sailors were exhausted by their march and had to sleep somewhere, so two of them went into the next room, and two remained downstairs. They were awakened in the middle of the night by a slight thud. Looking cautiously to see what was the matter, Tsutsumi came face to face with a soldier, Murakami, who had become separated from his unit and was following down the same track as themselves. He had gone upstairs in the dark, and stumbled over the sleeping sailors. They all went to sleep again, but when Tsutsumi looked at Murakami the next day he saw that sleep had changed to death. He had really gone to the limit, thought Tsutsumi, looking at the exhausted skinny frame — every ounce of physical and spiritual strength had been used up.

Now enemy aircraft began to be active again. But, curiously, they did not come down to strafe. Propaganda leaflets — as Tsutsumi took them to be — fluttered down from the skies: 'Japanese soldiers! The war has come to an end. If you stop for a moment under the trees, you will notice the flowers in the silence of the evening — it is like old times. If you stay out in the open in Burma you will catch malaria, so come in as soon as possible. The war is over.' There were many such leaflets lying along the track and in the forest, but Tsutsumi was not to be fooled – he could recognize propaganda when he saw it, gave a grim smile, and walked on.

By 9 September, they had reached their intended crossing point, and passed over to the other side of the Shwegyin Chaung without mishap. There were any number of log boats in the water, so there was no need to set to and make a raft. Close by the crossing point, they saw some fruit which reminded them of mandarin oranges, growing in profusion, but they proved too sour to the taste. It was a disappointment, because Tsutsumi had anticipated replenishing the body's supplies of vitamin C from the luscious yellow objects and put them to his mouth at once. Once over the *chaung*, they joined up with about a dozen soldiers who were making south through the rubber plantations like themselves. The following day, they were startled to hear a loud voice echoing through the rubber trees, from a long way off: *'Butai oran ka?'* 'Are there Japanese troops here?' The call was repeated at intervals. They lay down on the grassy verge. 'There's some odd character wandering around,' was Tsutsumi's inner reaction to the voice, but he said nothing as they waited for its owner to show himself. After a while, he spotted two men wearing Japanese uniform approaching through the trees. The one in front was carrying the Japanese Rising Sun flag, the one behind a white flag, and they held both of them on high as they walked up.

'These are prisoners,' Tsutsumi thought at once. 'They've been taken, and they've been sent out again under enemy orders to bring in stragglers.' Swiftly he gave his men orders to fix bayonets – if anything untoward occurred, they were to run these two men through. Tsutsumi grasped his pistol, and walked towards them, stopping twenty paces away. They saw him, and came to a halt. Neither of them wore a sword, he noticed, and they seemed to be unarmed. They stared at each other, and the one in front spoke. 'My name is Major Wakō. I am a peace envoy from Burma Area Army, and I have come to inform you that the war is over. Here is the rescript of His Majesty the Emperor.' He shouted this, to cover the distance between them. But the phrase 'the war is over' had never entered Tsutsumi's head as a possibility, not even in dreams – not even the idea, let alone the phrasing of it – and he simply thought the two were enemy agents. He signalled to his men to work round the two strangers and surround them, went forward, took the document which Wakō handed to him, and gave it a cursory glance.

Suddenly he was not so sure. Half doubting, half believing, he looked at them. They did not give him the impression of being spies or enemy agents, now he was closer and could read the expression in their eyes. But he was taking no chances. He began to question them, and was, in spite of himself, impressed by Wakō's obvious sincerity and the pain his mission was causing him. Tsutsumi paraded all the men, and had them listen to the rescript and the Army order Wakō carried as well. The order was dated Moulmein, 1400 hours, 18 August, and said, briefly, that an imperial order had been received putting an end to hostilities in East Asia on 14 August. It commanded all Japanese troops in Burma to cease hostile action, with the provision that if they came under attack from Burmese, they could defend themselves, but were to undertake no offensive action. The order was to be distributed by telegram, messenger, and, if necessary, from the air. It was signed by the general officer commanding the Burma Area Army, Kimura, and attached to it was an order from Lieutenant-General Sakurai of 28 Army, giving more detailed instructions to his own men. From Paan, about 17 miles north of Martaban, at 1200 hours on 7 September, he repeated that the war was over, that 28 Army had concentrated in the area between Martaban and Thaton, and that

those soldiers of 28 Army and its subordinate units who were
still moving south along the east bank of the Sittang were to
cease hostilities. *Gunshi* – peace envoys – were being permitted by the British to search the area to bring them in.
When they were ordered to lay down their arms, they must
do so. His order was to be distributed by messenger, or,
relying on British co-operation, dropped from the air.

But there was more than the order. Knowing full well how
such a message would be received, Sakurai had taken the
precaution of adding something over and above the formal
military command. The text ran:

This is not a hoax by the British. The army is sending out a number of
envoys in an effort to reach all of you. The reason the order is coming
to you in this way is that signal communications have broken down.
The enemy is continuing reconnaissance flights, but there is to be no
more bombing over the entire front. The fact that you cannot hear it
any more will seem very strange, but it is a proof that the war is at an
end. It is imperative you trust this order, dismissing all doubt from your
minds. Pass the news along to units near you. It is necessary for the
future of the Empire and the Imperial Army that you bear the
unbearable with patience, repress rebellious feelings, and carry out
orders with sincerity. All officers are to return to their original
attachments as soon as possible. A report has come from higher
authority to the effect that those who lay down their arms after the
Imperial Rescript will not be considered as prisoners-of-war.

For Tsutsumi, and indeed for many like him, that last phrase
was vital. The ugly fate of becoming a prisoner, of being
handed over to one's enemy without a fight and being cut off
from the patrimony of the Japanese warrior tradition for
ever – this fate had been removed.

Nonetheless, there were still those who refused to believe
the war was over, or who took the other way out, finding the
unbearable *really* unbearable, and opted for suicide. Tsutsumi
talked on and on with Wakō, and could see more and more
clearly that he had not been lying in any way, his whole
speech and behaviour showed this. So he called over the

army warrant officer who was the man of the most senior
rank among the soldiers accompanying them, and persuaded
him to obey Wakō. But there was still something in his own
situation he had to clear up. He was an officer in the Japanese
Navy, and should really make for Naval headquarters
(wherever they were by now) as fast as possible to report. He
could not, therefore, go back with Major Wakō, even though
he had begun to accept the news of the surrender. 'This puts
me in some difficulty,' Wakō answered, 'but I understand
you perfectly well.' Of course he did – there was a tacit
understanding between them, an unspoken realization of
what would be correct behaviour for the *bushi*, the traditional Japanese warrior, which both felt themselves to be.
Tsutsumi handed the soldiers over to Wakō's care, and took
his leave. Wakō gave him two cigarettes from the packet he
had been given by a British officer before starting off into the
jungle – two *Players*, whose aroma Tsutsumi never forgot.

The leave-taking proved abortive. On the afternoon of 12
September, Wakō was waiting for him on a narrow mountain
road between two hills. The reason was simple. He had made
a mistake in letting Tsutsumi move south on his own. The
duty laid upon him by the British had been to bring in every
single Japanese to Shwegyin, and the British were not
concerned whether the men were army, navy, or civilians.
Tsutsumi went over his reasons for wanting to reach Naval
headquarters, but Wakō was adamant. 'Burmese have come
with me,' he pointed out. 'They've been sent to carry my
rations and escort me. You can't see them from here, but
they're waiting for me back along the path. Even if I could
pretend I'd not come across you, they're sure to talk when
they get back, and the British will know at once what's
happened. It's a question of my responsibility now, you must
see that. I know exactly how you feel – and you know I feel
the same. But the end of the war is a fact, we have the
Emperor's order. You *must* come with me.' Tsutsumi was
still unwilling, and the question and answer started up again

and went on and on. 'I understood his reasons all right,' Tsutsumi remembers, 'but I had my own reasons, and they seemed right to me.' Wakō kept him talking, and as evening approached, and they had reached no conclusion, it was agreed they should all spend the night in a nearby hut which belonged to one of the Burmese Wakō had brought with him.

The following morning, 13 September, Wakō asked Tsutsumi to come with him to the top of a little hillock. He agreed, and when they got to the top his eye followed Wakō's pointing finger. In the distance he could see a village where about 1,000 Japanese troops were assembled, or were moving about in little groups across an open space. There could be no doubt about it, then, Tsutsumi realized — so many Japanese in one place, like this — the war must be over. He had a sudden sensation that his sword was missing and an intense feeling of poignant regret ran through him at the same time. It was a complex sensation, impossible to describe. But he knew that it signified acceptance of what Wakō had been urging upon him, as they both went down the hill, back to the native huts.

Later in the day, a boat pushed out from Shwegyin, and crossed the *chaung* to Winkanein. A young British army lieutenant was in it and came up at once from the river bank. He seemed to know Wakō, indeed to be on fairly good terms with him, and he saluted Tsutsumi and greeted him in Japanese. It was fluent but ungrammatical enough to make Tsutsumi wince. He accepted from Wakō that the young man was a British officer, but it took some doing — he wore nothing but a Burmese *longyi*, and a pair of wooden Burmese sandals, no shirt, no badges of rank. The lieutenant looked curiously at Tsutsumi. By this time his jet-black hair had grown long and shaggy, his beard was matted, his clothes in tatters, and there was still an angry light of resentment in his eyes. He looked for all the world like Robinson Crusoe. Tsutsumi got up, finally, and went over to the boat. He began to declaim angrily that it was American economic imperialism which had begun the war — was the lieutenant aware of this? — and that Japan would never have surrendered in normal circumstances. 'No, I'm sure you're right,' the lieutenant answered. 'A new kind of bomb has been used in the past few weeks, which is different from any other kind that's ever been dropped. I daresay the Japanese would never have surrendered otherwise.' They climbed into the country boat and were soon out in the middle of the *chaung*.

It was late afternoon by now, and extraordinarily peaceful. The *chaung* ran down to the Sittang like a silver knife cutting through the green luxuriance on either side, and the warm sunlight broke down through the clouds and irradiated the surface of the water, making the gleaming trees even more brilliant. The lieutenant was evidently taken with the scene, and began to whistle a few bars of the Pastoral Symphony. Tsutsumi listened for a while, felt his anger diminish and then surrendered to a change of mood. He too began to whistle the symphony. There were many friends and comrades he would never see again, and his country was, even now, beginning to know the agonies of defeat; but life was still coursing along his veins, he had survived an almost impossible odyssey. He had come through.

NOTES

Introduction

1 S. Woodburn Kirby, *The War Against Japan*,V, p. 45.
2 Ibid., p. 528.
3 *Nansō (Window on the South)*, No. 31, July 1965, p. 31.
4 Bisheshwar Prasad (ed.), *Indian Armed Forces in World War II, The Reconquest of Burma*, Vol. II, Orient Longmans, 1959, pp. 459-60.

Part 1

Chapter 1

1 The details on Hanaya are mostly drawn from *Senshi (Death in Battle)* by Takagi Toshiro (Asahi Shimbunsha, Tokyo, 1967). I am deeply indebted to Richard Storry, of St Antony's College, Oxford, for the loan of this book.
2 Ba Maw, *Breakthrough in Burma*, p. 179.
3 Ibid., p. 264.

Chapter 2

1 Aida Yuji, *Prisoner of the British*, Cresset Press, London, 1966, pp. 131-2.

Chapter 3

1 *Sittang; Mei-go Sakusen (Sittang; Operation Mei)* published by Asagumo Shimbunsha for Defence Agency, Tokyo, 1969, p. 413.
2 Aida, op. cit., pp. 1-2.
3 Aida, op. cit., pp. 167-8.
4 Aida, op. cit., pp. 11-12.

Chapter 4

1 *Sittang; Mei-go Sakusen*, p. 273. Fukudome was Tsuchiya's opposite number, responsible for operational planning; later, in the post-war era, he became commanding officer of the Self-Defence Forces A/A School at Chiba.

2 The name is Japanese, not Burmese, and was used as a code-name for the conference site.

3 He is now a general in the Japanese Ground Self-Defence Forces.

4 The *Kikan*, or 'organization', was named after the mediaeval warrior hero, Kusunoki Masashige.

5 A tributary of the Sittang, which rises in the Yomas and crosses the Mandalay Road just south of the village of Kanyutkwin.

6 The Japanese official historian of the Sittang Battle has been unable – rather understandably – to find this village on the map. It is presumably a local amplification of Ingon, north-east of Kanyutkwin.

7 In fact, the highest ranking prisoner ever taken was a captain. Several captains were captured in these few weeks of the break-out.

Chapter 5

1 Prasad, op. cit.,p. 458.

Chapter 6

1 Okamura's account is given in the magazine *Nansō*, July 1965, p. 36.

2 Major-General S. Woodburn Kirby, *The War Against Japan*, Vol. V, *The Surrender of Japan, H.M.S.O.*, 1969, p. 37.

Chapter 7

1 *Sittang*; *Mei-go Sakusen*, Tokyo, 1969, p. 343.

Chapter 8

1 *Defeat into Victory*, p. 528.

2 The terms 'captain', 'lieutenant', etc., when used in this chapter of 12 and 13 Naval Guard Forces, are *naval* ranks.

3 War Diary of 12 Guard Unit, in *Sittang; Mei-go Sakusen*, Asagumo Shimbunsha, Tokyo, 1969, pp. 451-3.

4 The dispositions were as follows:

    13 Overland Unit (680 men)

        Main Unit: 550 men under Fukami

        Rangoon Land Combat Unit (130 men under Sublieutenant Fukui. Later merged with main unit in Yomas.)

    13 Toungoo Ack-Ack Unit (4 men)

        Survived, after crossing with army units.

    13 Sea Route Unit (220 men)

        Torpedo Boat Unit (100 men under Sublieutenant Nakamura)

        30 of these, including Nakamura, survived.

        Landing-craft Unit (120 men under Sublieutenant Hirose)

        29 men survived, under Sublieutenant Morimoto.

    Naval Post Office (4 men under Morimoto)

        No survivors

    12 Overland Unit (190 men)

After Captain Kōno's death in battle, 190 men under Lieutenant Nonaka were merged with Tsutsumi's unit. 4 men under Sublieutenant Yoshida survived. (Some others fell into British hands.) About 1,000 men in all, then, of these naval units, lost their lives before the summer was out.

5 Not to be confused with the small town of Taikkyi, on the Prome Road, where 28 Army had had its headquarters.

6 Later still, the unit was to come under the command of Major-General Matsui and his Kani Force, but no liaison was ever established between them – and by then it was too late to matter anyway.

7 There are two villages of this name, quite close to one another, as frequently happens with Burmese place-names, due north of the bend in the Sittang at Milaunggon.

Appendices

THE BRITISH FORCES FACING 28 ARMY
AND THE CAPTURED OPERATION ORDER

On 1 June 1945, the British-Indian Army in Burma underwent a major face-lift. What had been the prestigious XIV Army continued to exist, but some of its proudest units—5, 7, 17, and 19 Indian Divisions — were incorporated into a new formation called XII Army, under the command of Lieutenant-General Sir Montagu Stopford, formerly the Commander-in-Chief of XXXIII Corps. XII Army consisted of the divisions of IV Corps plus two divisions (7 and 20) and 268 Brigade in the Irrawaddy Valley. Most of 255 Tank Brigade was quartered at Pegu and between Pegu and Yamethin were two divisions operating under the command of IV Corps: 17 Division between Pyinbongyi and Pyu and 19 Division between Toungoo and Yamethin. In the low-lying area of the Sittang Bend was 5 Division, later succeeded by 7 Division. 19 Division was not merely guarding the main road south to Rangoon; it also had feelers pushed out along the road to Mawchi from Toungoo, and another on the road to Kalaw — both of these cutting across the southward escape routes of the defeated Japanese from north and central Burma, leading ultimately to Siam. That was the east side of the cordon round the Pegu Yomas. The west side was taken up by 20 Division, deployed between Paungde and Hmawbi along the road between Rangoon and Prome; and 7 Indian Division, with 268 Brigade temporarily under its command, controlling the area between Thayetmyo and Prome. The forces were, of course, fairly thinly spun out, and their duties were heavy. Between Toungoo and Pyu stood 98 Brigade of 19 Division; between Pyu (or rather just to the north of Pyu) and to a point south of Kanyutkwin was 64

Brigade.

At this point 17 Division's territory began, with 63 Brigade from north of Penwegon to north of Nyaunglebin, 48 Brigade to south of Daiku with feelers out to the Sittang at Shwegyin. Three brigades of 7 Division covered the Sittang Bend, the Pegu area, and the area between Payagyi and Daiku. With these forces Stopford was to maintain security in Burma, re-establish law and order and civil government and help in the projected reconquest of Malaya by providing 5 Division from Rangoon in August and two other divisions (7 and 20) in the late autumn. There had been some changes in personnel, too. Cowan had been succeeded in the command of 17 Division by Crowther, a brigadier from 89 Brigade of 7 Division. It must have been quite a break for Cowan, who had served for over three years with 17 Division, and had seen it in the depths of the bitterest defeat and in the euphoria of mechanized triumph. But Crowther was no amateur, and no stranger to the forces 17 Division was facing. As a brigadier in the Arakan he had fought Sakurai's men before. He seemed less subtle than Cowan in some ways — tall, beefy, red-faced, but quite clear in his own mind how he intended to cut Sakurai's break-out into ribbons. The Corps commander had changed too, and here there is no doubt that there would have been a fitting paradox if Lieutenant-General Sir Frank Messervy had remain-ed a few weeks longer. Early in July Messervy went on leave and was replaced by Major-General F. I. S. Tuker who had commanded 4 Indian Division in the Western Desert and Italy. Tuker's experience of warfare was considerable and his interest in the Indian Army was passionate and deep, as his writings later showed, but Messervy was the general whom 55 Division had caught with his pants down at the 'Admin Box' in the Arakan in 1944, and there would have been some poe-tic justice if he had remained to command the corps which was to annihilate the Japanese Army responsible for his own discomfiture.

The British generals had an almost perfect picture of what

Sakurai was about. On 2 July 1945, at a point in the eastern foothills of the Pegu Yomas just north of the village of Myogyaung and a few miles south-west of 17 Indian Division headquarters at Penwegon, a patrol of the 1/7 Gurkhas bumped a small Japanese force and a brisk battle ensued. From the Japanese dead – nineteen in all – the Gurkhas picked up the usual souvenirs and a despatch bag, the leather of which was soaked from the monsoon rain which had clearly dogged the unfortunate Japanese since they set out. The Gurkhas knew about the value of captured documents and in a very short time the leather bag was lying on a table in 17 Division headquarters, its contents being gingerly removed and dried. They were worth the effort. One of them, bearing the signature of Nagazawa Kanichi, was dated 14 June 1945. It was the operation order for the entire force to move across the Sittang in accordance with the plans of 28 Army. No date for the break-out was given on this document, but the area of movement of the force was clearly defined as bordered by a line drawn through Kintha, Penwegon and Kyaukkyi to the north and Myogyaung, Mukh Ram and Hill 852 to the south. The Force's front of advance was to be between those lines. The operation order went on to describe the distribution of the Force into three columns, with the names of the units attached to each column, the routes to be taken by each column from the Yomas assembly area and to the area where the break-out was to begin, in great detail: the left break-out column was told, for instance, to proceed by the same path as the centre column up to the closed contour height 2½ miles west of Hill 1221, then to a river-crossing point 2½ miles north-west of Hill 1221, then to pass between the letters S and F in the name Aingdonkun Reserved Forest, on the map, and lastly to high ground on the west side of an unnamed lake at the western end of the Daingtaya Reserved Forest. (The Japanese were still using British maps, and where there were not enough to go round they made tracings from the Ordnance Survey on to rice paper and glued the squares together.)

Those points which would have to be attacked and held were then described. The bridge on the railway by the Kun Chaung was to be held by the left column and the centre column was told 'to secure Penwegon' while the main body advanced to Kyaungwa. Points where demolitions were to be carried out were noted. At a point 2 miles north-north-west of Kyauktaga the embankment road was to be destroyed and any attacks by British armoured vehicles were to be repelled and the enemy prevented from repairing the road. In the advance party of each column would be elements of the *Kamikaze Tai*. Movement along the Baingda and Yenwe Chaungs was forbidden in order to conceal the Force from enemy air observation. No firing was to be permitted in order to prevent confusion among the columns and, wrote Nagazawa, 'Cold steel will be the order of the day.' As they moved out from the first assembly points to the plain, well-known routes would be avoided, and a feint in the direction of Toungoo would be made by all three columns. There was to be no wireless communication until the Sittang had been crossed, only visual signals and runners were to be used. Rations were to be on C scale for seven days (including three days on B substitute). All salt and dried and salted fish would be carried even if this meant cutting down on rice. Lastly, when the Force headquarters reached the Shan Plateau, it would send up two red signal shots 1 mile east or west of its position.

The order made it perfectly clear how difficult the Sittang crossing was likely to be. *Kamikaze Tai* was detailed to collect country boats at crossing points on the Sittang, but each column was responsible for its own crossing, and three-to-four-men sampans were to be constructed of bamboo which the men would bring to the river with them, together with motorcar tyres, tubes, drums, and cans. More than twice the usual amount of ammunition was to be carried as far as the Sittang, and no weapons were to be destroyed or abandoned without permission from the column commander. Bullocks and horses were to be taken across the river as time permitted — priority was to be given to casualties and stores. Each horse was to have with it a spare set of shoes and fifty nails, and one week's fodder on the basis of 1 kilogramme per day. For the British readers of this document, it was quite a haul in itself. But there was more in the little leather bag: several other operation orders of a more specific kind, authorizing reconnaissance along certain tracks. A scribbled message to *Kamikaze Tai* asked for the investigation of the road from Alegin to Ananbaw via Zayatkwin, the marshy ground on both banks of the Sittang, the condition of the road to Kyaukkyi, the width of the Sittang, its speed at certain points, the depth of the water, the condition of the banks, the presence or otherwise of country boats, the narrowest part, the part of the opposite bank it was easiest to reach by using the current, whether there was jungle near the villages, the height of miscanthus, whether or not it was possible to pass through the swampy ground on foot, whether the villages had a landmark such as a pagoda which might be of use, whether the village names corresponded with the readings on the map, what they were called in the vernacular and so on.

Where demolitions had to be carried out — on the bridge south of Mukh Ram — it was essential to know the materials of the bridge, whether iron, concrete, or wood, with the number of bays, where the signal lines were, and where it would be suitable to destroy them, how far it was possible to go down the Kun Chaung by raft, how wide it was, its speed of current, the state of its bed and banks; the roads which linked the routes to be used on the left bank of the Sittang, what they were made of, if they flooded at the height of the monsoon and how much, the width and shape of the road surface, the places where it had collapsed; details of the enemy on all the roads and paths to be used by the columns, and on the attitude of villagers, whether it was possible to get food such as rice and salt from the villagers on the Shan Plateau once the columns had reached that far. The Force also wanted to know the frequency and timing of enemy aircraft activity in the Sittang Plain, the areas where dense mist occurred, and when it cleared up. And the password for one of the columns was spelled out – rather unoriginally, it was *Kami,* and the countersign *Kaze.*

That document was drawn up and issued by Colonel Nagazawa on 14 June 1945. It was captured eighteen days later, on 2 July. By 7 July, it had been translated and distributed from 17 Division headquarters. A fresh and more accurate translation was carried out at IV Corps headquarters in Pegu on 10 July; and the document was finally vetted and retranslated at Mountbatten's Rear Headquarters in Delhi on the 16th. The British and Indian forces had plenty of warning about who they were to meet, and where. The day of the break-out was not clear from the documents, but became so some days later. At any rate, a fortnight before the break-out was to start, its entire course of development along the Shimbu Force front was totally known to the enemy through whose thinly held line it was proposing to pass.

It was not long before other documents were taken which completed the picture – maps showing where reconnaissance parties had encountered our patrols – or which noted down a Burmese National Army position, tables of strength of the break-out columns, listing every unit, its officers and men, the weapons carried, down to the number of rounds per man, and the number of horses and bullocks available to carry the guns.

Before he left IV Corps headquarters, Messervy pondered this mountain of information and decided to reinforce the area between Pyu and Nyaunglebin where the main break-out effort was clearly to be directed. The sector between the Pyu Chaung and the Kun Chaung was to be the special preserve of a unit called Flewforce, named after Brigadier Flewett who, with 64 Brigade headquarters – and later a battalion from that brigade – three battalions of infantry, a tank detachment, a detachment of medium guns, and two artillery batteries, sat right across three of the routes for the break-out. It was assumed, rightly, that neither 20 Division nor 7 Division would be unduly hard-pressed during the weeks to come, and three battalions were taken from them and handed over to 17 Division as reserves.

In the light of hindsight and our knowledge that the war was to come to an end a little over three weeks after the break-out battle began, it is difficult to realize that it was by no means obvious to the officers and men of IV Corps that the end was near. Many of them were reconciled to spending several more years in East Asia, and many saw their immediate future as being still very much occupied with the reoccupation of the rest of Burma and a move across the mountains into Siam, to face other formations of Japanese troops. It was therefore a matter of simple necessity to catch and kill as many Japanese as possible before they could escape the net. Messervy intended to do just this: he envisaged two main areas in which the Japanese could be brought to a killing ground — one between the Pegu Yomas and the Sittang, and the other between the mouths of the Sittang and the Salween. The discovery of Nagazawa's plans, and by extrapolation, the likely movements of Sakurai's entire 28 Army, almost guaranteed the fruition of the first killing ground.

But not all Messervy's subordinate commanders agreed with the detail of where the Japanese were to be caught. Crowther introduced a vital change of plan when he took over 17 Division. Up to the middle of July the division by and large allowed Japanese to cross the line of the Mandalay Road, had them followed to the Sittang by patrols and then attempted to destroy them on the line of the river with artillery fire and air strafing. Those who managed to reach the river were left for the Patriotic Burmese Forces, which was the name given to groups of Burmese guerrillas acting under the command of British officers from Force 136. The men of the Patriotic Burmese Forces watched the likely crossing points on the river and disposed of small Japanese groups or individuals as they made their way towards it. For small groups, in fact, this was a perfectly feasible procedure. But Crowther had his doubts whether it was an appropriate method for dealing with the forthcoming break-out which was clearly − the documents showed this − going to be on an unprecedentedly large scale. So he issued an operation instruction to his division which said that, in *his* view, a better plan would be to destroy the Japanese either as they crossed the Mandalay-Rangoon Road or as they came within range of the road from their shelters in the foothills; then, and only then, should the remnants be followed up to the Sittang. He realized that his division could not cover every single crossing place in force: it had 74 miles of road to guard. He ordered likely places to be selected and strong ambushes to be laid by night, on the assumption that the Japanese would cross in the hours of darkness. Based on information brought in by V Force and local agents, ambushes would be laid on likely crossing points every night of the battle, and the Japanese were to be fired on as soon as they came within gun range.

JAPANESE CASUALTY FIGURES IN BURMA

1 The Imphal Campaign

Unit	Before Imphal	After Imphal
15 Division	20,000	4,000
31 Division	20,000	7,000
33 Division	25,000	4,000
Rear Units	50,000	35,000
TOTAL	115,000	50,000

2 The Irrawaddy Battles

Unit	Before	After
15 Division	7,000	3,000
18 Division	15,000	5,000
31 Division	10,000	6,000
33 Division	7,000	4,000
53 Division	5,000	3,000
Rear Units	30,000	25,000
TOTAL	74,000	46,000

3 The Break-out over the Sittang (figures supplied by Major Yamaguchi in Payagyi Camp, 1945)

Unit	Before break-out (end of April 1945)	After break-out (end of August 1945)
28 Army headquarters	660	370
54 Division	9,400	3,423
Shimbu Force	6,757	2,943
Kanjō Force	2,338	1,140
Units under army comd.	7,544	3,798
105 I.M.B. (Kani)	4,173	2,279
TOTAL	30,872	13,953

The above statistics do not include Kantetsu Force, which broke out ahead of the main body. 28 Army's numbers at the time of its formation (29 January 1944) were 59,000. It should be pointed out that these figures were considered by the British staff at the time to be exaggerated. Revised figures were produced by the Japanese for a history of their operations printed by XII Army headquarters (Rangoon, December 1945) and these are as follows:

Unit	Before	After
Headquarters, 28 Army	680	512
54 Division	9,300	3,963
Shimbu Force	6,751	3,113
105 I.M.B.	4,173	2,279
Kanjō Force	1,358	533
Forces Under Command 28 Army:		
Shini Butai	2,993	1,500
Baba Butai	2,603	1,085
Sei Butai	1,778	905
Mukai Butai	1,568	920
TOTAL	31,204	14,810

The footnote to these figures by the British staff states:

The Japanese give the strength of their forces in the Pegu Yomas as over 31,000 of whom approximately 14,800 are said to have escaped across the Sittang. They have little or no evidence to support these figures, and in point of fact the whole of 28 Army which was concentrated in Payagyi Camp, 10 miles north of Pegu, after the surrender, included only 7,621 officers and men who had taken part in the break-out battle.

Our estimate at the time of the breakthrough of the forces involved was approximately 19,000 of which over 11,000 were claimed in killed and prisoners-of-war, and 500 remained sick in the Pegu Yomas, leaving only some 7,500 who made their arduous way to the east of the Sittang, where our waiting guerrilla forces accounted for more of them. It appears therefore that the figures given here by the Japanese are considerably exaggerated and that our estimate was much nearer the truth.

The variations are, then, considerable, between a Japanese total of roughly 30,000 at the start, and a British total of 19,000; and a Japanese total of roughly 14,000 at the finish, and a British total of 7,000.

The Japanese made another reckoning of the strength of 28 Army which appeared in *Nansō (Window on the South*, July 1970, p. 49), an old comrades' association magazine run by Lieutenant-Colonel Tsuchiya on behalf of the *Sittang Kai*. The break-down is by rank, and shows the figures of those in 28 Army in the surrender camps in 1945; and of those who are listed as killed or missing:

Rank	Numbers surrendered in 1945	Killed/Missing
Lieutenant-General	1	0
Major-General	4	0
Colonel	12	0
Lieutenant-Colonel	4	0
Major	34	4
Captain	247	44
Lieutenant	207	80
Second Lieutenant	242	126
Cadets	0	12
Total Officers	751	266
Warrant Officers	133	34
N.C.O.s	2,174	1,307
TOTAL	2,307	1,371
Other Ranks	4,835	9,974
TOTAL	7,893	11,607
Senior Civilian	1	3
Junior Civilian	6	5
Civilian	22	50
TOTAL	29	58
GRAND TOTAL	7,922	11,665

JAPANESE CODE-NAMES

Japanese Forces used the conventional distribution of units, with classifications not dissimilar to those used by the British:

buntai	squad
shōtai	platoon
chūtai	company
daitai	battalion
rentai	regiment
ryōdan	brigade
shidan	division
heidan	force/group
gun	army
shūdan	army group

In addition to this formal classification, every Japanese unit had a code-name and was also, to its soldiers, very often known by the name of its commander. Which commander's name was used depended on the size of the unit involved and the degree of attachment felt by the soldier to his formation. For example, 112 Infantry Regiment of 55 Division was at one time sent out to act independently of the division, under the direct command of 28 Army. In this role, it was given the name of *Kanjō Heidan,* or Kanjō Force, the term *Kanjō* having a martial significance: *kan* being the character for 'shield' or 'defender', and *jō* that for 'castle'. The commanding officer was Colonel Furuya, and to the troops it could be, and frequently was, referred to as *Furuya Butai* or Furuya Unit. *Butai* is the Japanese for 'unit' when a battalion or something larger is referred to; when the unit is smaller, the word *tai* is used. Thirdly, Kanjō Force bore the general code-name for all Japanese units in Burma, *Mori* ('Forest'), since *Mori* was the code-name for the unit in overall command, Burma Area Army, and each unit under its command could be known by the code-name *Mori* plus an identifying number. Burma Area Army would send out signals as *Mori* 9410, 54 Division headquarters as *Mori* 10109, and so on.

The lower a man's rank, the lower would be the formation to which he would regard himself as being personally attached. It would be more likely for a Japanese private of the 112 Infantry Regiment to refer to himself as belonging to *Hosokawa Butai,* Hosokawa Unit, since Hosokawa was the name of the first battalion commander; or to *Otsubo Butai,* Otsubo Unit, since Otsubo was the name of the commander of the the second battalion. Hosokawa and Otsubo were majors, and would represent the 'ceiling' of command of most private soldiers. So on down the scale.

These names would not necessarily be used for official signals or transmitting orders, save for brief signals scribbled in a notebook and passed rapidly by messenger from company to battalion and vice versa. For wireless signals and orders of any consequence the name *Mori* would be used with an identifying number.

The larger formations in Burma all had a single word or character by which they could be briefly referred to. Usually the word chosen, as in the case of *Kanjō*, had some extra significance. 18 Division was known as *Kiku,* 'Chrysanthemum', that flower being one of the most frequently used patriotic symbols in Japanese iconography. 54 Division used the archaic word for 'warrior', *Tsuwamono.* 55 Division at first used the word for 'shield', *Tate,* the implication being that on the coast of the Bay of Bengal it was acting as the buckler of the Empire in the most far-flung of its conquests. Later its name was changed to *Sō,* meaning 'magnificent', 'vigorous', 'strong' – a more magniloquent choice, possibly, but less precise in its function.

The name selected for 28 Army was *Saku.* This was not, despite appearances, an abbreviation of the general's name, though the syllables no doubt recalled him to the troops' mind when it was used. But there was a set of meanings in this word. The character *Saku* forms part of a compound *sakuryaku,* meaning 'stratagem', 'ruse', 'artifice', the *saku* element implying 'scheme', 'expedience', 'resourcefulness'. The implication was not over-subtle: the Allied forces against which 28 Army would have to fight were no doubt superior in numbers and mechanical equipment, but this disparity would be overcome by superior planning, strategy and resourcefulness. To cap this implication the three words used for the other major formations making up the army could be read in another way to make up a phrase. 2 Division's name, *Isamu,* 'brave', could be read *Yū.* 55 Division's *Tate* was changed to *Sō.* 54 Division's *Tsuwamono* could be read *Hei.* The combination provided *Yūsōhei,* 'a courageous warrior'. Courageous warriors under the command of a resourceful strategist – this, then, was the plan of action for 28 Army.

Code-names were also in use for the headquarters, rendezvous, and other important names in and around the Pegu Yomas. Some of these are mentioned in the chapter dealing with Shimbu Force.

CHART OF ORGANIZATION OF JAPANESE ARMY

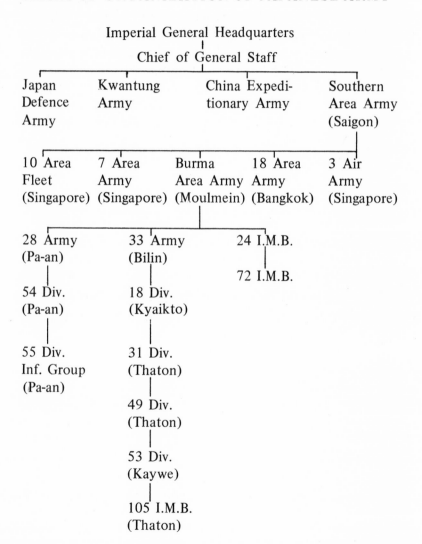

Imperial General Headquarters

Chief of General Staff

| Japan Defence Army | Kwantung Army | China Expeditionary Army | Southern Area Army (Saigon) |

| 10 Area Fleet (Singapore) | 7 Area Army (Singapore) | Burma Area Army (Moulmein) | 18 Area Army (Bangkok) | 3 Air Army (Singapore) |

| 28 Army (Pa-an) | 33 Army (Bilin) | 24 I.M.B. |

72 I.M.B.

| 54 Div. (Pa-an) | 18 Div. (Kyaikto) |

| 55 Div. Inf. Group (Pa-an) | 31 Div. (Thaton) |

49 Div.
(Thaton)

53 Div.
(Kaywe)

105 I.M.B.
(Thaton)

This chart shows the relationships obtaining at the time of the Japanese surrender in August 1945. Subordinate commands are only shown for Burma Area Army. The places bracketed show the headquarters of the formation at the time of the surrender. 105 Independent Mixed Brigade ('Kani Force' in our narrative) is shown under 33 Army. Southern Area Army had further reorganisation in view when the surrender order arrived, including the dissolution of 28 Army. 55 Division was already split in two, part ᴏ. it remaining in surrender camps in Burma, part having reached Phnom Penh in Indo-China.

28 ARMY ORDER OF BATTLE, JANUARY 1944

General Officer Commanding: Lieutenant-General Sakurai Shōzō
28 Army headquarters
2 Division (from Southern Region Order of Battle)
54 Division (from Burma Area Army Order of Battle)
55 Division (from Burma Area Army Order of Battle)
14 Independent Anti-Tank Battalion
71 Field A/A Battalion
44 Field Machine-gun Company
1 Bridge-building Company (9 Division)
26 Bridge-building Company (15 Army)
10 River-crossing Materials Company (15 Army)
55 Independent Motor Vehicle Transport Battalion (15 Army)
236 Independent Motor Vehicle Transport Company (15 Army)
10 Special Motor Vehicle Transport Company (15 Army)
51 Independent Battalion (Armour) (Burma Area Army)
101 Field Road Company (Burma Area Army)
20 Field Road Company (15 Army)
118 L of C Hospital (Burma Area Army)
70 Casualty Transport Section (Burma Area Army)
71 Casualty Transport Section (Burma Area Army)

Attached Units

1 Battalion, 213 Infantry Regiment (Kubo Battalion)
2 Company, 3 Heavy Field Artillery Regiment
11 Shipping Engineer Regiment (less 1 company and 1 section)

3 Company, 4 Shipping Engineer Regiment (Asanaga Company)
3 Marine Transport Battalion
Part of 38 Anchorage headquarters
Main body of Burma Branch, Southern Army Fortifications Department
38 Water Duties Company
93 Land Duties Company
101 Company, Fortifications Duties (2 sections)

Local Units

Part of Burma Area Army Signals
Part of *Hikari Kikan*
Part of each of Burma Area Army supply depots

Weapons of 28 Army before break-out

Rifles	18,600
L.M.G.s	454
H.M.G.s	108
Grenade-launchers	298
Trench mortars	23
Infantry guns	11

(from figures given by the Japanese to XII Army, December 1945)

BIBLIOGRAPHY

British and Indian Sources

Ba Maw, *Breakthrough in Burma. Memoirs of a Revolution, 1939-1946,* London, Yale University Press, 1968.

Tim Carew, *The Longest Retreat*, London, Hamish Hamilton, 1969.

Lieut.-General Sir Geoffrey Evans, *The Desert and the Jungle*, London, Kimber, 1959.

K. K. Ghosh, *The Indian National Army*, Meerut, Meenakshi Prakasan, 1969.

Major-General S. Woodburn Kirby, *The ·War Against Japan,* Vol. IV, *The Reconquest of Burma*, London H.M.S.O., 1965.

Major-General S. Woodburn Kirby, *The War Against Japan*, Vol. V, *The Surrender of Japan,* London, H.M.S.O., 1969.

Compton Mackenzie, *Eastern Epic*, Vol. I (all published) (*September 1939 – March 1943. Defence*), London, Chatto and Windus, 1951.

Frank Owen, *The Campaign in Burma*, London, H.M.S.O., 1946.

Bisheshwar Prasad (ed.), *Official History of the Indian Armed Forces in the Second World War, 1939-1945. The Reconquest of Burma*, Vol. II, Orient Longmans, 1959.

Field-Marshal Sir William Slim, *Defeat into Victory*, London, Cassell, 1956.

Japanese Sources

Aida Yuji, *Prisoner of the British*, translated by Louis Allen and Hide Ishiguro, London, Cresset Press, 1966.

Impāru Sakusen – Biruma no Bōei ('The Imphal Operations

— *the Defence of Burma'*), Asagumo Shimbunsha, Tokyo, 1968. (Ed. by the Defence Agency, Historical Research Section.)

Sittang; Mei-go Sakusen (*'The Sittang Battle; the Coup de Force in French Indo-China'*), Asagumo Shimbunsha, Tokyo, 1970.

The Japanese Account of their Operations in Burma, Headquarters Twelfth Army, Rangoon, 1945.

Morita Yoshio (ed.), *Hiroku Dai Tōa Senshi* (*'Secret History of the War in East Asia'*), Tokyo, Fuji Shobō, 1953.

Payagyi Interrogation Reports: Burma Command Intelligence Summary No. 1 (2), 'The History of Japanese 28 Army'; Twelfth Army Intelligence Summaries, No. 10, "A Short History of Japanese 54 Division" (Rangoon, 1946).

SEATIC Historical Bulletin, No. 240, Singapore, 1946.

SEATIC Historical Bulletin, No. 242, Singapore, 1946.

Takagi Toshiro, *Senshi* (*'Death in Battle'*), Tokyo, Asahi Shimbunsha, 1967.

Tsuchiya Eiichi (ed.), *Nanso* (*'Window on the South'*), privately printed for the Sittang-Kai at 59 Shūcho, Bunkyo-ku, Tokyo. (Issues used: Nos. 27 to 37 inclusive.)

Tsuchiya Eiichi, *'Shi no tekichū ōdan Biruma hōmengun no higeki'* ('Breaking through the enemy—the tragedy of Burma Area Army'), in *Nihon Shuho*, No. 441, 25 April, 1958, pp. 33–41.

Tsuchiya Eiichi, *"Getsumei ni kieta nikuhaku tokkōtai"* (*'Special attack unit vanishes in the moonlight'*)—an account of Shini Butai, *Maru*, No. 244, September 1967, pp. 237–270.

Tsutsumi Shinzō, *Tenshin* (*'Withdrawal'*), privately printed for the author, Tokyo, 1967.

Uzumaku Sittang (*'The Swirling Waters of the Sittang'*), (*History of 121 Infantry Regiment, Tottori*) published by the Nihonkai Shimbunsha, Tottori, Japan, 1969.

INDEX

Note: Japanese names are given in Japanese sequence,
i.e. with the surname first.

I4